Assessment in Higher Education

ASSESSMENT IN HIGHER EDUCATION

Politics, Pedagogy, and Portfolios

PATRICK L. COURTS
AND
KATHLEEN H. McINERNEY

PRAEGER

Westport, Connecticut
London

Library of Congress Cataloging-in-Publication Data

Courts, Patrick L.
    Assessment in higher education : politics, pedagogy, and
portfolios / Patrick L. Courts and Kathleen H. McInerney.
        p.   cm.
    Includes bibliographical references (p.) and index.
    ISBN 0–275–94426–3 (alk. paper).—ISBN 0–275–94427–1 (pbk. :
alk. paper)
    1. Universities and colleges—United States—Examinations.
2. Portfolios in education—United States.   3. College students,
Rating of—United States.   I. McInerney, Kathleen H.   II. Title.
LB2366.2.C68   1993
378.1′6′71—dc20   92–41612

British Library Cataloguing in Publication Data is available.

Library of Congress Catalog Card Number: 92–41612
ISBN: 0–275–94426–3
        0–275–94427–1 (pbk)

First published in 1993

Praeger Publishers, 88 Post Road West, Westport, CT 06881
An imprint of Greenwood Publishing Group, Inc.

Printed in the United States of America

The paper used in this book complies with the
Permanent Paper Standard issued by the National
Information Standards Organization (Z39.48–1984).

10 9 8 7 6 5 4 3 2 1

Copyright Acknowledgments

The authors and the publisher are grateful to the following for granting the use of material:

All-Bright Court by Connie Porter. Copyright © 1991 by Connie Porter. Reprinted by
permission of Ticknor & Fields/Houghton Mifflin Co. All rights reserved.

The Woman Warrior: Memoirs of a Girlhood Among Ghosts by Maxine Hong Kingston.
Copyright © 1977. Vintage Books.

In memory of John and Eleanor Courts,
and to Jayne and John McInerney—my first and best teachers.

Contents

Acknowledgments

First and foremost, I wish to thank the members of the General College Program Assessment Committee of the State University College (SUC) at Fredonia, New York, whose dedication, hard work, and careful thinking helped me begin to shape the parts of this book for which I am responsible. I borrowed freely from the reports cowritten by members of this committee and feel fortunate to have worked with such a fine group of scholars and teachers. Second, more specifically, I owe a deep debt of gratitude to Minda Rae Amiran who, as Dean of Special Studies at the time, involved me in the assessment project and whose editorial feedback on this manuscript while it was being written made it better than it otherwise would have been. She is, of course, responsible for none of the weaknesses herein, but her cautions, sound advice, and expertise in assessment most certainly helped Kathleen McInerney and me strengthen and clarify certain parts of the text.

Next, much that engendered the conception of this book derives directly from the often startling and straightforward statements students wrote for parts of the Fredonia Assessment. Since these statements were anonymous, I will simply thank the students in general, who, I believe, care more about their educations than we sometimes realize, and who, by and large, have already assessed the system as they experience it. Likewise, I thank those students who are named within the text and whose comments about peer-tutoring and their own learning experiences as tutors add, we believe, powerfully to the least represented voices in the assessment movement—the voices of students. Indeed, some of these tutors actively assisted in providing editorial feedback for Chapter 1 when it was in its infancy.

Of course, I also thank Penelope Deakin, Director of the Learning Center, for a broad variety of assistance, including providing me with written reports from student tutors that might add to the tone of the book. At least equally important, I offer her thanks for reminding me to "find my voice" at the very beginning of the writing project.

I also appreciate the research support I received from the staff of the SUC–Fredonia library, who, as underfunded as they are, continue to try to help those of us who research and write. Thank you also to Cathleen Henning for her work on the index.

I must also express my deep gratitude to the wonderful assistance and support I received from my coauthor, Kathleen McInerney. Her intellectual and emotional commitment to excellence in teaching and to the inclusion of "the other," prevents the book from becoming distanced from those the assessment movement is about—our students.

Thanks also to Kim, Ingrid, and Patrick whose interest in my work and whose willingness to share their own opinions about testing and education helped keep me moving when the project sometimes began to seem too big. And finally, deepest appreciation to Karen Mills-Courts who sees more than most in a leaf of grass.

Patrick L. Courts

Thank you to all who have been and continue to be my teachers—especially Jim Marshall and John Conner at the University of Iowa for their support and their unflagging commitment to students as well as scholarship. Thanks also to the students in my classes and in the Reading/Writing Center at Augustana College. Working with them has helped me to understand the richness and complexity of learning.

Thanks also to the wonderful people at the Augustana Library for their patient and expert assistance and especially to Barbara Doyle-Wilch for shepherding me along in this project—as if she did not have enough to do. Pat and I are very grateful to Christina Johanssen for her generous assistance as midwife in the final stages of this book. Thanks also to Joan Robinson for her enthusiastic help, despite an enormous workload, with the preparation of portions of the manuscript. And thanks to Kathy Stout for helping me understand computers better.

To all the folks in the Reading/Writing Center at Augustana—Deb Hartley, Carol Pressley, Katie Hansen, and all the tutors—I owe much for their generous support. Char Hawks, the mother of the Center, and Bea Jacobson, who orchestrates the Center with grace, clarity, and love, have contributed more to this book than they will ever know. And I appreciate the patience of all those who listened to and read various sections of this—Charlie Mahaffey, Mike Jerin, Mary Beth Hines, Walt Kurth, and Chuck Hyser.

To the other mother in our family, Joanne Madson, I will always be grateful for the loving and expert parenting she gives to my younger daughter. Without the knowledge that Katie was in such good care, I could not have written much.

To Pat Courts, my gratitude, for convincing me of many things, including, most importantly, that I had something to say here. Without his belief in the urgency of adding students' voices to inform assessment policies, this collaboration never would have found form.

My daughters, Morgan and Katie, daily reinvent the world for me. Their curiosity, patience, and love of Happy Meals contributed to the completion of this book. And, most of all, thanks to my husband, Michael Halstead, for his sociological imagination and abiding support.

Kathleen H. McInerney

Introduction

This book is intended to help anyone who is embarking on the process of assessing students' learning, school curricula, and educational programs. Although we focus primarily on the use of student *portfolios* (collections of selected written work produced by students) and the role they might play in assessing programs and in teaching students in colleges and universities, we believe that the ideas and issues we explore should be relevant and adaptable to those involved in assessment across the entire educational spectrum. Additionally, our emphasis on student portfolios is not intended to minimize other kinds of qualitative, "authentic" approaches to assessment. Rather, we believe that portfolio assessment of programs and individual students involves many of the most complex aspects central to most qualitative assessment approaches, and therefore serves as concrete examples intended to guide anyone engaging in assessment. Most important, however, is our belief that educational assessment *must* contribute to improving the lives and learning processes of students and teachers. Otherwise, why bother?

THE REVOLUTION

The American educational system appears to be poised on the edge of a revolution, but "revolutions" being what they are, they often entail considerable suffering and confusion for all involved. The educational revolution we refer to entails a variety of fashionable buzz words: *performance-based education, outcomes, value-added teaching, Time Quality Management, National Assessment, state-imposed mandates, standardized testing, accountability, portfolios.* . . . And depending on one's understanding of these terms and one's knowledge about teaching, learning, and assessment, this revolution may be symbolized by either a guillotine threatening any and all who choose to dispute the sense of imposed assessment mandates; or, if we educators take charge of our own profession as we approach the twenty-first century, the revolution may be symbolized by a new educational constitution that details the rights and responsibilities of teachers and learners.

Many states have already begun to explore avenues of change in their educational systems, and their work has already begun to suggest exciting possibilities for the future. The State of Vermont has begun massive implementation of student portfolios as part of the teaching-learning-assessment process. Pennsylvania is moving toward outcomes-based education. California is engaging in broadly based experimentation in performance-based models of education. And depending on who is talking in these states, some teachers are excited and energetically embracing the changes while others feel confused and threatened.

In New York, Commissioner of Education Thomas Sobol presented A New Compact for Learning: Improving Public Elementary, Middle, and Secondary Education Results in the 1990s, a document that describes the direction that much of the anticipated educational change will probably take. As such it serves to illustrate what the future appears to hold as well as the aspects that may appear threatening to teachers long accustomed to grade levels, standardized exams, and things as they have been for the last many years in American education. Perhaps, more than anything else, the document illustrates the enormous amount of work that must be done before constructive change can take place.

As part of this new compact, schools will establish "performance standards" intended to mark student "progress, [but] not as 'promotional gates' " (Sobol 1991, 4). The skills, values, and knowledge that students are expected to acquire as they move from elementary through high school will be specifically described. Moreover, "statements of desired outcomes will be specific enough to ensure that all students acquire a solid core of skill and knowledge in the use of the English language; in mathematics and the natural sciences; in the social sciences; and in the humanities and the arts. However, they will be broad enough to permit interdisciplinary studies and local variations in specific content" (Sobol 1991, 4). Underlying the entire project will be a qualitative system of assessment that will move beyond standardized exams to the use of student portfolios and evaluations by teachers based on their observations of students' accomplishments. Additionally, "School and school-district achievement will be reported through annual Comprehensive Assessment reports (as in the Regents Action Plan and the Excellence and Accountability Program) and through periodic School Improvement Reviews, as well as through annual statewide... reports" (Sobol 1991, 6).

Colleges and universities, for their part, will define the abilities, knowledge and thinking skills students need in order to begin their studies in higher education. Likewise, they will assist in "developing measures for assessing" the acquisition of these abilities and skills (Sobol 1991, 15).

Clearly, this is heady stuff. Questions and confusions abound. How will all this change come about? Who will specify the specific kinds of performances expected of students? How will such specification escape the trap of identifying discrete, fragmented skills or bits of information precisely because they are the easiest to assess? How will teachers be (re)trained to work constructively within such a system? And where will the money come from that will be necessary to support such massive change?

At the same time that many states appear to be undertaking such major changes in their educational systems, state legislatures, college administrators, and parents are demanding that higher education begin to hold itself accountable. How much and what are students learning in those four (very expensive) years of college? What do students really learn in those general education programs? How successfully does higher education help students become more literate, critical thinkers? Which colleges should receive the greatest public financial support?

Finally, underlying all this turbulence at the local and state levels of education is a call for National Educational Standards and National Assessment. Patrick Courts' participation in the "Higher Order Thinking and Communications Skills Study Design Workshop" sponsored by the National Center for Education Statistics (November 17–19, 1991) helped us both gain a better understanding of the movement toward national assessment, though we are not always encouraged by all that we understand. This particular working conference was populated by about sixty people, all of whom had different relationships to the assessment movement. Some few, like Courts, had actually been involved in creating and implementing assessment projects. Others seemed primarily interested in obtaining research grants, and some appeared to be promoting particular instruments for assessment. By and large, however, everyone worked hard and in good faith toward the charge: that is, to create a plan to assess college student–learning in support of National Education Goal 5.5. Goal five states that "by the year 2000, every adult American will be literate and will possess the knowledge and skills to compete in a global economy and exercise the rights and responsibilities of citizenship" (*America 2000* National Education Goal 5.5).

We were encouraged, to some extent, about the areas of agreement that grew out of this first phase of the development process. As Sal Corallo, workshop coordinator, wrote in his letter to participants (March 12, 1992): "Most considered a useful assessment not an end unto itself but a means of diagnosing and correcting problems in the teaching/learning process." Many participants favored "institution-specific or bottom-up development and administration of the instrument(s)." At the same time that we found such sentiments encouraging, however, we were concerned by a subtle undercurrent that seemed to guide much of the discussion. Few, it seemed, had questioned the reasons or sense motivating a national assessment. With the exception of some powerful statements made by Ted Marchese, Trudy Banta, Ed Morante, Pat Courts, Ernest Benjamin, and Peter Ewell (in fact, by many of the people who made up "Group 2"), there appeared to be tacit agreement that a national assessment is a good idea.

But National Goal 5.5 calls for helping citizens to become literate, productive members of a global economy, and to some of us, the idea of beginning with assessment seemed to be a little backwards. First, or at least simultaneously, we must find ways of helping people become more literate, more creative/critical reasoners, and more knowledgeable, an effort that is enough to make one dizzy.

At any rate, the workshops reemphasized our concern that assessment be directly tied to improving instruction and to improving the quality of the lives of students and teachers. And it is this concern that causes us to repeat, throughout this book, that assessment tools and approaches must be controlled locally by teachers, that they must be informed by attempts to better understand the needs and abilities of students, and that their purposes must be constructive rather than destructive.

Of course, we do not pretend to know what will happen as a result of this educational revolution. Given the fact that educational systems are notoriously impervious to change, perhaps nothing will happen, and business will be conducted as usual. But given the additional fact that American schools, teachers, and students are suffering through tremendous difficulties these days, perhaps this will be the educational revolution that actually occurs. And if we, including all of you, can be a part of articulating what needs to occur and of implementing constructive changes, the future looks exciting. One thing is for certain—some future is clearly ahead.

Our own immediate concerns, however, focus on the assessment movement in American education, particularly at the college level. Although we have hope for the constructive possibilities that appear to be inherent in performance-based models of education, we are also concerned—deeply concerned—that the teaching and learning process will be subsumed by assessment, that teaching and learning will become even more test-driven than they presently are. Because we favor qualitative, authentic approaches to assessment, because we believe that local control of assessment is essential, and because we want to keep teachers and learners at the center of the enterprise, we have written this book.

Our book, then, begins with a highly critical examination of multiple-choice, standardized testing, then moves to a discussion of the human beings who populate the world of higher education and the psychosocial constructs that surround them. In Chapter 2, this discussion is firmly based in the belief that respect for diversity of all kinds is essential to the creation of a healthy society, and it grows out of a concern that national assessment movements may accidentally (conveniently?) "forget" the human beings who are being assessed. Chapters 3 and 4 will explore the nature and use of student portfolios in assessment, the steps that might be taken to make the implementation of portfolios less troublesome than it may be, and, more importantly from our point of view, the role that the portfolios might play in improving programs, instruction, and the quality of students' learning. Finally, we will offer a broad variety of approaches to teaching and learning across the curriculum that we hope will be helpful to those who wish to be a constructive part of the changes that are ahead.

_____

CHAPTER 1

Testing, Anyone? Rhetoric and Realities

Support for using standardized tests to reform our public schools is mounting rapidly. Such tests are increasingly used to measure students' achievement and to make decisions about the placement of students, the competence of teachers, and the quality of schools. President Bush's "America 2000" plan proposes to extend that thrust to the federal level by establishing a national test for students at different points in schooling, from the elementary grades through high school.

A growing body of research, however, indicates serious problems with American testing, at least with how it is currently conceived.... "[O]ur testing policies have failed to achieve many of their intended positive effects, while creating some clearly negative consequences for the quality of schools and equality of educational opportunity." (Darling-Hammond and Lieberman 1992, B1)

New state proposals for common outcomes testing are coming forward again. On top of them, a *national* assessment effort has unfolded with astonishing consensus, force, and speed. These developments, I believe, return us to some old, basic issues about the role of assessment in public accountability. (Ewell 1991, 12)

To say that assessment is a "hot" topic in education from elementary school all the way through undergraduate and professional education is an understatement. No country is as committed to ongoing testing, measuring, and assessment of its students as is the United States. In the following discussion, we intend first to address the testing, measuring, and assessing that characterizes elementary and high school testing (from IQ tests, kindergarten screening tests, Iowa Tests, Stanford Achievement Tests, to SATs (Scholastic Aptitude Tests) and PSATs (Preliminary Scholastic Aptitude Tests); we will focus primarily on standardized, multiple-choice tests. After briefly examining the sense and nonsense of these kinds of tests, we will address the assessment movement in higher education, the desirability and efficacy of "off-the-shelf" tests used in many of these assessments, and the movement toward locally controlled, faculty-developed systems of assessment. Finally, we will make a case for "starting over," arguing, first, that the assessors themselves must examine their reasons for assessing anything and, second, that they need to define, exactly, what or who it is they are assessing. We agree with Laurel Blyth Riegel who writes,

> The evaluation and assessment system in public education must become more individual-referenced. It must rely on sensitive assessment to detect individual needs in a variety of areas, all of which are not simply academic. We need to define the "learner" as one who needs to know, and then proceed with the identification of what that encompasses for each learner. Needs may shift as our nation and the world changes. Our system must be flexible enough to accommodate evolution *and revolution*, and not incarcerate itself in outdated ideas of personal excellence. (1992, 23)

All too often, it seems to us, those who create the tests are far (entirely?) removed from the specific programs, curricula, and students to be tested. This lack of connection results in "generic" tests—tests that simply (or complexly) engage in assessing something, but what exactly the nature of that "something" is often remains clouded in jargon: that is, while the tests may "clearly" state that they are assessing a given program, ability, or skill, the specific elements within the program to be assessed are often fuzzily articulated; or, while a given skill (reading, writing) may be identified, the complex nature of the skill is often poorly delineated and unrelated to the genuine nature of the ability or skill to be tested (Paris et al., 1991, 12; Marzano 1990).

Consider the new, state-of-the-art SAT II Writing Test. Appearing to recognize the shortcoming of its past attempts to report scores indicating students' "aptitude" as writers, the Educational Testing Service (ETS) created this new test for college-bound students. Because of its potential popularity (and the power that college admissions offices have granted ETS), this test "will have a potentially greater impact on high school teaching than the current English Composition Test with Essay," another weak testing instrument (Hilgers and Marsella 1992, 8). Since it is an unfortunate truism of assessment that we teach what we assess, what is it that the new, improved writing test will cause high school teachers to teach? "Essentially, error detection and correction, stylistic awareness, and drafting impromptus under pressure in twenty minutes—hardly what most people would consider composing an essay" (Hilgers and Marsella 1992, 8). And as Hilgers and Marsella correctly suggest, this whole effort is backwards because tests—often inappropriate, invalid tests—handcuff teachers by dictating curricula and focusing the educational system on high test scores rather than on student learning.

As Russ Edgerton, President of the American Association of Higher Education (AAHE), points out, however:

In a poll taken in September [1991], 82 percent of Americans agreed that the nation "needs common national standards of performance that all schools should be expected to live up to." And 80 percent agreed that "this country should know how American students perform compared with world-class standards." This is a movement, it seems to us at AAHE [American Association for Higher Education], full of consequences, dangers, and new opportunities for higher education. We can sit by and watch, and wake up later to the consequences. Or we can engage the issues now and try to shape the course the movement will take. (1991, 9–10)

Let us begin, then, by suggesting that the only good reason for assessing either programs or student learning in education is to revolutionize—to change radically—what presently constitutes education in America. If the assessment movement cannot or will not lead to major changes and improvements in the teaching/learning enterprise, it has no good reason for being. Of course, such a position obviously suggests an explicit bias: education at all levels has become overly bureaucratized, devoted primarily to maintaining itself as an institution rather than to the teaching and learning of students. Elementary and high school systems succeed primarily as conveyor-belt systems intent on moving students from one grade to the next with little emphasis on any real learning. Colleges and universities too often focus on research and the transmission of information with little explicit attention paid to genuine learning.

STANDARDIZED EXAMS: OBJECTIONABLE OBJECTIVITY

First, then, an examination of standardized tests and the role they play in schools and assessment begins with this direct assertion: there is no good reason whatsoever for using standardized tests of any kind in assessing the developmental stages, abilities, and/or progress that students are making as they move through elementary school, high school, and college. But let us immediately qualify that statement by saying that this is not so much an argument against legitimate assessment of growth and learning or of curricula as much as it is an argument against standardized, multiple-choice exams (and surrogates like the SAT II Writing Test). We are particularly concerned about the potentially invidious, destructive role that standardized, multiple-choice instruments will play in any kind of national assessment [Report of Committee C (1991), 54]. Likewise, we agree with Liz Darling-Hammond and Ann Lieberman who point out:

Rather than supporting the American traditions of experimentation and local control, the proposed national tests would create a *de facto* national curriculum, and a limited one at that. By stifling further reforms aimed at creating curricula that emphasize thinking skills, and by failing to involve teachers or principals in a more sophisticated local assessment process, the national tests would foreclose the pervasive educational chance that we need. (1992, B2)

In fact, the only conceivable reason we can see for continuing to use standardized exams (aside from the profit motive of the testing services) is to guarantee that an already monolithic, intractable educational system will be impossible to change in any constructive ways because all change is geared toward producing better scores on meaningless tests. The test scores become the system's *raison d'être*: programs, funding, curricula, staffing—everything depends on standardized-test scores. The primary job of students is to take standardized tests and earn high scores. Ideas, activities—learning in general that is not directly related to the tests—are attacked as frivolous and unnecessary. Knowing that we teach what we assess, the system looks to the assessment instrument (a standardized test) and teaches to the test, over and over, for years (Paris, et al. 1991).

In some cases testing begins as early as kindergarten, but almost no one moves beyond third grade without having undergone some major form of standardized testing. It may seem ludicrous to argue that a first grader is already educationally behind his/her peers, that s/he must be assigned to a prekindergarten, followed by a pre–first grade, and so on. But many school systems use standardized reading tests, IQ tests, and similar instruments that will actually label students in this manner, relegating them to what must seem like a lifetime of always being "pre-" everything (Perrone 1992). Moreover, this kind of labeling is dependent on the notion that we know what we mean by a first- or second- or tenth-*grade level*— a notion based on a belief that everyone of a given age should, for some reason, be able to do and know the same things. Offhand, outside of school, we can think of no place that a notion like chronologically based grade levels would ever be allowed to function.

Of course, although one might argue that it is important to identify "problem students" early, to identify students who are not "up to grade level," so that we can help these students, the result is often destructive. Using standardized tests for the early identification of students with problems usually results in labeling them "remedial," learning disabled, or some such equally offensive label. Aside from the potentially devastating news that a perfectly normal five-year-old is already "behind" (behind what? the educational eight ball!), such early identification of problems almost certainly creates more problems than it solves. Instead of actually helping such students and allowing them to learn at their own pace, the system normally relegates them to special classes seldom designed to do much other than keep them together in a classroom and guarantee that they will remain remedial for most of their formal schooling. The self-fulfilling prophecy of school failure is established immediately. And the fact that the initial identification of the individual student is based on a standardized test of highly questionable validity seems to bother almost no one except, perhaps, the parents and their children who are victimized by such decisions (Paris et al. 1991).

The system has succeeded by blaming the learner (who simply does not have what it takes to succeed) and proceeds to label the child "remedial." Likewise, at the same time that the system purports to indicate its sensitivity to the learner's unfortunate problem by trying to remediate the learner, it takes itself off the hook by officially designating these students as unlikely to succeed in school because, after all, they are remedial. Jill Sunday Bartoli describes the "art of being stupid":

> Once a label of incompetence is conferred, and the equilibrium of the school system is restored (with respect to the "normal" others, the child's continued [and expected] failure . . . confirms the scientific diagnosis and the label becomes official. The school personnel dismiss the possibility that the fragmented curriculum or subskill teaching may be part of the problem (after all, the child has the problem— the label proves that), and the teacher feels nothing can be done. Fewer demands are made on the child, more exceptions are made, and the failure to learn is tolerated along with other deviance appropriate to the label. (1986, 18)

The child, writes Bartoli, learns to excuse herself from school. Thus it is that standardized testing and the use of such test scores to label and place students genuinely represents a solipsistic protection of the system by the system and for the system. It is a system in which teaching and learning are lost. The exciting road to being and knowing is blocked by the decision that a given individual is behind in being and knowing and will probably remain behind because s/he is a remedial "be-er" and and "knower." Indeed, it genuinely looks as though the purpose of such systems of testing is primarily devoted to maintaining the concept of grade levels rather than to serving the learners: such tests enforce a new reading of the timeworn cliché "a place for each and each in his/her place" with a vengeance—and an apparently cost-effective vengeance, at that.

So it is, then, that schools continue to test regularly throughout the school years, labeling students, placing them in groups from which it is difficult to escape, either intentionally or unintentionally, and deciding that some students will succeed because they are in the groups we expect to succeed while others will not succeed because they simply are not able to do so (and we usually feel very badly about those who are unable to succeed, but that is just the way life is). And if these opening remarks seem too radical, extremist, or unjust, we defy anyone to explain the underlying sense of the systems used to establish reading levels or grade levels as determined on standardized reading tests, the tests most often used to pigeonhole students. What exactly is a seventh-grade reading level? A twelfth-grade level? What are the criteria used to establish these levels? And what do standardized tests have to do with the actual process of reading anyway? How do multiple-choice tests based on single-word analogies, punctuation, grammar, and usage assess someone's ability to read or write?

Standardized Assessment in Reading and Writing

Standardized tests of reading (like those of writing) seldom have anything to do with any kind of normal reading (or writing) process and are notoriously unrelated to actual individual reading performance, especially when one considers extended texts and complex, critical thinking. Most of the tests consist of short pieces of prose followed by a set of multiple-choice questions. Weak test takers do poorly because they follow the directions ("Be sure you read the entire passage before answering the questions, and do not guess if you do not know the answer.") Good test takers ignore the directions, read the questions first, find the answers and guess when they cannot identify an answer—or even ignore the text altogether: "One study found that, when given the questions without reading passages, students did just as well as those who read the passages" (Beach and Marshall 1991, 224). Indeed the worst thing one can do on one of these tests is make the mistake of being interested in whatever it is the reading passage is about because this will take up time and cause the reader to think about what s/he is reading instead of merely identifying the "correct" answer.

In fact, good test takers know intuitively that test taking and thinking are not necessarily related activities. It is at least possible that those students who have already become totally cynical and accepted the inherent nonsense of the system are the ones who do best, and those who are still trying to make sense of the system and/or the test are the ones who will do worst.

But even at that, what is "best" and "worst" if it has little to do with real reading? The fact is that this kind of assessment probably does a good job of identifying those students who are good at, and will continue to be good at, taking such tests, an ability that may have much to do with success in the American school system, but little do to with much else. And why are we doing this kind of assessment in the first place: what is the purpose of this obsession with standardized testing? What does all this achieve? The answer is that we use these tests in order to "objectively" compare the performance of one group of students with the performance of another group so that we can make judgments about the success, failure, or quality of a given school or given program in relationship to other schools and/or programs. But since the tests assess nothing of importance, why would we want to make such comparisons in the first place— especially at such great cost? Of course, the answer is all too clear: this kind of assessment puts the overseers—boards of education, state and federal governments—in firm control of curriculum and what goes on in schools and keeps decisions out of the hands of students and teachers and parents. And such a system also guarantees that education will be directed at teaching students to perform well on these tests rather than at helping them to become active, articulate, literate learners. Instead of *improving* teaching and learning, this system supports a fraudulent sense of accountability and an outdated, "surface level" view of learning (Beckwith 1991, 17–19).

"Surely," you say, "things must get better as one moves up the rungs of the educational ladder." But consider the SATs and the ACTs (American College Testing) and while you are considering them, remember that the agencies that make and score these tests do so for money, just as did the agencies that sold those standardized reading comprehension tests that were given in first grade, fourth grade, seventh grade, ninth grade, and eleventh grade. The federal government invests heavily in testing, and the testing industry profits: A $1.4 million contract was recently awarded to American College Testing in Iowa City for the construction of tests to determine how well America's youth are prepared for the workplace ("Company Contracts" 1992, A10).

A brief visit to Princeton Testing quickly evidences that a considerable amount of money is involved in the testing business. As Paris et al. point out:

> [C]ommercial publishers reap large profits from the sale of achievement tests, scoring services, and data reports. Many districts routinely test all their students in Grades 2–12 every year, and the National Commission on Testing and Public Policy (1990) estimates that the equivalent of 20 million school days are spent each year by American children just *taking* tests (and perhaps 10–20 times that many days are spent in preparation for the tests). The commission estimates that direct costs to taxpayers of purchasing and scoring state and local tests may exceed $100 million per year. Adding in related services pushes the bill to nearly half a billion dollars annually, and even that does not include the cost of curriculum materials that publishers produce to fit the tests. No other country in the world has as much achievement testing as the U.S.A. nor allows such extensive commercial profiteering. (1991, 13)

And those interested in assessment have not really lived until they have had the experience of having someone from American College Testing try to "sell" them the ACT COMP (College Outcomes Measures Project) as the best off-the-shelf assessment tool available for measuring growth in higher education. After showing the buyers the shiny new test, these salespersons walk them through the array of scores and subscores they will be able to send: "It's all very easy and quick and you don't even need to know too much about assessment to use these tests." (Indeed, the less you know, the better the tests look.) These salespeople seldom say much about what is actually being tested or how given test items measure what they purport to measure. No one talks much about the appropriateness or sense of the test itself, but they sure have lots of scores and subscores. And anything that produces that many scores and subscores must be legitimate. "You want numbers? We got numbers." "What do the numbers mean?" you ask. And the reply: "Simply look at the title of the category the numbers come under and you'll understand. See, that number is for critical reasoning, so that's how well this student reasons critically. Get it?" "Got it." "Good!"

Indeed, even as we were writing, we received an invitation to meet in the hospitality suite of the creators of *COLLEGE BASE*, an instrument that is advertised to be singularly capable of measuring students' success in the "core" curriculum. If we will go to this hospitality suite, we are told, we will relax with friends, partake of refreshments, learn all about the test, and even receive a poster full of important terms and definitions having to do with assessment. Note that we do not intend to criticize the test here: the point is to remind everyone that this is big business that is involved here. These tests are products that are marketed just like other products. One might reasonably ask, however, how any off-the-shelf test could accurately measure mastery of an institution's core curriculum without first considering the specific elements that comprise any given curriculum? At the college level, we suspect that gullible administrators long divorced from teaching and students and interested primarily in cost-effective, quick solutions are easy prey for the salespeople of Testworld U.S.A.

But as we all know, the ACTs and the SATs are the most used tests for determining whether or not a student will get into a given college and, in many states, whether or not a student will get into college at all. And given the fine, open, liberal minds that characterize most college faculties, registrars, and administrators, one would naturally assume that these tests are valid determiners of . . . of what? If they are valid determiners of one's potential to succeed in a given college, then they represent the single most critical comment one could possibly make about what it is that colleges are doing. That is, if your ability to perform exceptionally well on a standardized, multiple-guess test indicates your likely success at college X, then it is likely that college X rewards people who do well on standardized tests. It is likely that college X relies on multiple choice tests in many of the courses its students take. It is likely that college X is like too many colleges and universities in the United States and pays relatively little attention to what students are actually learning (or not learning).

Reconsider what the acronym SAT stands for and what these tests purport to test. Because SAT stands for Scholastic *Aptitude* Test, these tests presumably assess one's aptitude for success in college. Consequently, a decline in scores suggests that students have less aptitude than they used to. Perhaps you know what that suggestion means, but we confess we do not—unless, of course, it means that students do less well on these tests than they used to, but we do not know why that matters in the first place because no one appears able to explain why the tests are worthwhile assessment instruments except insofar as they correlate with success in college. As we have already suggested, that these tests correlate at all with success may be more a critical commentary on higher education than evidence of the quality of the tests. And if this all sounds circular and silly, it is because it is circular and silly (Crouse and Trusheim 1988).

Of course, the fact is that these tests are useless as predictors of a student's likelihood of succeeding or failing in college. Taken alone, high school–grades are as good a predictor; high school–grades viewed along with such test scores are only slightly better predictors. Even more devastating is this information: these tests operate as negative predictors for minorities and students of color, a fact that is especially true in relation to the verbal scores. But anyone who knows anything about sociolinguistics and nonstandard dialects could hardly be surprised by such information.

Interestingly, though again not terribly surprising, the math scores on the SATs are also weak predictors of a student's potential for doing college-level mathematics. One is left with this rather serious question: if the SATs are intended to indicate a student's aptitude for success in college, and neither the verbal nor the math scores effectively predict success or failure, then why are these tests being used and what are they for (Crouse and Trusheim 1988; Greene 1988)?

That the tests predict so poorly is, of course, ironic, highly problematic, and clearly destructive, given the fact that many institutions use them to decide whether or not a student will be admitted. Equally important, however, is the fact that student scores on these tests are used by politicians and educators alike for the basis of apocalyptic pronouncements about the state of education and as support for undisguised attacks on elementary and high school–teachers, professors, and the world of the intellect.

Apocalypse Now: The Heart of Darkness

We doubt anyone who reads could have escaped the recent furor over the national "declines" in scores on the math and verbal sections of the SATs. A brief examination of the kinds of comments reported in the press surrounding this apparently devastating drop in scores is revealing. Prominently featured on the front page of the *Buffalo News* (August 27, 1991) was the following included in an article by Lee Mitgang: "Math averages also declined for the first time in eleven years: down 2 points from last year to 474. . . . Scores on the verbal section averaged 422—the weakest showing since national data were kept in 1969. Verbal averages had risen from 424 in 1980 to a recent peak of 431 in 1985, but have since eroded steadily." In the same report former U.S. Secretary of Education Lamar Alexander comments on this dire situation as follows: " 'The simple fact is that even our best students generally don't know enough and can't do enough to assure success in tomorrow's world.' " (How this would be evidenced by an aptitude test is beyond us, but one also simply has to question the truth of the assertion.) The fact is that our best students are extraordinarily good and capable. But people like Lamar Alexander and others are able to make disparaging remarks about American colleges and college students because the U.S. sends approximately "66 percent of its kids on to higher education" while "Germany and Japan weigh in at 32 percent and 30 percent respectively," restricting the college experience in ways that make it available to "openly the most academically gifted students" ("Why We Still Live Best" 1991, 90). In short, anyone who wishes to bother with relatively silly and poorly documented comparisons of U.S. college students versus those of other major industrial countries like Germany and Japan should be comparing the top 30 percent of our high school–graduates and the top 50 percent of our college graduates with all those of the other countries. On the other hand, aside from the desire to bash American higher education and mislead the public, why would anyone want to make such comparisons in the first place?

In the same *Buffalo News* report, it was stated that "Donald Stewart, board president, warned that SAT results signal a growing gulf between a top scoring 'educational elite and an underclass of students academically ill-prepared for the demands of college in the workplace.' " Echoing this relatively obvious fact about American Society, an editorial in the *Buffalo News* [September 1, 1991, F8] points out that the decline in SAT scores indicates a "growing gap in pupil preparation hurts America." The writer continues: "It isn't so much the decline of a few points in the average results of the 1991 Scholastic Aptitude Tests that ought to worry school leaders, although that's disappointing. More frightening is that a chasm may be widening between a high-scoring 'educational elite' and a growing group of the academically ill-prepared."

Keeping in mind that the essential uselessness of the SATs continues to underlie this discussion, the above quotations are significant because they identify an educational elite who are in training to run the country and an educational underclass who may well be entirely locked out of the mainstream of education and society in general. But while these statements suggest a terrifying reality, did we need SATs to tell us about an educational elite and the gap between them and the ill-prepared?

The *Buffalo News* editorial further asserts: "A fundamental purpose of common public education in our democratic society is to pry open the doors of knowledge to produce useful citizens and opportunity for all youngsters." But again one must ask, while agreeing with the assertion, how does testing of any kind contribute to achieving this desirable end?

There are, of course, those who defend the tests and want to emphasize the implications of the results. And it can come as little surprise that one such defender is the highly conservative Dinesh D'Souza. In his editorial, "Standardized Tests Are Imperfect But Necessary," D'Souza argues that although there are problems with the SATs, it "serves as a kind of academic thermometer. It is no remedy to stomp on the instrument and call for a new device that would register a more congenial temperature. Such a strategy seems to evade real problems that lie in the area of performance, not measurement" (1991, B3).

But these tests have little or nothing to do with important areas of performance or measurement, and D'Souza fails to recognize the irony and contradiction inherent in his position: if the SATs are the "academic thermometer," is the temperature really worth taking? If the thermometer used reveals little about the individual's condition and/or the nature of the disease, what is the point? And what problem will be solved if we simply teach to these tests? Perhaps the patient will begin to exhibit the correct temperature, but will this indicate genuine health? In fact, D'Souza falls into a trap that is relatively easy to fall into when discussing standardized tests of any kind: if one begins with the cliché that "it may not be perfect, but it is the best we have," one may be led to believe that, imperfect as they are, these standardized tests are worth using. But such a position is absurd given the fact that, perfect or imperfect, these tests are essentially valueless: what exactly they test is almost impossible to determine, and they clearly victimize people and block their opportunities to move out of the underclass (Crouse and Trusheim 1988; Paris 1992; Perrone 1992).

On the other hand, what we have said here suggests that D'Souza argues in good faith and believes what he writes: is it possible that he is simply playing another role in what is now a twelve-year-long attack on teachers, students, and the world of education? An attack that has consistently operated from a negative, destructive point of view, pointing to "failures" in public education at the same time that those who do the attacking always assert that real support in the form of funding will not solve the problem. That is, as the news articles already cited suggest that "throwing money at the problem will not solve it," one wonders whether or not just a little of that money might not relieve the overcrowding in inner-city schools, perhaps allowing high school–teachers in Queens, Watts, or the Southside of Chicago to teach fewer than five sections of thirty-five students each per day; perhaps allowing computer instruction in mathematics and word processing to take place with fewer than three students to each computer (in the few schools that have any computers at all); perhaps allowing teachers to participate in faculty development workshops; perhaps allowing libraries in these schools to buy some books.

It is an inescapable irony and shame that we so readily seek funds from most of the major industrial powers of the West and most of the Arab world in order to have a good, "new-fashioned" war with "smart" weapons, but the war on poverty and illiteracy is to be fought with little more than goodwill and the blood, sweat, and tears of the teachers and students who struggle against incredible odds to escape the world of the so-called underclass. Apparently it's a good idea to "throw money" at wars and machines of destruction. It is just bad to do it to help people. (Smart weapons rather than smart kids? Which would you choose?)

D'Souza, however, wants us to attack the "root problem," which he identifies as follows:

> The gap in mean test scores tells us that there are serious problems to address, such as terrible neighborhoods, ineffective public schools, inequitable access to resources. Unfortunately, instead of addressing the root problems and taking up hard questions such as illiteracy, lack of motivation, and social pathologies in our elementary and secondary schools, critics and activists have decided to fault the test. (1991)

This view incorrectly suggests that test scores have something to do with "taking up those root problems" and unjustly suggests that the critics simply wish to attack the tests. Quite the opposite is true, however: as two of those critics, we want everyone to rethink the reasons for all the testing and focus the assessment movement on improving teaching and learning. Forget all these test scores, and address the revolutionary socioeconomic and political decisions that must be made in order to change the "social pathologies" that are engendered by the poverty, crime, and racism that typify major segments of our society and particularly the segments that appear to have lower scores on the tests. The problem lies not with the tests' critics who fault the tests. The problem is caused by the false prophets and politicians who want to suggest that the tests mean something concrete, but who do not want to do anything about righting the wrongs that D'Souza correctly identifies as part of a "root problem" (1991, B3).

Certainly one of the most bizarre comments on the entire issue appears in Muriel Cohen's news report that "Diane Ravitch, deputy U.S. education secretary and a noted education researcher and writer, said the decline among the best students reflected a deficit in vocabulary and reasoning power."

" 'There is too much TV, not enough reading; the results are confirming everything we know about kids' and parents' behavior. *TV is written in short declarative sentences,*' said Ravitch" (Cohen 1991). Because we have been long interested in linguistics and discourse theory, we were fascinated and puzzled by Ravitch's claim. Surely we had been missing something about the language on TV. Knowing that almost no one reads TV scripts except those in the television business, and knowing that defining a "sentence" in oral language is more than a little complex, we decided to look into the matter more closely. Of course, we knew from our own delight in viewing TV soap operas and sitcoms, news, specials, movies, and so on that Ravitch's comment could not possibly be applied to most of these shows, and that left us the need to revisit children's shows.

Since the comment does not apply either to "Mr. Rogers' Neighborhood" or to "Sesame Street"—shows in which perfectly normal language is used, we assumed Ravitch must be referring to the language of Saturday morning cartoon shows. Having subjected ourselves to several of these shows ("Captain Planet," NBC; "Ninja Turtles," CBS; "Addams Family," ABC), we find ourselves still puzzled by what Ravitch might have meant in her condemnation of TV. The language of television shows is, by and large, normal language consisting of independent and dependent clauses, if-then structures, declarations, interrogations, commands, and so on. And this focus on language does not even begin to examine the fact that many of the children's shows "teach" kids about many of the same plots, myths, conflicts, and thematic issues that inform medieval romance and Shakespearean comedies. Indeed, the results of Susan Neuman's research on television and its affects on the literacy of younger viewers directly contradict the opinions expressed by Ravitch. Neuman writes:

> Television is a wonderful nemesis for those inclined to fret over the education of the young. It has been accused of robbing youngsters of childhood, reducing attention spans, and impairing children's ability to think clearly. Critics blame television for the decline in basic traditional academic skills and for problems ranging from dropping SAT scores to illiteracy. Young viewers are presented as bleary-eyed addicts, incapable of the mental effort needed to sharply focus on ideas in a sustained manner.

This chapter has found no evidence to support these claims. While television is clearly not an educational panacea, the charges against the medium have been unwarranted. Television viewing has replaced neither book reading nor homework, and has not lessened the desire for achievement. Rather, the medium is used selectively by children to serve their functional needs. And what they and their families chose to do with television is closely interwoven with expectations for future achievement and overall educational goals. (1991, 158–159)

Consequently we are left with the conclusion that this kind of comment from Ravitch is simply another political ploy using the old game of TV-bashing to suggest that problems would be solved if we simply stopped kids from watching television instead of actually facing the depth and complexity of the problems facing learners and teachers in most major city school systems.

Of course, the newspaper articles and ballyhoo continue, though much that is in the popular press is seriously repetitious. As we read the attacks on education and students that are primarily based on results from standardized tests, however, a little refrain keeps echoing in our heads. It is something a friend of ours often says, usually referring to his own life: "What's it all mean?" And the answer is that it probably does not mean very much in terms of any real information about students, teachers, and education, but even if it did, we would be hard put to figure it out. What it may mean, however, is this: while many of us are aware of the massive problems facing students and educators in this country; while we know that poverty, crime, racism, ethnocentrism, inadequate teacher preparation, underfunding, and the like contribute to causing the problems; while we can identify the complex socioeconomic factors that make illiteracy endemic among certain groups and assure that they will not be able to escape the poverty in which they are immersed and that the present system of education will never allow them to get into a college let alone succeed there; we argue about the importance of slippage in scores on standardized exams.

At some point, everyone must reject the diversionary tactics exemplified by someone like former Vice President Quayle who pretended to blame societal problems on television shows like "Murphy Brown." Quayle apparently wished us to believe that television has eroded long cherished family values (like valuing a good education); that it is not homelessness, unemployment, poverty, crime and drugs that cause problems; it is television and some anomalous group called the "cultural elite." It is these kinds of attacks, operating from the most twisted logic, that allow people to suggest that Rodney King, lying on the ground being beaten by Los Angeles police, was the person in control of the situation. What, one wonders, were the television shows that shaped the values of the police involved in that beating? What television shows did those responsible for the savings-and-loan debacle watch? What were their SAT scores?

Likewise, the political response to the total failure of society to meet the needs of many learners is to fault the learners and the teachers (or television or rap music) as the causes of weak performances on standardized tests, suggesting that if we can improve their performance on these tests, the problem will have been solved (especially if we also remove dangerous television shows like "Murphy Brown"). In these terms, assessment is a facade used by those in power to assure that the real problems and the genuine causes of these problems will never be confronted. And the rhetoric of the politicos in this forum is to attack the teachers, who say they want us to stop emphasizing testing and start emphasizing teaching and learning, to stop saying how badly everyone is doing and start giving them the tools to do a proper job so that they can engage problems of teaching and learning in complex society.

Hidden Truths?

But if you do not particularly believe this rhetoric, if you agree with D'Souza and you remain disturbed by the decline in standardized test scores, even then, you must consider that the population taking the tests has changed radically over the past two decades. More and more minority students, students from impoverished school systems, students whose lives are lived out in the carnage of the inner cities are taking the tests. So the scores go down a little. What is new? Where is the surprise? Did we need these scores to show us that most major cities are failing miserably in the area of education and that their failure is the result of a complex set of socioeconomic factors? Anyone who has taught in such schools or who has read about them knows full well that they are characterized by a poverty of the spirit as well as a physical poverty. Children and young adults in these schools see failure all around them; they often suffer from poor health, sometimes a lack of food, often terrible living conditions. Crime is rampant, and fear is everywhere. We ourselves taught students on the Southside of Chicago who liked school because it represented a clean, warm place where they received warm food at lunchtime. Nevertheless, the doors to the school were locked after the students arrived, not to keep students in, but to keep criminals out.

Apparently we need a national assessment program to determine that these students are not likely to do as well, not likely to learn as much, not likely to be the same kinds of fine thinkers as their well-fed counterparts in the private schools and suburbs. And what do we assert after assessing such students: schools are inadequate in these areas; teachers are frustrated and sometimes in a state of despair; drugs are the problem; certification requirements are too weak and teachers are not well-enough prepared to teach these students; television is ruining everyone's minds; and the popular culture, in general, is less "good" than it used to be—of course, that mythic time when the popular culture was "better" and when schools did a better job of preparing students for school was a time that was actually characterized by the racial and economic prejudices that worked together to allow a nation to ignore entirely students of color and students who lived in abject poverty. We find it ironic that our politicians seem to care most about these students and their problems only after the tests show us that there is a problem. We find it disgusting that the solution to the problem could be envisioned in newer, "improved" standardized tests.

Okay, that opinion still may sound like liberal claptrap. The fact is that the test scores went down and it sounds like nicely finessed *political correctness* to revise the facts and say that they only went down because a new population is taking the tests. The fact (and we use the term *fact* very loosely here) is this: test scores show that students in general are not as strong as they used to be, do not perform as well on these tests as they used to, do not have as much aptitude for college as they used to, and things are really getting worse. But even if we stay within the claustrophobic circle of the tests, for the moment, one would be hard put to support the negative point I have just stated using the SAT scores reported in the newspapers. Even in the solipsistic, isolated world of standardized tests, anyone familiar with the SAT knows that most people who consider the scores on the tests look at a 50-point plus-or-minus "soft spot"; that is, a change of 100 points might actually indicate that something dramatic has occurred. What exactly would have changed would still remain much of a puzzle, but if you choose to get seriously concerned over this kind of thing, wait until the change is 100 points and then get hysterical.

And what was President Bush's response to this state of affairs? What did the "education president" do about all this? You probably already know or have guessed. The first part of his new education agenda was to mandate more testing and measuring—more assessment. We needed, say Bush and his advisors like Diane Ravitch and Chester Finn, to test more and more widely so that we might compare all these populations. Now we ask you, what do you think we will find out through such comparisons? That students in Detroit do not fare as well as those in Ann Arbor? That students in the Chicago public schools do as poorly as students in the Los Angeles school system? That students surrounded by illiteracy, poverty, and crime do not score as highly as those raised in highly literate, upper-middle-class households? And as we say this, we ask you to remember that we are not talking about comparisons about good or bad people, smart or dumb people, innate or learned intelligence—we are referring only to what this system of testing reveals. At best, standardized tests reveal what we already know. Put more directly, why would anyone begin educational reform with more standardized testing? We suspect that at least part of the answer is that it is cheaper and easier to focus on testing than it is to focus on changing what is going on in major public school systems in the United States.

We repeat, however, that the only reason to participate in any kind of assessment process is to use assessment as a means for radically revolutionizing education, to use assessment as a means of refocusing education on the students and their learning rather than on meaningless test scores. Since we know the machine is "broke," we need to stop testing it and start overhauling it.

So far this may sound like an attack on the mistreatment of minorities that is caused by standardized testing. And even though that would be a perfectly reasonable attack, though it is nothing particularly new, the problem we wish to address goes well beyond such a specific focus. Given the concerted attacks launched against teachers and students in the elementary schools and high schools of the United States, and given the aggressive attacks on intellectuals, liberals, humanists, and professors that characterized William Bennett's tenure as secretary of education, it is little surprise that "assessment mania" has entered the world of higher education at a gallop. It is less of a surprise (though quite a disappointment) that assessment in higher education is sometimes characterized by many of the same ironies and blindnesses that characterize all the testing and measuring that preceded it.

Assessing the Ivory Tower

The momentum for assessment in higher education is fueled by powerful calls for national assessment in the schools: Thomas Kean, former governor of New Jersey, leads an organization called *Educate America*, "which has asked Congress to establish a mandatory test for all high school seniors. The National Educational Goals Panel itself has spawned a *National Council on Education Standards and Testing*, which will report on " 'the feasibility and desirability of a national testing system' " (Edgerton 1991, 9).

In higher education, the push for assessment often begins with a mandate of some sort. In 1986 the National Governor's Association called for the implementation of assessment programs in higher education that would genuinely measure what it is that undergraduates are learning. Governor John Ashcroft of Missouri, chair of the National Governors' Association Task Force on College Quality said, " 'The public has a right to know and understand the quality of undergraduate education that young people receive from publicly funded colleges. . . . They have a right to know that their resources are being wisely invested and committed. . . . We need not just more money for education, we need more education for the money' " (Hutchings and Marchese 1990, 16).

Additional external pressure comes from the federal government as "accrediting agencies face U.S. Department of Education (1988) and Council on Postsecondary Accreditation (1987) rules that stipulate, as a condition for their own approval, that they must require information about learning outcomes from the institutions and programs they review" (Hutchings and Marchese 1990, 16). That such pressures have significantly affected colleges and universities is evidenced by the fact that "82 percent of all colleges now report 'assessment activities underway,' " and this figure represents an equal mix of public and private institutions (Hutchings and Marchese, 1990, 14). And, in 1992, driven in large part by President Bush's "Education 2000," we experienced tremendous pressure to create a national system of assessment, an assessment system, as suggested by the following quote from a *Buffalo News* editorial, that will surely improve American education:

Imagine President Bush's domestic policy adviser, teacher unions leaders, a head of the national school boards association, governors, education experts, and business leaders agreeing on anything. Yet a panel made of those elements has agreed on something not only important but sweeping: national tests and standards for America's school kinds.

The congressionally appointed National Council for Education Standards and Testing . . . recommends that the United States create voluntary curriculum standards and tests. That could mark an important turning point in American education. ("National Tests Can Help" 1992, B2)

As this discussion now shifts from an examination of the assessment of elementary and high school students, teachers, programs, and school systems (and the attacks associated with such assessment), the first step is to look at the nature and goal(s) of assessment in higher education. Second, such an examination should reveal to what extent assessment in higher education falls into the same traps that characterize assessment of lower levels of the education establishment. And third, such an examination must confront this question: how can the assessment of higher education function constructively and avoid being used by politicians and bureaucrats to conceal the need for major changes that move beyond simplistic fix-it programs that blame learners and make it impossible for them to obtain a college education?

In their excellent article "Watching Assessment: Questions, Stories, Prospects," Pat Hutchings, first director of the AAHE Assessment Forum, and Ted Marchese, editor of *Change*, say:

Our view of assessment is mixed. As a phenomenon, it is at once powerful, scary in the wrong hands, increasingly a matter of law, and home to the day's most provocative discussions of teaching and learning. As a movement, it tilts at the deepest structures and habits of academic culture; its practice on campus is marked by tricky beginnings and important accomplishments. The one sure thing is that assessment warrants close attention. (1990, 12)

Of course, sometimes one suspects that the mandate for assessment grows out of a governor's or state legislature's desire to take the heat off of the decrepit highway and bridge system that threatens the lives of the citizens and decides to focus attention on the laziest, least accountable group of people who waste the taxpayers' dollars—college teachers. Or perhaps a governor whose economic programs have resulted in a major deficit wants to look tough in his/her attempt to cut that deficit and decides to use assessment to show how the "expensive" state university system does a poor job of educating its students and should, therefore, have its budget reduced, class sizes increased, and programs cut. Or maybe an academic vice president wants to begin an assessment program so s/he can move on to a better job using the assessment credentials to show how much some other institution needs him/her? It happens.

Conspiracy Theories Aside

We do not intend to suggest that the motivation for assessment is always fraudulent and cynical, for such is not necessarily the case. It is perfectly reasonable for someone to ask us to be accountable, but we must respond by aggressively rejecting fraudulent systems of accountability. We must insist that teachers maintain local control of assessment. Regardless of where the mandate originates, the possibility for well-intentioned and even successful assessment programs exists, though the potential validity and success of assessment relies almost entirely on the extent to which good teachers involve themselves in "owning" the process—and this alone does not guarantee a good assessment program. For one thing, even a faculty with the best of intentions needs to know something about assessment, potential pitfalls, and ways of avoiding such pitfalls before engaging in assessment projects. This all means, however, that faculty cannot contemptuously dismiss calls for accountability and, at the same time, complain about imposed systems of assessment.

In order to see the complexities surrounding assessment in higher education, and the ways in which it can fall into the same kinds of solipsistic entrapment of the assessment that precedes it in elementary and high school, one need only examine some relatively early major attempts at assessment.

In a well-known and not terribly unusual case, assessment demands were imposed on Northeast Missouri State University (NMSU)—a mandate that went so far as to stipulate that certain standardized tests had to be used. In the process of meeting these demands, NMSU used several tools for the assessment: (1) a "value-added" component comprised of "successive administrative [sic] of the ACT and the ACT COMP;" (2) "a nationally recognized and administered test, such as a GRE [Graduate Records Examination] field examination or a professional certification test;" (3) a "variety of questionnaire surveys;" (4) "the ETS placement examination; the ACT COMP writing examination; the ACT COMP speaking examination; other national exams, such as the ACS [American Chemistry Society] national chemistry exam; numerous local outcome measures within programs . . . and instruments such as the Myer-Briggs Personality Inventory" (Halpern, Krueger, and Heisserer 1987, 49–50).

By its own admission, the assessment project at Northeast Missouri State University was an incredible success:

> At NSMU, assessment has increased the involvement of students, faculty, staff, and administrators in improving learning outcomes and student attitudes toward the university and its function. Through assessment, the university has been able to document its positive influence on students and have a demonstrable impact on their total development. (Halpern, Krueger, and Heisserer 1987, 56)

For example, students indicated that they were "spending more independent time on learning" (Halpern, Krueger, and Heisserer 1987, 50). Additionally, these students engaged more frequently in "discussion with other students on serious topics," and they worked harder and longer on improving their writing (Halpern, Krueger, and Heisserer 1987, 51). Furthermore, students cared more about educational issues at the institution, and their satisfaction with the institution had increased (Halpern, Krueger, and Heisserer 1987, 51–52).

On the faculty side, the results were equally positive. Faculty emphasized "correct writing" more than in the past, using writing as a vehicle to enhance the higher-order thinking processes, a change recognized by students and faculty that added "integrity" to the degrees students earned (Halpern, Krueger, and Heisserer 1987, 53).

Likewise, the psychology department improved its curriculum, "implemented higher standards," created "more valid in-class assessment," provided "for a comprehensive exit review of the basic content of the discipline, and provide[d] generous encouragement to individual students who achieve" (Halpern, Krueger, and Heisserer 1987, 54). Indeed, the faculty became "actively involved in improving all aspects of their courses" (Halpern, Krueger, and Heisserer 1987, 54). Results in the major disciplines?

> In most of the majors, the results of the senior tests, along with the survey data and the experience of the faculty, have caused faculty to reevaluate all courses and sequencing of courses in the majors so that the essential elements of the discipline are being taught, and to ensure that the curriculum is sufficiently rigorous for graduates to be nationally competitive. (Halpern, Krueger, and Heisserer 1987, 54)

As for staff: "The admissions office, registrar's office, financial aid office, career/placement office, student activities office, and so on" focused more on satisfying student needs and supporting the university's central goals (Halpern 1987, 55). In fairness to NMSU, however, as one somewhat skeptically notes the rather incredible success of the assessment project, it is important to keep in mind that the assessment and even the tools of assessment were imposed on this institution. Under such pressure, it is probably wise to use assessment to identify solvable problems and then miraculously solve them. It is likewise important to note that, over the past few years, NMSU has moved away from such heavy use of standardized exams and begun to incorporate "more qualitative approaches such as portfolios" (Hutchings and Marchese 1990, 35).

While Northeastern Missouri appears to have escaped relatively unscathed from the imposition of assessment (though the claims for improvement may be somewhat exaggerated), in Florida, the situation has been considerably more destructive. There is some similarity insofar as assessment was imposed by the state legislature (as in many other states), but instead of focusing only on programmatic/institutional assessment, Florida focused on the assessment of individual students. One significant piece in the Florida scenario begins with the literacy concerns of State Senator Jack Gordon, a Democrat from Miami Beach, whose efforts resulted in the "Gordon Rule": students in community colleges must "write 24,000 words before their junior year. Another aspect of Gordon's effort is that a student in a composition course must write 6,000 words and in a literature course must write 3,000 words. The result has been massive protest by the teachers in the system who find it impossible to read the amounts of writing that have been mandated" (*Composition Chronicle* April 1991, 7).

As the *Tampa Tribune-Times* points out, given the teaching loads carried by these instructors, the requirement is absurd: "In a year, that amounts to more than 1.3 million words, twice the number of words in a King James version of the Bible" (*Composition Chronicle* April 1991, 7). Related to the "Gordon Rule," Florida institutions of higher education have been subjected to "the external imposition of tests to regulate individual student progress," and this has also had relatively disastrous effects (Hutchings and Marchese 1990, 24). Another result of the Florida Plan is a "rising junior" exam that students must pass in order to enter their junior year of college. While initially envisioned as a way of guaranteeing that students would be adequately prepared for their junior and senior years of college, the exam has had a terribly destructive effect on minority students who find themselves locked out of the four-year college experience.

The exam used in Florida is Florida's College-Level Academic Skills Test (CLAST) designed to ensure "in principle" that "each student who enters the upper division has mastered a certain level of reading, writing and quantitative skills" (Ewell 1987, 11). Referring to the Florida exam as a "gatekeeping" exam intended to ensure basic academic competencies in all graduates," Diane Halpern points out that these models are "roughly analogous to industry's quality assurance models. The rationale in 'gateway' models is that deficient students need to be screened before they begin upper-division course work, in much the same way that deficient widgets are screened out of a production line" (1987, 8). Aside from the fact that such models tend to focus on minimal competencies as somehow being adequate, they also interfere with "equity" because minority groups often do not get through the gate and are therefore unable to complete four years of college. Halpern specifically mentions Florida's Spanish-speaking students in this respect (1987, 8; see also Curry and Hager 1987, 57).

Robert McCabe, president of Miami-Dade Community College, speaks even more directly to the serious problems resulting from the Florida approach. Citing the use (and abuse) of the College Level Academic Skills Test (CLAST), which all students must pass before they can begin upper-level college studies, McCabe points out that "half of our 50,000 credit students have a native language other than English" and that, given the mode of holistically scoring the exam, "there is virtually no prospect for a second-language student to meet the 1991 standard. The situation makes it very tempting . . . to turn the English curriculum into a program to teach students" how to pass the test, driving faculty to create a curriculum that they cannot support, that is academically fraudulent, and that is clearly "not in the best interest of the students" (Hutchings and Marchese 1990, 24). McCabe further asserts that CLAST has had a "particularly devastating impact on minorities" (especially African-American students), denying these students access to upper-level course work and, of course, a four-year college degree, even though there is evidence that "a substantial percentage of those being denied upper-division access would be successful" (Hutchings and Marchese 1990, 24).

It should be obvious that what is most disturbing in assessing the assessors of higher education, particularly in terms of these last two examples, is this: all too often, assessment projects have used the same kinds of tests that were used in elementary and high school, the same kinds of standardized tests that have been used all along to label and abuse students—the same kinds of exams that have been used to misrepresent and ignore any kind of real learning. When most people think of assessment, they think of the computer-graded multiple choice, standardized test—but most of these were not specifically designed for the purposes they are used for—and even some that are supposedly so designed do very little to assess what they propose to assess. As has already been indicated, in addition to something like Florida's CLAST, testing agencies provide a range of standardized tests of general knowledge and skills. As Peter Ewell points out, the ACT is used to make decisions about college admissions, CLEP (the College Level Examination Program) created by ETS is used for giving academic credit through examination, the GRE (Graduate Record Examination) created by ETS for admission decisions in graduate schools, the PPST (Pre-Professional Skills Test) intended to assess student growth resulting from instruction.

Various and significant problems are associated with such tests, however. For example, standardized tests created by testing agencies cannot directly engage the content of a given curriculum: if one English department emphasizes genre or psychological approaches to literature, but another emphasizes postmodern philosophical approaches, and yet another emphasizes a multicultural approach to literature, what kind of a standardized GRE test does one construct? How does ACT COMP engage and assess specific elements of curricula at a broad variety of institutions? And what do the scores resulting from such exams mean? Do normative scores, like those resulting from the GRE, reflect the performance of an institution's entire graduating class (Ewell 1987, 17–18; Report of Committee C 1991, 55)?

What Ewell does not mention, and the alarm that must be sounded here, is that these exams share exactly the same kinds of faults typical of other standardized exams: they essentially assess a student's ability to take a given exam and little more. Often such exams are used because they happen to be easily available, easily administered, easily scored, easy to compare across institutions, and they make few demands on faculty time for the creation of valid assessment instruments (Ewell 1987, 17). Indeed, they pretty effectively escape all the constructive possibilities that the assessment movement has to offer.

The End of the Beginning

One need simply look at some of the major assessment programs in higher education to see what occurs as such programs are imposed from the outside and implemented by groups who have not had the time or expertise to think through a project carefully. Nevertheless Hutchings and Marchese make the important point that more recent assessment projects have begun to move away from such a heavy reliance on potentially abusive standardized exams and have moved toward more qualitative forms of assessment, though we remain concerned at the continuing appeal of such "off-the-shelf" exams. And although faculty have increasingly taken charge of assessment and engaged the difficult project of creating their own assessment tools directed at assessing the specific programs at a given institution, such successes appear often to be the result of relatively hostile negotiations with state agencies.

A concrete example of one such battle is presented by the University of Virginia's several-years-long war with the State Council of Higher Education for Virginia (SCHEV) (Hutchings and Marchese 1990, 17–21). A less hostile atmosphere surrounded the University of Connecticut's move toward assessment, but even so, in both the cases of Virginia and Connecticut, there have been some positive results: discussions of assessment and attempts to implement certain approaches to assessment have raised faculty consciousness about the importance of undergraduate education and caused many faculty to question what exactly it is they are doing and why they are doing it in terms of what students are actually learning (Hutchings and Marchese 1990, 25). The same positive results appear to characterize assessment programs at the University of Tennessee at Knoxville, Kean College of New Jersey, and King's College in Wilkes-Barre, Pennsylvania (Hutchings and Marchese 1990, 29–34).

Though Tennessee was forced to use ACT COMP, in each of these cases, faculty involvement appears to have been relatively high from the beginning, and this situation appears particularly true for King's College. While most of these assessment programs seem to result in higher degrees of consciousness and caring about undergraduate instruction, some seem to result in more specific changes in the actual teaching of courses. This is perhaps most true at King's College where assessment began "in the late '70s—before the rash of reform reports and considerably before any 'assessment movement' " (Hutchings and Marchese 1990, 32). Different in important ways from most of the other programs that we have been discussing, King's College assessment is "first and foremost a *pedagogical* strategy," focusing on student outcomes (Hutchings and Marchese 1990, 21). In the case of King's College, an emphasis on writing-across-the-curriculum led the faculty in intensive discussion about the broader aims of their courses, eventually resulting in a core curriculum in which courses were to "contribute to student learning of eight 'transferable liberal learning skills': critical thinking, creative thinking and problem-solving strategies, effective writing, effective oral communication, quantitative analysis, computer literacy, library and information technologies, and values awareness" (Hutchings and Marchese 1990, 32). What is particularly interesting about this fact is that it is so different from what appears to normally result from assessment, particularly as Marchese and Hutchings review major assessments in the *Change* article. While many assessments seem to result in raised consciousness, heightened awareness, and greater concern about undergraduate education, assessment at King's College appears to have resulted in new and different courses and classroom approaches. To some extent, the same may be true of the New Jersey assessment (we have heard conflicting stories), but by and large, one is hard put to find concrete results that have an immediate impact on student learning growing out of assessment projects.

Unfortunately, there is good reason to believe that qualitative assessment projects focusing on actual student performances may be losing in the battle with standardized tests. In summarizing some of the more recent events occurring in the assessment arena, Peter Ewell writes:

> As always in assessment, events took place in bewildering variety. In South Carolina and other states, legislative or board proposals for common postsecondary outcomes testing were narrowly defeated. In Missouri, they were not; all sophomores in the university system will complete the standardized "College Base," examination beginning next year. In Tennessee, debate raged all summer [1991] about whether to retain the ACT COMP examination as a key element of the state's "performance-funding" mechanism, fueled by institutional contentions that the exam was inappropriate for this purpose. In Texas and Minnesota, similar "results-based" funding surfaced as a major component in proposed legislative budgeting approaches for the coming year. Finally, in Virginia—the original home of discretionary institution-centered assessment under state auspices—institutions appeared more than willing to use this discretion to cut back or eliminate their assessment programs as funds got tight—until explicitly warned off this course of action by state authorities. Last, but far from least, this past summer New Jersey closed down its controversial, innovative, and expensive General Intellectual Skills (GIS) assessment—ironically, just as a national advisory panel recommended that exactly this kind of "performance-based" examination be developed for use in assessing collegiate progress on the President's National Education Goals. (1991, 12)

Finally, although we will discuss the assessment project conducted at the State University of New York College at Fredonia in some detail in Chapter 3, it is appropriate here to present a brief overview in order to place it in the context of the other assessments we have been discussing. At SUNY–Fredonia, a group of faculty, led by Dr. Minda Rae Amiran and funded by the Fund for the Improvement of Postsecondary Education (FIPSE) *voluntarily* conducted an assessment of its General College Program a few years ago. The members of the committee began as novices and ended as beginners. We worked very hard. We created some fascinating qualitative instruments (tests). We found that we did not have enough money to do many of the most important things that we wanted to do and should have done. We continued to work very hard. We ended with interesting results, guides to assist those assessors who will follow us, and a well-written report that the U.S. Department of Education (USDOE) agrees is interesting and well written. Did constructive changes result? Absolutely. Individual faculty have implemented changes in their courses in order to confront some of the disturbing findings in the Fredonia assessment; a few departments have begun to work through committees and workshops to address some of the issues raised in the assessment, but not nearly enough has happened (and given the incredibly harsh budget cuts we have been experiencing, one's optimism fades).

There it is; that is the end of the self-congratulatory part of the results. Unlike NMSU, we cannot claim that our findings have resulted in a massive overhaul of the General College Program. Like many institutions in SUNY, instead of improving anything, especially a General College Program or classroom instruction, we are essentially trying to move through serious, often debilitating budget cuts without entirely destroying our reasons for being. On the other hand, we are not personally convinced that things would be much different even if the economic situation was significantly better, and the reasons are these: (1) our assessment suggested a need for a major overhaul of the ways in which we think about higher education; (2) it suggested that programs and curricula are not working very well; (3) it suggested that much of what goes on in most courses has little to do with achieving the effects we pretend to cherish; and (4) it suggested that teachers in general seriously overestimate the amount and quality of what their students are learning. As one examines these kinds of assessments, one is reminded of the senior honors student at King's College who said to Academic Dean Donald Farmer, "There's a lot more teaching going on [in this college] than learning" (Hutchings and Marchese 1990, 32). Furthermore, follow-up activities have suggested that the likelihood of changing what already exists will be very difficult. One sometimes has the feeling that simply having completed the assessment itself was enough to please almost everyone in some perverse sense. Oddly, however, people who seem quick to accept the sense and validity of tests like ACT COMP are even quicker to reject more qualitative kinds of assessment that actually examine what it is students think and are able to do in certain areas of thinking and reasoning.

As we have already noted, at Fredonia, hardworking, committed, creative faculty have taken it upon themselves to address problems revealed through the assessment; however, other faculty, who see that the assessment indicates relatively little growth in various student thought processes and abilities, use the results to argue for the elimination of the General College Program. Still others argue for structural changes within the program. Finally, budget crises provide the need and rationale for increasing class sizes and large lecture sections in the face of evidence that clearly suggests the need for much smaller classes, more writing, and more individual attention to students. In short, one does not have the sense that either faculty or administrators recognize the clearest implications of the assessment: major changes need to occur in curricula and what goes on in our classrooms. As our next chapter clearly indicates, many students are quietly sick and tired of what they experience, and to no small extent, pretty much ignore what goes on in their classes because they are good enough at taking multiple-choice tests to pass their courses with minimal involvement and minimal learning.

Another major irony is this: many of us who conducted the assessment have a good, solid sense of the shortcomings of our tests. We know that the writing test barely begins to assess what is happening with student writing at our college. We know the results of the reading test surprised and confused us, especially in relationship to the writing test results; and we know that the reflexive thinking test, our attempt to begin to look at metacognition, analogizes well with the relationship between alchemy and modern chemistry. But we also know that what we did remains at the forefront of assessment in higher education. We know that the most important thing we found out is that assessment must become learner-centered. We need to backtrack and find out what it is these students are learning, why they care about it, what they want to learn, how they think they learn best, what we think about what they tell us, and how it matches up with what we think they are learning and should be learning.

There is much more that will be covered in following chapters, but by way of a short, quick summary of this chapter and an introduction to what is to follow, let us end with these assertions: As long as we teach what we assess, the assessment movement as it presently exists is a threat to the search for any kind of truth, even the most fleeting of truths. Until we examine what we teach and what (how) students learn, we cannot sensibly assess anything. Valid assessment must grow out of a cooperative venture centered on active interrelationships between students and faculty. The only valid reason for doing assessment of any kind is to improve the teaching/learning enterprise. Any national assessment that is not preceded by a national emphasis on changing and improving what is currently going in the nation's schools and colleges is absurd. And any local or national emphasis on change in education that is predicated on the idea that "throwing money at the problem will not help" is predicated on a vicious lie. When highways and bridges need repair, the government throws money at the problem. When the post office cannot operate efficiently within its budget, postal rates go up. If education is to improve in this country, we must stop simply throwing well-shaped, political rhetoric at the problem: it is long past time to engage the problem with all its complexities—teacher preparation programs, certification requirements, in-service training for teachers, class sizes, and so forth. We already know a considerable amount about what needs to be changed and even what kinds of change need to be implemented. A system of national tests is simply an expensive diversion that, we believe, in and of itself will result in no change whatsoever. And an imposed system of standardized tests represents one of the most destructive possibilities on the assessment horizon.

For the moment, however, let us turn our gaze toward the human beings who are at the center of this entire issue. Let us consider the students and what they have to say.

CHAPTER 2

Dehumanizing Norms

... A test? And you want to know what we think?

—college junior

I'm glad someone cares about how well we are learning instead of just how much.

—incoming first-year student

The approaches to assessment we choose to adopt, adapt, or create will reflect our assumptions about the nature of learning and the roles of the participants. The students quoted above suggest that conventional testing in school fails to account for human beings who learn; they are surprised to be asked what and how well they think. It seems, from the student narratives about college that we will discuss here, that not only do we not ask students at that level to reflect upon their learning very often, but we have estranged college students from their own learning. We are beginning to recognize the implications of students' "otherness" to the academic community (See, for example, "A Stranger in Strange Lands: One College Student Writing Across the Curriculum, McCarthy 1987; "The Friendly Stranger: Twenty-five Years as 'Other'," Neuleib 1992). To understand the other, we need to do better than to employ more short-answer evaluations such as multiple-choice tests, alumni surveys, and placement records. Assessment can, and ought to, include students in the conversation, to better examine what it is they are learning, how they believe they learn, and what components of the educational system assist or prevent them in coming to know. Geertz writes: "We measure the cogency of our explications not against a body of uninterpreted data, but against the power of the scientific imagination to bring us into touch with the lives of strangers" (1973, 16). If we fail to examine the nature of learning in college in our efforts to construct assessment procedures, we then ignore the essence of the discussion. Assessment is, then, an opportunity to examine learning by including students in the conversation and to better see how our models of learning play out in teaching and assessment conventions.

First, let us imagine a classroom characterized by practices encouraging a narrow range of student behaviors such as correct performance (writing for the teacher), getting the right answer (saying what the teacher "wants to hear"), exhibiting the appropriate role characteristics (sitting quietly, not talking to a classmate, filling in the right bubble, not forgetting information until after the test). Teachers thinking about evaluation of students' learning, beyond conventional midterm and final exams, are likely to participate in the assessment conversation with the same language that they use to describe learning: covering the material, getting all the chapters in, maintaining standards. The professor is the neutral transmitter of knowledge; the student is the receiver. This is the transmission model, or what Paulo Freire calls the "banking" model of education:

> The banking concept distinguishes two stages in the action of the educator. During the first, he cognizes a cognizable object while he prepares his lessons in his study or laboratory; during the second, he expounds to his students about the object. The students are not called upon to know, but to memorize the contents narrated by the teacher. Nor do the students practice any act of cognition, since the object towards which that act should be directed is the property of the teacher. (1971, 67–68)

The students' accumulation of knowledge is judged by tests designed to extract bits of memorized material asked in contexts dislocated from typical occasions for learning. If this approach permeates the institution so profoundly that it is tacit knowledge and practice, then that college will probably adopt a framework for discussing, and measures for documenting, learning that reflect these conceptions and artifacts of education. Assessment, then, becomes a simple, unambitious, unreflective, and disempowering process to ensure the status quo.

Similarly, imagine an administration discussing programmatic assessment so that they may at least appear to be responding to accreditation requirements or state mandates. "We'll do it just to get it done," said one dean. If the rest of the college community remains unaware of, and uninvited to, this discussion, then assessment fails to have true function or meaning—it becomes a reactive, bureaucratic maneuver. The off-the-shelf tests will provide an easy solution to the pressures to assess.

Yet, as we have noted, that solution is dishonest and hollow; quick answer approaches to assessment reflect little, if any, genuine concern for learning and offer no substantial information about learners and teachers to teachers and learners. "Formal testing has moved much too far in the direction of assessing knowledge of questionable importance in ways that show little transportability. The understanding that schools ought to inculcate is virtually invisible on such instruments" (Gardner 1991, 134). Furthermore, short-answer assessments as gateway tests suggest the bankruptcy of the entire system. Gateway testing implies as well as condones the notion that faculty understand their students' abilities only in surface, impersonal, and remote ways and that students are entirely unwilling or sufficiently disabled to be concerned or articulate about the quality and meaning of their learning.

Reductive assessments requiring no reflection, generating little investment from faculty and students, and offering no ownership of or affinity to knowing simply further alienate students from their educations and selves as learners. Ken Macrorie invokes the notion that teaching should not frighten "learners out of their unconscious selves" (Macrorie 1984, 231). Assessments such as the ACT COMP and the GRE, occurring in a communicative void, do not even presume that learners have selves, that reading and writing are social constructs, that learning and curriculum are negotiated in local contexts, or that assessment is always a "human event, influencing and influenced by the dynamics of school life. It is a complicated social, linguistic, and cognitive process with great potential to impact the functioning of the school community" (Loofbourrow 1992, 26).

In *Savage Inequalities*, Jonathan Kozol describes the strangely unhinged relationship among testing, teaching, and learners, in which students are only distantly connected to, or subjects of, evaluation:

> Clark Junior High School is regarded as the top school in the city. . . . "We spend the entire eighth-grade year preparing for the state exams," a teacher tells me in a top-ranked English class. The teacher seems devoted to the children, but three students sitting near me sleep through the entire period. The teacher rouses one of them, a girl in the seat next to me, but the student promptly lays her head back on her crossed arms and is soon asleep again. (1991, 34)

Kozol's investigation into education in the United States leads him to move beyond the political rhetoric surrounding education and to listen to learners:

> It occurred to me that we had not been listening much to children in these recent years of "summit conferences" on education, of severe reports and ominous prescriptions. The voices of children, frankly, had been missing from the whole discussion.
>
> This seems especially unfortunate because the children often are more interesting and perceptive than the grownups are about the day-to-day realities of life in school. For this reason, I decided . . . to listen very carefully to children and let their voices and their judgements and their longings find a place. (1991, 5–6)

It is this listening stance, expanding our notion of the subjects and content of our teaching and testing, that will alter the grounds of our work. Meaningful assessment efforts must uproot the power disparity between the unclad "emperors of testing" (Mayher 1990, 261) and the rest of us—we who are in classrooms daily as students and teachers. "Situated" (Stallman and Pearson 1990, 41), "grounded" (Parker 1990, 75), and performance-based assessments are examples of alternatives to psychometric models, alternatives that grant primacy to understanding individuals learning and teaching. Assessment, writes Robert B. Parker, involves "philosophical questions . . . assessment, is, inherently, a subjective process because it involves persons, as *subjects*, making and using judgements about other persons" (1990, 81). If we choose to develop approaches to assessment that attend to the "passionate contribution of the person knowing what is being known" (Polanyi 1958, viii), and include the voices and experiences of all the participants in the academy, in particular contexts, that magnify rather than reduce students' learning, then we have initiated a process of dialogue and collaboration that can lead to engaged learning and growth for individuals and substantive change and renewal for the college community.

ETS GOES TO COLLEGE

The challenges posed by assessment and the conversations about these efforts clarify and reflect polarizing tensions in pedagogy, curriculum, and testing across levels, yielding particular difficulties for the academy and its traditional notions of education. The arguments seem focused most clearly around whether learning/knowledge is a mechanical, information processing accretion of objective knowledge or if learning/knowing is socially constructed by active, meaning-making learners, negotiating their own processes of knowing in various contexts. In the latter conception, the learner's relationship with knowing is emphasized. In the former, the learner is essentially unheard/invisible, an unobtrusive recipient of our well-wrought notes.

We have tended, in the academy, not to direct our gaze to students' learning nor pursue inquiry into our teaching with the rigor or regard we apply to our own scholarship. At a small liberal arts school devoted to excellence in teaching, a professor commented, "No, I'm not teaching summer school, thank God. I've got *much, much* more important work [research] to do than that." The devaluation of teaching is not only acceptable, but privileged; in reality, at most colleges and universities, merit and tenure are awarded for publication. Inexperienced teachers, shabbily paid part-timers, and/or graduate students perform the bulk of the second-tier work of introductory courses—basic disciplinary socialization. Too many faculty ignore most of their students, bemoaning their students' ignorance and ill-preparedness and teach to the one or two most "capable" in their classes—a practice college teachers would not countenance from high school–or elementary school–teachers. Deans have become less like academics and more like fiduciary managers, students less like learners and more like mobile capital. But the assessment conversation calls our attention to our postures. The organization of the academy and the questions we ask and do not ask about teaching and learning and students signify our worldview and our ideological stance of what it means to be educated in a course, in a discipline, and in college. These questions and their absence are crucial in understanding why or what we assess.

While our college mission statements and other public assertions may present honorable goals (e.g., the stimulation of intellectual curiosity, a breadth of understanding of the liberal arts, a commitment to teaching with frequent interaction between faculty and students), classroom practice may involve little more than lecture, objective tests, and teacher-directed recitation of material that will be quickly forgotten after, or well before, graduation. Curriculum committees may spend years debating and constructing course requirements and sequences, while little, if any, attention is paid to how students might best learn and how teachers might best teach. Miles Myers (1987) describes the "Gas-N-Go" model of education: students stop at some courses and fill up, pass by others, or just "top it off"—as if the process of learning were simply a series of quick stops at various isolated gas pumps bearing no relation to one another or to the customers. Yet college faculties and administrations are the architects of these structures. To have ignored learners, and to continue to do so, in the conversations about education, simply to lecture in (or fuel up) and test out, hoping that students' "skills" are filled up along the way to graduation, is both untenable and unethical.

Unfortunately, the model perseveres. In 1990, 80 percent of colleges who reported having assessment procedures in place used purchased, standardized measures (Blumenstyk and Magner 1990, 11) such as the ACT COMP, a test offering little information about how, when, what, and why students learn. Few faculty read the results of this test, and students take it in the same spirit in which they pay library fines. At some colleges, students earn chances to win VCRs and gift certificates by taking the test. A professor referred to ACT COMP as "absolutely meaningless. It doesn't mean anything to me, and it doesn't mean anything to my students. The results are a joke—it's a waste of time and money."

In one school, curricular improvements correlated negatively with students' ACT COMP scores; ACT directed the school to throw away that year's results, but not the use of COMP (Vaughn 1992). Many people in the current assessment movement would ask us to scrutinize this kind of trivialization of, and complacency about, our testing practices—which would be no small or simple task. Andrea Lunsford asks:

> What would recognizing the ideological freight of our tests cost us? . . . We would have to give up a naive faith in objective, externally verifiable and knowable and measurable and replicable reality. We would have to produce tests that allow for the social construction of knowledge, to place students in interactive, collaborative settings. And we would have to allow for pluralistic and multiple ways of knowing and being. (quoted in Belanoff and Dickson 1991, 248)

If we are to participate in assessment, or in any educational reform, it seems essential to listen and attend to the human beings centrally involved well before test items are constructed or purchased and programs devised: this is the central premise of the kind of assessment we propose in this book. Otherwise, the good intentions of assessment may be defeated by our failure to examine both our own and our students' expectations and beliefs about, as well as their experiences of, learning in college.

Anne DiPardo's recent study of educational equity programs in college provides us with moving insights into students' experiences within a peer teaching program designed to enhance learning in college, but a program that failed to examine how this played out daily in students' lives and how they learn (1991). DiPardo examined the educational dynamics of small group tutorials, groups organized under the rubrics of collaborative learning and individualized learning (as well as the economic motive to make tutoring more cost-effective) on participants' experiences in this program.

Even within a program designed to provide support, linguistic minority students continued to be marginalized and excluded from participating fully in the academy through the program's failure to attend to the complexity of learning in social contexts and the persistence of institutionalized racism:

> These students' struggles with academic discourse must be seen as part of a larger grappling that is at once cognitive and social, personal and public. While the final products of this struggle might be reflected in test scores, grade reports, and retention figures, its vicissitudes are played out upon a more elusive territory—in its daily unfolding and, particularly, in students' ongoing attempts to make sense of the dialectic between self and other. The job of all instructors . . . is not simply to provide useful background knowledge or skills, but to invite students into this dialectic—a dialectic both intellectual, and, because of its social nature, also charged with feeling. (1991, 5)

This multidimensioned dialectic is rarely made explicit in most academic settings. Further, DiPardo's study of the intricacies and imperatives of teaching and evaluating linguistic minority students offers a way of talking about assessment issues as well—to scrutinize and understand what we do before claiming to have met the challenges of assessment:

> At times, we're moved to wonder at the audacity of institutional good intentions, at policies and programs that promise to cherish diversity and promote the academic success of these students—this, often, in the absence of any fine-grained understanding of who they are, of their past and current struggles, of the sorts of support that might help. Ironically, we come to realize that the language of policies and programs can become a sort of shield, a veil which obscures the many ways we're missing the mark—that if we're to begin closing the recalcitrant gap between goodwill and substantive action, we need to still the public rhetoric, to take a long, perhaps disconcerting look at the knotty complexities of what *is*. (1991, 91)

A LISTENING STANCE: WHO ARE THESE PEOPLE IN OUR CLASSES (AND WHAT ARE THEY SAYING ABOUT US)?

DiPardo's work brings into prominence the voices of learners and attends to the multiple social and political contexts constraining the students' learning. The perspectives and methodologies of many feminist and ex-centric (Lather 1991, 33) theorists, teachers, and researchers involve explicitly valuing the interpretations of the other, reciprocity, and social change (Oakley 1981; Gilligan 1982; Belenky et al. 1986). To listen to learners, especially "others," often silenced in the academy, offers perspectives largely ignored in assessment. (While alumni surveys and satisfaction questionnaires are examples of student assessment, their data seem disembedded and thin in contrast to classroom and portfolio assessments. Consider the following survey item, typical of such instruments, to which a student responds on a Likert scale: "I understand and appreciate people from other cultures better." How many students would disagree?)

A feminist view of assessment and learning offers a way of listening, and one way of examining "what is." While not monolithic, feminism is an inclusive framework, focused on those who typically have been marginalized and silenced by institutions and who occupy subordinate positions in the hierarchy, in this case, of education. John Willinsky notes that "gender is but one source of difference and meaning, yet one that has profound political and personal implications for the world at large, for the young coming of age, and for the community known as the classroom" (1990, 114–115). Feminist approaches, Willinsky argues, can be characterized by a "sensitivity to difference . . . a difference in gender, certainly, but also one that works across a number of dimensions, each with its own social meaning, in anyone's life" (1990, 115). Further, in our inquiry into students' learning via assessment, a feminist analysis marries the architecture of assessment with its subjects, as in research paradigms: "Through dialogue and reflexivity, design, data, and theory emerge, with data being recognized as generated from people in a relationship" (Lather 1991, 72). First, we will examine what students have to say about learning in college, and then look specifically at minority students' conceptualizations of, and responses to, school experiences.

Students describe learning in school with energy and clarity—as anyone who asks for narrative course evaluations or eats lunch in the college dining hall well knows. Unfortunately, the students' appraisals of their learning sometimes yield discouraging results. For example, consider Patrick Court's study of written comments made by Fredonia students who participated in the Fredonia assessment (see Chapter 3 for a fuller discussion of the test). In addition to the statements students made on the writing test and the reflective thinking test, students also had the opportunity to write about the test experience. The following quotations, from students in the Fredonia assessments as well as students at other colleges, are representative of what the learners have had to say about their learning in school.

The most common criticism from students focuses on the quality of the education they are receiving, the way teachers teach, and the level of performance expected of the students. First, by far one of the most common remarks made by students focuses specifically on the tendency of teachers to rely primarily on lectures and/or workbook exercises in order to "transmit" information, on the absence of interaction, and on the lack of what student after student refers to as "hands-on learning":

> The teacher lectured from an outline of key words on the overhead projector. Several people commented that his lectures were hard to follow, but I thought they weren't too difficult because he followed the book. In fact, at times he read straight from it! . . . I observed, "Five people walked out of the lecture early. I assume that from the time that had elapsed that it was after they'd copied the outline. I noticed people who simply copied the outline of key words and then just sat there in a kind of stupor." One day . . . as I counted the twelve people who left early, the girl to my left did homework for another class, the guy in front of me ate yogurt, and the guy to my right organized his Franklin Day Planner. One girl's notes consisted of "Boring>>>>>Big Time!" (Anderson et al. 1990, 19)

Clearly, the significance of the "key words" in this sociology class eluded the professor's students. Another student, whose comments are elaborated on later, says that "the problem most students have is . . . trying to understand why they are getting all those disjointed facts. I don't know a better way, but there has to be one."

We find it impossible to avoid joining in with the student's voice in that last opinion, because s/he is so clearly correct. And while we may not know a "best" way, surely we can implement "better" ways. But this last quotation is particularly interesting because the student emphasizes the lack of attention given to "relationships" and "the flow of one section to another."

The problem described by this last student appears all the more serious when one considers statements made by different students about the tests of scientific and mathematical thinking. Although all of the tests were directed at assessing students' thought processes and their abilities to deal with certain kinds of problems, and none of the tests was focused on content, some students were clearly unfamiliar with the possibility of successfully solving a problem they had not specifically studied. For example, one student mentions that s/he could not answer the scientific reasoning exam because s/he had "never taken a course in biology," even though the test asked for no specific biological information whatsoever. Another mentions that s/he could not handle a math problem-solving question because it has been a "long time" since she had a math course, though the question demanded no specific computational ability. Here are a few additional comments: "I don't think the test accurately tested the General College Program because they both [the scientific reasoning tests] seemed to be concentrated quite heavily on biology, and some students may not have even elected to take biology" said one student. Another student recommended that tests should be given closer "to the time when a student took a General College Program course," because one might "forget" the information.

These students are not confident, self-directed learners. They are not confident in their ability to approach a problem and figure it out on their own. They appear to feel they can complete a task only if they had been recently taught how to "do it" in school, but if they have not recently been taught almost exactly what is asked of them, then they appear to assume that they will be unable to succeed.

In addition, while the students do not appear to be fully conscious of the relationships among their criticisms of schools, curricula, and teachers who emphasize discrete bits of (apparently) unrelated information and their own abilities to perform successfully on tests, the students evidence a powerful sense that they are not learning as much as they should be. Moreover, it is particularly important here to recognize that the criticisms of the students are related to the kinds of things they are not able to do well on the exams; they do not feel that schools, in general, help them to reason independently and see relationships among ideas/subjects. One would think that if these young people can recognize the inherent faults of the present emphasis (in most testing and much teaching) on discrete bits of information and unrelated, isolated acts of "learning," then the educators might also recognize and do something about the problem.

Student complaints about classroom approaches to teaching present a fairly clear picture of the causes underlying weak student performances on test areas demanding constructive, critical-analytical thinking and reasoning:

Professors reading straight from the book is terrible; you get nothing out of it and it is very boring.

Student participation is important, presentations, discussions groups, etc., rather than simple lecture. All too often professors don't ask "What do you think?"

True learning can't be defined by an opscan sheet or by memorization. . . . Classroom lectures and information lay the groundwork for learning, but it all comes down to whether or not you can do what you've supposedly learned. . . . Straight lecture and testing without instructor interaction do not help the learning process.

What is least helpful about the school learning experience is that teachers are generally too concerned with covering a curriculum and not concerned enough with making sure that students really gain new understanding from coursework.

Students get bored with the same routine everyday. They don't like to sit passive and they really shouldn't be. They should be able to move around. The teachers should use their natural aggression and focus it into projects and discussions, the teachers should let them create, instead of harnessing them in chairs and lecturing at them. All students learn in different ways, but I think they all would learn better by doing and getting actively involved in their learning.

I spent so much time cramming and memorizing for tests and quizzes, I do not feel I learned as much as I should have.

I believe all of us have had the teacher who simply copies the information from the book to the board (or from their head to the board) with expectations of understanding from the students. We need teachers with a here's-why philosophy not just the here's-how. How and why must be taught together. That's what teaching is.

I closely observed the teacher because I was so disgusted with his technique. The professor was more concerned about the texts that about the students, either as a class or individually. This surprised me, considering the small size of the class. ... He brushed my comments aside because they "weren't what he was looking for." I decided that it's not worth the trouble if the professor wasn't going to listen (Anderson 1990, 35).

Many of these students' comments voice an attitude that is common among the essays: the writers feel that their high school and college teachers do not really care much about them, their learning, or interacting with them. What is also relatively clear is this: students do not engage fully or energetically in learning something they do not want to learn or see no reason for learning. At the same time, they do want to engage and be engaged by their teachers, and they repeatedly assert that such interpersonal engagement helps them learn and be interested in learning. Unfortunately, it appears to be a relatively uncommon part of most school experience.

Even so, the solution is not so simple as it might initially appear; that is, student comments of this sort suggest we teachers need "simply" do two things: (1) foster better student-teacher relationships (i.e., show them we care about them and their learning); and (2) motivate them and facilitate their interest in whatever it is we are involved in teaching. Of course, as any teacher knows, any suggestion that the second point is simple or even consistently possible to achieve is laughable. While some might argue that students come to school ready and willing to learn, this is true only in some world that has not already turned them off to the experience of being open and curious. The fact is that many of the students most of us deal with have had bad (or at least boring) school experiences, and they are not coming to us with quite as much energetic curiosity as we would hope. The fact is that they are tired of being "talked at," "read at," and ignored as human beings. But the first point (establishing better interpersonal relationships with students), though hardly simple to achieve and clearly demanding enormous amounts of teacher time and energy, certainly suggests a sensible, humane, beginning point. It further suggests that it is not enough for teachers to be "good" or even "excellent" in their disciplines.

These students want to be involved in their own learning; they want to be more than passive observers who move through a predetermined set of rituals as they move toward achieving their degrees. What perhaps is most exciting is this: They genuinely appear to want to learn something. What is most disturbing is this: they do not appear to believe they are learning very much.

From here, we can also look to students whose experiences have been more explicitly erased from academic landscapes. While all the students commenting above express their alienation from school and classrooms, attributes of class, race, age, and/or gender have further reduced the access of many students to the system we are talking about assessing.

It is perhaps most essential to understand what we do in college through the voices of the "other(s)," those excluded from its social, political, curricular, and pedagogical structures. The marginal person, of course, offers a unique and revealing perspective on the ethos and climate of an institution or culture. And perhaps it is only through the eyes of the other that we can begin to understand a system that has, for the most part, worked well for most of us in it. When I talk to peer tutors about their work, in the Reading/Writing Center, I tell them that the hardest part of tutoring is to be able to see where and why others are challenged; students are often recruited to be tutors by faculty because these students are successful. Because of their success, the students' procedural knowledge of studying and learning is mostly subterranean. We work, then, to make their knowledge more explicit, by mining their learning experiences, good and bad, and by listening carefully to students who encounter difficulty in school. As teachers, we too were the good students, well-acculturated into school ways; we may need, as do our tutors, to listen better and more closely.

The typical patterns of school ways, androcentric and hierarchically arranged, do not recognize the educational and social histories of students. And such blind spots are powerful enough to preclude learning. A teacher of English as a Second Language (ESL) with advanced degrees in Scandinavian reports that she cannot get newly arrived Japanese students to converse in class; the teacher is unaware that most English instruction in Japan consists of rote paper and pencil exercises. A professor complains to a writing center director about the "laziness" of his Asian student who keeps falling asleep in class; the director asks, "Is she tired?" The professor has not considered the multiple and overwhelming demands on this exchange student and the "refugee syndrome" with its characteristic exhaustion.

Other kinds of racism and classism operate in institutional politics, elevating a monolithic image of the ideal college student. An administrator, choosing to cancel language proficiency assessments for international students, rationalizes his decision by saying most of these incoming students are "from Europe anyway, not from the black holes of South America." An English teacher is puzzled by a student's unusual difficulty writing a composition in response to the departmentally required reading, E. B. White's "Once More to the Lake." This essay narrates a father's confrontation with his mortality as he recalls childhood summers at the family lakefront cabin, measuring these against his observations of his own son's growth. The teacher fails the student's essay because of its incoherence and lack of textual reference. The teacher did not know that the young woman was fatherless, the daughter of a drug-addicted mother, and homeless—certainly unable to find any reference to her reality in the essay and sufficiently silenced to forego a critical response to the values and beliefs encoded in the essay and the assignment. A pedagogy predicated upon the imagined ideal, or what Audre Lorde calls the " 'mythical norm' . . . white, thin, male, young, heterosexual, Christian, and financially secure," (1992, 497) diminishes all of us rather than enriching any of us.

LISTENING TO (OTHER) LEARNERS

When I went to kindergarten and had to speak English for the first time, I became silent. A dumbness—a shame—still cracks my voice in two when I want to say "hello" casually, or ask an easy question in front of a checkout counter, or ask directions of a bus driver. . . . During the first silent year, I spoke to no one at school, did not ask before going to the lavatory, and flunked kindergarten. . . . It was when I found out I had to talk that school became a misery, that silence became a misery. I did not speak and felt bad each time I did not speak. I read aloud in first grade, though, and heard the barest whisper with little squeaks coming out of my throat. "Louder," said the teacher, who scared the voice away again. The other Chinese girls did not talk either, so I knew the silence had to do with being a Chinese girl.
                                        —Maxine Hong Kingston (1977, 191–193)

Silence and tension. Words and fury. These are connected for me. When there is a lull in the class discussion . . . or when silence is discussed, I feel like I'm going to explode. . . . I battle with myself whether or not to speak. "I should plan out what I'm going to say," I'll sometimes think to myself. After all, I don't want to take up class time making stupid comments. Sometimes, I'll even make a contract with myself before class that I'll have to speak in class that night. Usually I'll wait until almost the end of class when my tension is built up. I'll open my mouth and, like a firecracker set off, my words will come.
                        —University of Massachusetts student (quoted in Annas 1987, 4)

My husband doesn't really know what I'm studying—he has never asked and I've never told him.
                                        —a returning student (in Castellano 1992, 383)

Women's narratives of learning in school reveal the stultifying and silencing effects of school for them. Their writings are permeated by metaphor of loss, burial, and robbery to describe the transformations of their voices and sense of originality. The words of Ann Marquart, a college senior, are representative: "I know I used to love to write, but through the years in school, I wrote less and less. I couldn't use my creativity anymore. But I know it's still in me—I just need to find it and get it out." Both males and females detail the suppression of their voices and insights to fit the academic voice of neutrality and authority their high school–teachers tell them is required in college. And neutrality and authority are not attributes our culture uses, of course, to describe women.

The risks of participating, of claiming conviction and self-possession, even in the everyday routines of class discussions and writing papers can be tremendous for women students. Adrienne Rich says:

> Look at a classroom: listen to the many kinds of women's faces, postures, expressions. Listen to the women's voices. Listen to the silences, the unasked questions, the blanks. . . . Listen to the voices of the women and the voices of the men; observe the space men allow themselves, physically and verbally, the male assumption that people will listen, even when the majority of the group is female. . . . Listen to a woman groping for language in which to express what is on her mind, sensing that the terms of academic discourse are not her language, trying to cut down her thought to the dimensions of a discourse not intended for her, *(for it is not fitting that a woman speak in public)*; or reading her paper at breakneck speed, throwing her words away, deprecating her own work by a reflex prejudgement: *I do not deserve to take up time and space.* (1979, 243–244)

Although women represent more than half of the college student population in the United States, during their time spent in college, female students' aspirations and expectations *decline* (Hall 1982, 1). While the percentage of women graduating in traditionally male fields has improved, female students continue to think of themselves as less able or deserving than male students. Isaiah Smithson discusses his experiences as a supervisor of graduate teaching assistants:

> These women did not think of themselves as intelligent and imaginative. Most of their male counterparts, whether or not they were as impressive, felt much more assured of themselves and their abilities and prospects. A study [Linden et al., 1985] of engineering students . . . confirms my informal observations. The study shows that the women in graduate programs have higher verbal and math SAT scores and higher grade-point averages than their male colleagues. Yet the women rated themselves less strong with regard to their science, math, problem-solving, and spatial abilities than did their male counterparts. (1990, 5)

This dissonance between the students' perception of "hard data"—test scores—and self-perception is important. Does it mean that women students, perhaps all students, recognize the dubiousness of these tests? Does it alternatively, or also, mean that these women students have been disabused, perhaps permanently, of their belief in themselves as students? Myra Sadker and David Sadker argue that persistent and prevalent gender bias in student-teacher interactions, from preschool through graduate school, negatively affects women's performance on standardized tests: Female [college] students are more likely to be invisible members in teacher-student interactions. Post-secondary instructors note, however, that they are generally unaware of these biased patterns" (1990, 178). In analyzing patterns of classroom interactions, Sadker and Sadker vivify the inequities in teacher response: Male students, when they perform poorly, are criticized by teachers for failing to apply themselves. The converse is true for female students: when girls and young women perform poorly, teachers "seldom attribute intellectual inadequacy to lack of effort. Male students are led to believe that, with greater effort, they can achieve success" (1990, 179). Female students learn to believe that they are not intellectually able. These inequities in patterns of classroom interactions "may result in lower levels of achievement, career aspiration, and self-esteem for women. . . . Girls enter school at a higher achievement level and leave at a lower achievement level" (1990, 180).

These test scores are the traditional hallmarks of ability, used to track students in kindergarten through senior year, in admission or denial to college and graduate school, in the awarding of student loans and scholarships. Clearly, however, even though test makers constantly address the issue of test bias, gender and "achievement" seem to be confounded. Given the long-standing and pervasive patterns of estranging women from their own potential—and certainly traditional teaching and testing practices are suggestive of a larger picture—it is difficult to imagine plotting such complexity along a normal curve.

The structures and formats of standardized tests themselves work against the ways in which women construct knowledge. Mary Field Belenky et al. in *Women's Ways of Knowing*, suggest that patterns of socialization influence the development of women's perspectives on knowing in ways that are markedly different from men's (1986). "Relatively little attention has been paid to modes of learning, knowing, and valuing that may be specific to, or at least common in, women" (1986, 6). Of course, there are women students who seem to fare just fine in school, despite their gender status. Reading researchers suggest, however, that these women tend to adopt more privileged, androcentric modes of knowing and reading, acting as "members of a muted group [who] are disadvantaged in articulating their experience, since the language they must use is largely derived from the perceptions of the dominant group. . . . In order to be heard, muted group members must learn the dominant idiom and attempt to articulate within it" (Belenky et al. 1986, 21). What is absent or remains untranslatable, then, is "unvoiced, perhaps unthought" (Belenky et al. 1986, 21). It may be that college, and all education, for these students, is a process of unlearning one's self.

The research presented in *Women's Ways of Knowing* also suggests that traditional modes of assessment do not account for women's responses to, or on, such tests:

> It is not evaluation per se that subverts the aims of instruction but evaluation in the separate (impersonal, objective) mode. Evaluation in the connected mode requires the standards of evaluation be constructed in collaboration with the students. Where impersonal standards are used, the students are turned into objects,

and the connection between teacher and student is broken. The "feminine world of subjectness" is abandoned in favor of the "masculine world of objectness" (Noddings 1984, 196). As [Nel] Noddings says, "Many of the practices embedded in the masculine curriculum masquerade as essential to the maintenance of standards," but in fact "they accomplish quite a different purpose: the systematic dehumanization of both female and male children through the loss of the feminine." In an educational system that placed care at its center, human development might take a different course. (Belenky et al. 1986, 208–9)

Some in education, particularly at the university level, may find an "ethic of care," or affiliation, one that characterizes women's moral thinking (Gilligan 1982; Noddings 1984; Ruddick 1980) falling far short of the "ethic of rights," involving competition and individualism (Gilligan 1982) that typifies male moral perspectives and the academy. (Of course, many women do not subscribe to an ethic of care, and, conversely, many men embrace this moral stance.) Despite the many caring and careful teachers, however, our hierarchical structures—evaluation in particular—institutionalize and valorize a meritocratic order—the "best" students "make it" and the rest do not. Yet in this view, we lose sight of our purposes and ignore who our students are. Some teachers have difficulty conceiving of careful, learner-centered teaching:

> We once heard a professor . . . remark that the students were passive because the teachers were "too nurturant" and that a more impersonal approach might produce more independent, responsible, and active learners. Presumably she meant that in "taking care," of students, we rob them of responsibility. . . . But surely there are forms of talking care that make the ones we care for stronger rather than weaker. Taking care need not mean taking over. (Belenky 1986, 213)

Indeed, "taking over" seems, to us, careless.

Students' narratives of life in school suggest that the "impersonal" approach leads to dehumanization, if not depersonalization. Mike Rose, in *Lives on the Boundary*, comments on the experiences of one student:

> "It was so weird," said Kathy. "I was walking down the hall in the engineering building and suddenly I felt really strange. I felt I was completely alone here. . . . I go for days and don't see anybody I know." The huge lecture halls, the distance from the professors, the streams of students you don't know. . . . Some will eventually feel the loneliness as passage. . . . But a much deeper sense of isolation comes if the loneliness you feel is rooted in the books and lectures that surround you, in the very language of the place. You are finally sitting in the lecture hall you have been preparing to sit in for years. You have been the good student—perhaps even the star—you are to be the engineer, the lawyer, the doctor. Your parents have knocked themselves out for you. And you can't get what some man is saying in an *introductory* course. You're not what you thought you were. The alien voice of the lecturer is telling you something central to your being, is after all, a wish spun in the night, a ruse, the mist and vapor of sleep. (1989, 174)

A Vietnamese student at Augustana College writes of his sense of being in school, how, as in Rose's description, school is a nightmarish illusion of some kind, a place where he is always an outsider: "In my life, I remembered that I raised my hand in class only several times. I felt scared when I did that. . . . That why in class, I always chose a passive role. . . . In school, I never felt right . . . I thought about the days I was there was a bad dream I had."

At another college, a Salvadoran student says: "Before, when I just came to college, I was afraid that I wasn't going to survive. Because my English . . . they said you have to write one paper, it was like I was gonna die . . . because I couldn't express myself to begin with. I was afraid" (Dipardo 1991, 2).

Olivia Castellano writes:

> I did not escape years of being told I wasn't right, that because of my ethnicity and gender I was somehow defective and incomplete. Those years left wounds on my self-esteem, wounds so deep that even armed with my books and stolen knowledge I could not entirely escape deep feelings of unworthiness. . . . I was so frightened by my white, male professors—especially in the English Department—they looked so arrogant and were so unforgiving of their knowledge—that I didn't have the nerve to major in English, although it was the major I really wanted. (1992, 379)

Students learn otherness, particularly linguistic marginalization, early on in school. Otherness is established not only in classroom expectations, but in the larger school community as well; it becomes a haunting and debilitating condition, constantly alienating students from themselves and from the institution. A senior at the University of Michigan says:

> When I'm walking to class, I feel defensive. Right off the bat, there's like an initial shock about you, to your presence. The white students are looking at you. . . . It's generally assumed by all whites that your presence is a product of affirmative action . . . they're wondering what you're doing here. And they're wondering if you're going to be as stupid as all the rest of them. The whites at the university struck me as so arrogant, so pompous, and so condescending, that I could not stand the sight of them. When I was finished with my classes, all I wanted to do was go back to my room, shut my door, and not have to see their faces. There was a cost because I shut myself off from people . . . and I felt as if it was eating me up. Very literally eating me alive. (from "Racism 101" 1988)

For other minority students, difference is a category to be avoided assiduously. One Chicana was angry to find her name listed with the names of other students of color in a campus multicultural resource handbook. "I don't even speak Spanish," she wrote. "What am I a resource of?" From that point on, she used an anglicized version of her name. Certainly, to have one's identity threatened by the culture of school, to be outside of the educational mainstream has profound consequences for students' relationship to themselves, the world, their learning, and their academic performance.

The costs are great, as the University of Michigan student said. The students' narratives eloquently describe the pain and price of acculturation and achievement in college. Both teaching and assessment practice, as well as institutional policies, need to attend to difference and educational inequity with methodologies more sensitive than comparisons and standardization. Madeleine Grumet, quoting Jean Elshtain, notes that "human bodies, human families, and human discourse present annoying obstacles to the creation of a . . . 'rationalist mericratic order that would require, namely, the application to, and assessment of, all human beings on a single set of formal and abstract criteria' " (1988, 169): Extended, qualitative, and contextualized inquiry represent ways to listen to and learn from rather than exclude these "annoying obstacles." In analyzing achievement tests and the education of African-American students, Asa Hilliard recommends that we gather much more information about the educational experiences of these students, and even then, says Hilliard:

> No matter how good such instruments [standardized measures] are, if they follow the present pattern, they are likely to be multiple-choice, paper-and-pencil tests. We need to hold out for more. There is a need to broaden the assessment process, for we need detailed information on the progress of our children in many areas. In particular, we need detailed information on their writing, speaking, discussion, and dialogue." (1990, 142)

Linguist Jim Cummins describes an approach to teaching and assessment that accounts for diversity as well as engages teachers as agents. We find his last two recommendations especially useful here:

> Students from "dominated" societal groups are "empowered" or "disabled" as a direct result of their interactions with educators in the schools. These characteristics are mediated by the implicit or explicit role to which . . . (3) the pedagogy promotes intrinsic motivation on the part of students to use language actively in order to generate their own knowledge; and (4) professionals involved in assessment become advocates for minority students rather than legitimizing the location of the "problem" in the students. (1986, 21)

DIFFERENCE AND DEFICIT

In educational testing practice, we too often not only silence diversity, but we recast it as irrelevant or deficient. For example, consider the dissonance between our theoretical knowledge of literacy and the constructs of literacy suggested in achievement tests. In reading and writing theory, there is a robust body of research about the importance of the reader's background and prior knowledge on comprehension of text as well as the significance of the rhetorical aspects of writing; yet test guidebooks warn the test taker about using "outside information" to answer questions.

Mary Trachsel, in her examination of college literacy testing, writes that on such tests the formal dimension of language eclipses the communicative functions, as shown in "recent efforts on the part of test makers to present texts as autonomous receptacles of meaning and to remain uninvolved in a communicative exchange by disavowing any necessary adherence to the value systems presented in reading passages" (1992, 150). The message of such a disclaimer to test takers is that "functional communication is a nonessential component of literacy skills allegedly measured by such tests" (1992, 150). Mary Trachsel also notes that this message is further established by test makers' declaration that the "essays will be read by impartial readers and [their] admonishing [the students] not to call upon any prior knowledge that they may have in connection with the substance of the reading passages in the test" (1992, 151).

One preparation guide for the LSAT, entitled *Cracking the System: The LSAT,* supplies hopeful law school–applicants with directives as to how they should tackle reading passages on the LSAT:

> FORGET ABOUT "READING COMPREHENSION"
> Your goal is to answer questions and to earn points, not to understand a handful of obscure reading passages. The less time you spend reading the passage, the more time you will have to answer the questions. You need only a superficial understanding of a passage to answer its questions. If you try to gain more than a superficial understanding, you'll waste time, become confused, and lose points (Robinson 1989, 17–18).

We are left to wonder, then, just what does the test test? Although awareness of the rhetorical dimensions of literacy, perceptions of relationships, and critical reflection are considered evidence of creativity, intelligence, and good scholarship, they will not garner any points on such tests; indeed, according to this genre of test guides, attempts to comprehend will confuse test takers and divert their time and attention away from the real task—racking up points. This presents a marked and serious gap between our teaching practices and understanding of learning/knowing and the constructs of knowing created by current test measures. We agree to rank, admit (or not), place (into "remedial," "regular," or honors curricula) students by their ability to fill-in-the-bubble of the correct antonym for, say, "frangible," in spite of "a growing body of pedagogical theory and practices encouraging teachers to consider the functionally, socially embedded aspects of literacy and to promote them in their students' learning" (Trachsel 1992, 176).

The formal, as well as epistemological, codes and conventions of the tests themselves, requiring decontextualized knowledge produced in competitive settings, militate against the deeply embedded cultural practices of many of the test takers. To not allow a peer to see one's answers would be offensive to Vietnamese students. To answer quickly would be poor thinking to a Navajo student (Brown 1991, 69). To score better than one's boyfriend might be thought unwise for a female student. To answer a question without group collaboration, "talking story," would be puzzling to an indigenous Hawaiian child (Au 1980). Narrative sequences can vary according to one's sociolinguistic community, differing greatly from the teachers' and the tests' "correct" discourse patterns (Michaels 1986). Shirley Brice Health's ethnography (1983) of rural southern children shows the high degree of discontinuity between the language of school and testing and the community, leading to a high percentage of failure of children from the "wrong" culture, the one missing on the test and linguistic codes of school talk.

Rexford Brown describes the pedagogical principles operating in the reservation classroom of a non-Native American. The social studies teacher asserts that "every teacher here has lowered standards . . . whether they'll admit it or not. We all bend over backwards to get these kids through. But they don't know very much" (1991, 63). Brown, responding to the classroom interactions and the teacher interviews in this school, notes:

> [This teacher] believes that most of [his students] can neither read nor write at the high school–level, but he carries on as if they could. He makes no effort to help them; thus, they do poorly, and he lowers his standards. It is apparently easier to lower standards than to teach what the students need to know in order to do the work . . . lecturing and recitation make a lot of sense when you are pretty sure your students can't read and write very well, and you don't feel your job is to address those deficiencies. You identify yourself as a "content" person, not a "skills" person, and you try to cram some knowledge into them and then test quickly . . . you give students an oral education. (1991, 63)

Indeed, traditional literacy instruction, the foundation of academic achievement, has symbolized deficit principles. The reading teacher's role, until recently, has been to diagnose and correct defects. Models of deficiency have, in particular, driven discussions of minority children's literacy: cultural deprivation, cultural "difference" (different than whom?) linguistic impoverishment, even the insidious "lazy lips" notion popular just a few decades ago. Because this kind of ethnocentrism is not as acceptable to discuss in public fora any longer, political response now finds other avenues to veil the same deficit theory. We have nervously elevated "our" cultural heritage and how many "facts" your first grader needs to recognize (easily packaged to translate into test materials).

Then there is the more technoscientific version of intrapsychic and asocial causes for difference—blaming the victim through sociobiology and individuals' chemical and genetic problems (the learning disability gene, the attention deficit gene, the illiteracy gene). The latter rationalizations offer the victims little hope for recovering from their malady and succeed in deflecting attention from the social and political realities: that schools as they are (employing, for the most part, a transmission model of education) cannot nourish a great number of our students; cannot acknowledge race, class, and gender as endowments of their students; and devalue "the contributions that students can make in terms of their own experience, interests, and methods of inquiry; thereby impoverishing the learning experience" (Wells 1986, 219).

The appalling overrepresentation of minority children in special education classrooms attests to the system's approach to "organizational irritants," (Thomas, in Bartoli 1986, 127) that is, the creation of educational ghettoes. Politicians' injunctions to "just read to your children" as a remedy for our educational ills ignore that school, library, and public transportation budgets have been gutted and that the poor can envision few incentives for participating in the American educational dream. Beneath the rhetoric of democratic schooling and individualized learning still exist the policies of educational Darwinism. The introduction of competition—as an avenue for school reform—among public schools for "desirable" students and even more desirable funding affirms this.

The language sometimes used to characterize students in college reinforces the notion that students have acute deficiencies and are outsiders to the elite culture of college. Mina Shaughnessy's pivotal analysis of basic writers (1977), those entering the college community with the inauguration of open admissions at CUNY (City University of New York), transformed writing teachers' ways of understanding error—by demonstrating that the puzzling (to teachers) syntactical structures, word choices, usage "mistakes" were really guided by a complex internal logic rather than laziness or illiteracy. Yet the notion of deficiency endures: we continue to hear the language of inadequacy and dysfunction in faculty rancor over "remedial" courses, writing "clinics," deteriorating admissions standards, and grade inflation.

College study skills books, a profitable segment of the textbook industry, are saturated with the language of deficiency as well as efficiency, reminiscent of the time-motion studies of the 1930s and of the production model derived from business. In this worldview, success in college is more a matter of management savvy than of reflective learning and epiphany. One text, *How to Manage Your Life,* is a compendium of Andrew Carnegie–like quick fixes: To avoid becoming "a nuisance on class discussion . . . identify a reasonable number of comments for you to make given the size and length of the class. Keep track of how many comments you have made (as well as noting their length), and spread your quota over the entire class period" (Williams and Long 1991, 165).

The title of a very popular study skills text, *Becoming a Master Student,* characterizes the position of students as colonial, aspiring to become owners of enough cultural capital (accrual of courses with passing grades) to possess the promise of lucrative credentials. Reading becomes a routinized task, overlaid with pseudoscientific steps which bear little resemblance to how or why real readers read. The advice of study skills how-to books suggests a kind of learning driven by mechanical behaviors or formulas, a matter of taking the proper kinds of notes in the proper kinds of notebooks. Curriculum and canon here are stable truths, not to be questioned or actively encountered with a critical stance or personal knowledge.

HOW DID WE GET HERE?

The emergence of the assessment mandate directed toward colleges enjoys concurrence with several other phenomena in the academy. The 1970s was characterized by growing heterogeneity among the college student population, following "open admissions" policies, increasing numbers of students entering college, changing demographics in the United States, and an influx of international students. Additionally, the devastating economic conditions of the last decade have forced colleges into fierce competition for a dwindling pool of applicants and funds and, thus, the subsequent lowering, or perceived lowering, of admissions criteria ("scraping the bottom of the barrel," in faculty vernacular). Widely read and watched media as well as some academics offered (and continue to present) dire tales of the decline of education and the graduation of "illiterate" students. It is within these circumstances that the mandate to assess arose.

Toni Morrison, in a keynote address to the Chicago Humanities Council (1992), spoke of the changing demographics our schools, the invisible becoming visible, and the minority becoming a majority. She argues that assessment is a political response of the educational system to the

> perceived threat of an unforeseen, unwelcomed change in both curricula, content and population . . . unconcealed rage over the perceived loss of a neutral golden age, a nonpolitical academy and society . . . a resistance [to change] predicated in claims of maintaining excellence, but based in fact on a sexist, racist, and culturally privileged will to maintain power. . . . Before, [the point] was for us to become more like them, or depending upon your point of view, to make them more like us, or to measure the growth by how close the grower came to a paradigm already agreed upon. [Populations seeking education today . . . are suggesting that] they want to say who they are, not be told. They want to participate in the measuring process.

The well publicized "decline" in standards and "crises" in education may be seen as a kind of political backlash to any increasingly diverse student body with increasingly diverse concerns. ("We don't have a *white* student union. Why should they get one?" or "We don't have *men's* studies. Why should they?" Or, "We're hiring a priest. What next? A rabbi?") The pressure to standardize educational outcomes and curricula is also a reaction to the educational legacy of the 1960s and '70s, when students' involvement and choice in their studies increased. As former Secretary of Education, William Bennett decried the apparent encroachment of "eccentric" studies onto the rightful ground of core knowledge, arguing that college students were being denied "an adequate education in the culture and civilization of which they are members" (Sims 1992, 9). Bennett's report, "To Reclaim a Legacy," authorized colleges to amend this disturbance expediently. The cultural anxiety that fuels Bennett's reclamation,

Hirsch-like lists comes at a time when being "American," (lazy or hardworking) seems up for grabs. We are asked, in education, to respond with an escalation in testing of this "core knowledge." Certainly, this is an anxiety that can lead to a constricted notion of academic success that threatens (1) our efforts toward educational equity, (2) the expansion of curriculum and canon, and (3) our attention to learners and learning rather than the sanctity of some imagined, static cultural text.

Mike Rose writes that "it's our cultural fears—of internal decay, of loss of order, of diminishment—that weave into our assessments of literacy and scholastic achievement" (1989, 7). The movement of the federal government has been to centralize educational outcomes and curricula through national assessments:

> Oppositional or alternative goals such as student empowerment, individuation, creativity and intellectual skepticism embodied in art and music . . . and unconventional learning styles and subject matter are to be excluded from approved pedagogical or curricular mandates. In short, the official policy is to wage an ideological offensive to persuade local school officials as moral agents of intellectual standardization (Aronowitz and Giroux 1991, 9).

Jenny Cook-Gumperz, Harvey Graff, and others have noted the historic rise of testing in response to the mass education movement in the United States: "We are firmly in the midst of a 'literacy crisis.' It is not the first such perceived crisis; at times of large-scale, rapid change and confusion about the condition of civilization and morality, 'literacy' has seemed to suffer a 'decline' almost generationally across the span of recorded history" (Graff 1987, 373). The pattern of testing, literacy testing, in particular, suggests a sinister agenda:

> The development of universal education in America was directed by a ruling-class desire to bring literacy under the control of a single, state-sponsored system of education. This desire was motivated by a fear that literacy's power to enact social transformation could be a dangerous weapon in the hands of members of the working class, were they not properly socialized to accept the authority of established social institutions (Soltow and Stevens 198).

It is not surprising that the mandate to assess follows similar perceived patterns in higher education.

Yet the impetus also emerges from within another sort of circumstances. Paradigm shifts in our disciplines have led us to look more closely and with more generosity at the social as well as the institutional; at the effect of the observer on the observed; at the individual in concert, rather than in isolation, from others; at the reader(s) composing the text(s) rather than an ideal reader combing through the "hidden meanings" of an autonomous, univocal text; at the social construction of knowledge rather than the monolithic canon. And it is these intentions that can inform and shape our beliefs and interpretations of student learning and assessment. Rather than responding to the pressure to assess with more narrowly defined, atheoretical testing instruments concentrated on ends rather than means, sorting populations rather then understanding students who are learning, the converse could also become policy and practice—(1) that assessments could disrupt the structures of excluding, ranking, labeling, and disabling students (and teachers); (2) that assessments could be reflective of, and shaped by, a "pedagogy of thoughtfulness" (Brown 1991); and (3) that, most of all, assessment could improve teaching, by carefully interrogating and understanding the experiences, expectations, and beliefs of learners and teachers.

What makes these issues even more complex is this: While it is essential for teachers to understand their own cultural worlds and those of their students, this knowledge alone does not offer us any simple way of assisting students. Who among us has not experienced the minority student who comes to us angry and defensive—intransigent silence interrupted only by "I don't know." Other such students, when forced into dialogue, tell us we are unreasonable and confusing. And still others smile and nod, pretending to understand for the sake of harmony in the relationship and in deference to our authority. Of course, they not only "don't know," they are often terrified, and their response, in many cases, is to disappear, stop coming to class, or leave school altogether.

At Fredonia one semester, I was advising incoming students who had not yet preregistered. In the midst of the relative chaos that often characterizes late registration, someone guided a Japanese female over to me. Happy to help her devise a schedule and speaking very slowly, I explained the general college program. She repeated over and over to me "Yes, I understand." When she told me she intended to major in English, I inquired about her proficiency, which I sensed was relatively weak at the oral level. She assured me haltingly that "talking no very good, but read and write, yes." When we were through, she smiled gratefully and thanked me "very much for kindness." Assuring me that she understood which building to go to next, she left the room. I followed, just to be sure, and watched her exit the building in the wrong direction and proceed to head off campus. Quick-witted as I am obviously wont to be, I suddenly realized that she had not understood most of what I had been saying to (at) her. I went after her, brought her back to the advising room, slowly and carefully began again, and finally found a student to escort her to various buildings and through the registration process. Later, of course, I would find out that her language proficiency was woefully inadequate for success in college-level literature classes. Fortunately, through a system of jury-rigged support services and the goodwill and energy of student tutors and a few colleagues, we managed to make her semester with us reasonably constructive. But I cannot help but wonder where she would have ended up if I had not followed her that day. I do remember, however, that she was headed west.

If we fail to learn about our students, then we fail to educate them. Assessments defining our students and our own selves and work in meaningless ways promote neither excellence nor equity, nor even goodness, in schools. But assessments inviting interaction, dialogue, reflection, and learning offer us a way to evaluate, respond, and promote learning. We move now to a discussion of portfolio assessment, first programmatic and second, focused on individuals. We suggest that portfolios are one of the clearest, and perhaps most complex, means of including students and their voices in our assessments of curricula and individuals.

CHAPTER 3

Qualitative Program Assessment: From Tests to Portfolios

For several years now, [with support from the Fund for the Improvement of Postsecondary Education], Fredonia has been assessing a new general education program, and they've chosen to go the local route in all cases, with faculty-designed exams to cover a variety of cross-cutting general-education outcomes. I think that's a right idea. . . . In [the final] report they set forth what they learned—and equally interesting, what they didn't learn.

They didn't, for instance, ever learn the "Truth" about their students. In fact, much of their work at the outset entailed discussion—and, I dare say, heated debate—about the soundness of this and that instrument, pilot testing, whether the results could be compared with this way or that, what was valid, what not . . . with the result, as I say, that no truth was learned. What the faculty *did* learn was that . . . students were taking and passing individual courses alright, but they weren't seeing connections; they couldn't put the pieces together.

The solution? No doubt there were (and should be) several. . . . [Fredonia faculty] are now working to develop a portfolio approach to assessment that will give them more in-depth information about each student's ability to put the pieces together, but also—and here's the beauty of the thing—help the student *develop* that ability. (Hutchings 1990, 4)

Indeed, the use of portfolios throws light on the very process of measurement or evaluation. For portfolio assessment occupies an interesting in-between area between the clean, artificial world of carefully controlled assessment ("Take out your pencils. Don't turn over your books till I say 'go'.") and the swampy real world of offices and living rooms where people actually write things for a purpose and where we as actual readers look at texts and cannot agree for the life of us (sometimes for the tenure of us) about what they mean and how good they are. Or to put it differently, use of portfolios highlights the tension between *validity* and *reliability*. (Elbow 1991, xii)

STORIES FROM THE FRONT: THE FREDONIA EXPERIENCE

As a teacher of English, I became involved with Fredonia's assessment project primarily because I believed then, and continue to believe, that program assessment and outcomes-based educational systems have potential for tremendous damage unless they are created, implemented, and controlled by *teachers* who understand what actually goes on in classrooms and who also understand how genuinely complex it is to quantify human cognition, cognitive growth, or "learning" in any but the most primitive terms. Everyone involved must resist the temptation to return to simplistic "competency-based" models of education that emphasize discrete, fragmented, and often irrelevant skills.

But regardless of my opinions about the issue, I feared that the State of New York was moving toward a demand for programmatic assessment at the college level and outcomes-based individual assessment in the public school system. Given that fact, I agreed to be a part of a group composed almost entirely of faculty, who would create a series of instruments designed to assess our General College Program. And lately, as I find the public media filled with calls for a national assessment, I am all the more committed to trying to short-circuit the foolishness that is sometimes associated with assessment. And I reiterate that, from my point of view, assessment of any kind that is not clearly and primarily directed at improving what we do in classrooms is a waste of money and time.

So let me begin at my beginning. I do not believe a detailed description of Fredonia's General College Program (hereafter GCP) is either necessary or particularly interesting for the general reader. Let it suffice for me to say that the program is not "competency-" or "skills-based" in any of the traditional senses of those terms. Students have a broad degree of choice among courses across disciplines that have been specially designed or redesigned to emphasize print literacy, metacognitive or reflexive thinking, problem solving, scientific reasoning, a sense of history, and an understanding of foreign cultures and the degrees to which ethnocentrism can inhibit an understanding of other cultures. The major point here is that we were not trying to find out if our students could write business letters, answer multiple-choice questions about a reading passage, fill in a chart of elements and their atomic weights, find India on a blank map, explain the importance of the year 1492, or itemize the basic tenets of Buddhism. Rather, we wanted to find out how much they had grown or improved as writers and readers, how much their mathematical and scientific thinking had matured, and how their ideas about human history and cultural diversity had been affected between their first and third years of college.

A committee was created of twelve faculty members representing a broad variety of disciplines, and we set about the task of boldly going where none of us had ever gone before; I use this Star Trek allusion purposely because for many of us, myself included, the whole endeavor smacked of science fiction involving uncharted space voyages into an investigation of dimensions we were not at all sure we could investigate.

Like typically good scholars, we began by reading everything we could find that had been written about assessment in the years immediately prior to our project. I would like to say that this reading solved our problems, but for the most part it did not provide us with a test or series of tests we might simply implement. Nor had we really expected it to. Instead, the research confirmed what most of us had expected in the first place: Standardized tests manufactured and sold by Educational Testing Service (ETS) or American College Testing (ACT) were of almost no use for several reasons, not the least of which being that they do not really test much of anything other than how well one does on a standardized test. The best assessment instruments are those created by the individuals intimately involved with students, the institution and the programs that are to be assessed (Aper, Cuver, Hinkle 1990, 476).

Consequently, it became immediately and painfully clear that we would have to create our own instruments, test our tests, so to speak, to find out if they provided the information we were searching for, teach ourselves to evaluate student performance on the tests, find a control group at another college, give the tests, score them, evaluate our findings, and make whatever follow-up recommendations we might wish. It was not so much a problem of realizing that we were "in over our heads" that frightened us, as much as it was the realization that this was going to be a long swim up river against a formidable current.

The Process

The full committee began by considering brief presentations from selected members of the group intended to highlight some of the key issues and potential problems we might encounter as we attempted to create assessment instruments for given areas. Immediately following this series of relatively wide-ranging discussions, we split into temporary subgroups in order to create itemized lists of specific skills, abilities, or processes that should be tested in a given area. The subgroup working with reading, writing, and reflexive thinking, for example, had not decided at this point that reflexive thinking would even be a part of the assessment. The importance of these initial discussions cannot be overemphasized: it was only through these initial discussions, as the group articulated relatively obvious items—things like "the ability to create a central focus in an essay," and "the ability to identify an author's central focus in an article," that we began to articulate more complex items (the ability to infer, or to identify underlying assumptions). And this investigation eventually led the group to items involving metacomprehension and metacognition (meaning the ability to recognize relationships between one's own experience and the experience represented in work produced by another author and consciousness of one's own learning style and ways of approaching learning something or learning how to do something).

The point here is that these subgroups were intensely involved in a discovery process that would lead to an articulation of the kinds of things the assessment would eventually assess. These lists were then reviewed and refined by the entire committee. This review was a particularly important step because it would eventually lead to a fully articulated set of "grids" on which all the skills or abilities to be assessed would be listed and, eventually, matched with the test question or exercise that would allow us to assess student performance (See Appendix A: Grid for Reading for an example). Although this grid would evolve as we more fully articulated the various assessment instruments, this beginning was of central importance as it helped us to engage in the process of creating the tests themselves.

Having established the grid and having agreed that we would create instruments that actively engaged students in "doing" whatever kind of thinking, reasoning, or languaging that we wanted to evaluate, we split into three subgroups: one focusing on reading, writing, and reflexive thinking; one focusing on mathematical and scientific reasoning; and one on historicism and ethnocentrism. Each subgroup then (1) created instruments that might assess growth in these areas (as specified on the grid); (2) identified which specific outcomes listed under the General Education Outcomes (See Appendix B) a given instrument might assess; and (3) submitted the "test" to the whole committee for discussion, refinement, and, occasionally, ridicule.

I say *ridicule* with good humor because anyone identified with such a process must become aware that the assessors (a much privileged class) might have tremendous difficulty succeeding on many of the instruments that a given assessment group is using. It was important for all concerned to see me and my sociologist friend laugh in embarrassment when faced with blank maps and told to fill in the names of countries (an instrument later rejected). At another meeting, of course, we had the fun of watching some of our prestigious colleagues fail at some of the problem-solving tasks that had been suggested for use.

As we worked together to examine the tests each subgroup was creating, we also continued to refer to the original grid, making sure that our tests were directly related to our defined purpose. Through this interactive process of examining potential test instruments, referring to the initial grid, trying the tests ourselves, and continual discussion, we eventually arrived at a set of instruments we felt we might use in the assessment. I emphasize these early steps because, without them, without giving them the time and energy they demanded, the project would never have been completed. Throughout the next two years, but especially as we worked together to refine and revise various test instruments, the grid operated as our stable center against which we might consider the value of a given test: (1) matters of efficiency (Does one kind of test allow us to assess more items on the grid than another?); (2) matters of relevance to the task (Does a given instrument assess something that is on the grid?); and (3) matters focusing on the quality of the instrument (Does it address the complexity of the item on the grid, or simply appear to do so?).

An absolutely key point, here is this: anyone engaging in programmatic assessment must be thoroughly familiar with the program that is being assessed and its stated objectives (Aper, Cuver, Hinkle 1990, 476). It was not unusual in our early discussions (and even some later ones) when were were designing the instruments, for one or more individuals to make strong arguments for inclusion of an instrument that would test geographical knowledge, foreign language competency, and so forth. The only problem was that these were not objectives of the program we were assessing. It is all too easy to get caught in the trap of trying to assess everything that some idealized program *should* do or that some group *should* know, regardless of whether or not the program being assessed happens to address all the everythings. It is important to remember that it is rather easy to identify what all educated people *should be able to do,* but we may want to ask whether or not we can do all the things we think that others should do.

At any rate, everyone on the committee tried to do the tests, critiqued them, offered suggestions for change and revision, and sometimes simply decided that a given test was either irrelevant or useless. Once the tests were approved by the larger committee, each group set about articulating the criteria by which degrees of success or failure would be measured for each instrument. Creating clearly articulated criteria and hierarchies of criteria ("outcomes," if you will) that might allow us to clearly differentiate one level of performance from another was much more difficult than creating the tests themselves. And this process, along with training ourselves to score the tests, took the most time and energy, aside from actually scoring the final tests. The first part of the process took place over the period of about one year. When it was over, we had nine tests and we were finally ready to "test the tests" by administering them to small groups of students so that we could find out if the tests gave us the information we wanted and so that we could begin to train ourselves to score the tests.

Once we began to examine the first set of student responses to the tests, we found that things were not going as well as we had hoped. Directions on one test had to be carefully refined so that students could not simply define historical events in terms of the last two years of their lives. Problem-solving tests had to be changed because some of them were so difficult that no one could do them at all: if a test is so difficult that no one can do it, one has no basis for examining change or growth; one simply finds out that no one can do it. On the reading test, some of the follow-up questions showed themselves to be either redundant or unnecessary, and the essay we had chosen for them to read proved to be a little too long for the time period we had allotted. In all cases, as we began to try to score the tests, we found ourselves refining scoring criteria in an attempt to make this subjective process of evaluation reliable and valid.

In a sense we began again. We revised the tests, discussed revisions, gave them again, scored them again, and only then felt that we might finally go ahead with the test itself. I will not even go into the problems we had finding another institution with a profile similar to our own that would agree to give the tests, but by the end of two years, we had found an institution to cooperate, we had given the tests, and spent the final year scoring them, evaluating our results, and writing final reports and recommendations.

The following discussion provides a brief description of the tests themselves so that they can be seen in a little better context. But it is important to note that this is simply intended to provide a perspective. If we learned nothing else (and I believe we learned quite a bit) through our involvement with assessment, it is this: qualitative assessment of the kind we are discussing here and the kind that is involved in a portfolio system demands that those doing the assessing create their own instruments, criteria, and scoring system. While a reader may borrow freely from what follows, the first step in assessment is to be sure that you are assessing your program and not someone else's or some fictional program that you have created in your own minds.

All of the following test descriptions are paraphrased and/or quoted from *The GCP and Student Learning: A Report to the Campus*, written by Minda Rae Amiran with The General College Program Assessment Committee, August 1989, and referred to as the GCP Report in the following discussion. (For a complementary discussion of the Fredonia assessment and related assessment projects at Western College at Miami University of Ohio, see Amiran, Schilling, and Schilling).

The Instruments

Writing Test. To test our students' writing ability, we asked entering first-year students, entering transfer students, and upperclass students who had not been transfer students to describe and analyze what they had found to be a major problem with the educational system in their high schools. We chose the subject because we wanted to be sure to present the writers with a topic about which all would have adequate background experience and knowledge to allow them to write concretely and, hopefully, with some engagement. The essays were first scored holistically, and then on the basis of separate criteria like the ability to create a clear central point, offer supporting evidence, analyze reasons, and write Standard English.

Reading Test. Because we desired to avoid the artificiality inherent in most comprehension tests and the multiple-choice questions that characterize such tests, we chose to give the students a twelve-page article from an introductory anthology in sociology. We chose the particular article because it focused on a community's response to two groups of young people, one of which was comprised of "good" kids, and the other of which was composed of rowdier kids. Our primary concern was that the students would have enough background knowledge to bring to the text to allow them to transact with it constructively and with some interest. The students were then asked to provide several sentences of response to a series of questions based on the reading. These questions asked them to identify the author's main point, his supporting evidence, the implications of his essay, his underlying assumptions, and the organizing principle used by the author. Further, in hopes of seeing to what extent students could place the reading in their own context and experience, measuring its sense or nonsense against their own experiences, we also asked them to explain why they agreed or disagreed with the author's main point, illustrating their opinion through a relevant personal experience. Students had ninety minutes in which to complete the test.

Reflexive Thinking. Before describing this particular test, a brief digression may help here. Initially, we had intended to call this test Metacognitive Thinking, but early in the design stages we knew that we could not begin to examine the complexities involved in metacognition through a single test. At the same time, we believe that metacognition is central and essential for the most proficient degrees of learning to occur. Since *metacognition* is a relatively new concept in education, easily oversimplified, some defining should help here. By *metacognition*, we do not simply mean the ability to structure one's own approaches to learning a concept or solving a problem (though this could be a part of the broader definition). Metacognition involves more than the self-knowledge that "I always approach a long writing assignment by making an outline (or by free writing, or whatever)." Metacognition suggests a *meta*-level of consciousness of one's own thought processes. As such, it involves an almost simultanenous, conscious degree of self-awareness:. "This is how I approach or think about a situation (problem, issue, concept)"; "this is how I might best approach this particular concept in order to more fully understand it"; "this is how I am thinking about this issue, and it is or is not effective"; "these are the other possible approaches I might take instead."

At its most basic level, a lack of metacognition (or *metacomprehension*) characterizes the learner who has "studied" the chapter for the test, believes that s/he "knows" the material, but is then completely baffled when faced with the test itself. Not only did this learner not know that s/he did not know, she does not understand how to go about knowing (Weaver 1988, 24).

Of course, at its most advanced levels, some kind of full consciousness of self and self's interaction with others, one might reasonably argue that no one is ever genuinely metacognitive. We certainly find it difficult to imagine this degree of metacognition. One is tempted to say that "it takes one to know one," adding that only a self-deceptive egocentric would claim to be fully metacognitive. Anything that involves thinking about one's own thinking presents us with the most serious complexities (and, some might argue, impossibilities). And yet, as difficult as it is to describe, some learners pretty clearly enjoy a higher degree of self-conscious awareness of their own learning processes than others. And it also appears clear to us that the most powerful learners are those who are best able to monitor their own learning processes: These are the learners who "know when they know" and are able to structure their own learning so that they can productively move on from that self-knowledge toward more and fuller knowing. Furthermore, these learners "know when they do not know," which puts them in the position of using a different approach to the problem or seeking help.

While our reflexive thinking test only scratches the surface of assessing students' metacognitive abilities in this more complex sense, it does, at least, approach the issue. But given the obvious importance of developing higher degrees of metacognition, we believe that portfolios most directly suggest ways both to develop and to assess this essential ability.

Likewise, our sense of the importance of metacognition is directly related to the importance we place on actively engaging students in the writing process, across the curriculum, in order that they might consistently attempt to use language to articulate and examine what it is they think: As a linguistic process, writing uniquely allows learners to be surprised by what they know, discover what they do not know, and use what they know to know more (Murray 1985, 7). More directly, writing is first and foremost a self-reflective process that is both regressive and progressive in the same moment. As writers use writing to discover what it is they are trying to say, they also discover more that needs to be said. In the moment of writing, the writer moves between the roles of writer, producing the text, and reader, reading what has been written:

> In the moment of author(iz)ing, the moment of writing, the writer is reading (using language to make sense of) that which is in there (inside the writer) in order to externalize it through the surface structures of language. . . . In the moment of externalizing the meaning, . . . the writer engages in the recursive process of reading what he is writing and writing what he is reading. The two processes are inextricably bound together. (Courts 1991, 110)

In the Fredonia assessment, hoping to find the extent to which our students are conscious of their own learning processes, we asked them to write a brief description of something they learned outside of school and then to answer follow-up questions examining what they had written. These follow-up questions asked them to identify the major factors influencing the learning event they described, to identify any pattern that characterized the learning experience, and to contrast that with any patterns they observed in school learning situations, to draw any conclusions they might about learning in general, and to comment on the ways schools structure the learning experience. They had one hour for the entire task.

Quantitative Problem Solving. We created two similar tests of four questions each

> to assess student problem solving. One question on each test could be solved through very simple algebra, once the equations had been properly set up. Another was an open-ended estimation problem, under realistic conditions of uncertainty.

Problems three and four were identical on the two tests, though their order was reversed: the first of the pair was supplied with prompts, the second was not; though the setting of each problem was different, the algebraic solutions were very similar (Amiran 1989, 13–14).

In addition to being asked to solve the problem, students were asked to state their assumptions and explain their reasoning process. For example, one question was as follows: John has a pail with 40 washers in it and finds the total weight to be 175 ounces. Sue weighs the same pail with 20 washers in it and finds the total to be 95 ounces. (a) how much does each washer weigh? (b) how much does the pail weight? (c) no matter how trivial they may seem, what assumptions did you make in solving the problem? (Throughout the assessment, it was questions like this last one, *c*, that were particularly important to us because we were trying to assess students' *thinking processes* rather than their knowledge of unrelated bits of information.)

Scientific Reasoning. Students had to do two tasks for this exam: First, they had "to design an experiment to show the relationship between hours of exposure to sunlight and rate of growth in spider plants," and second, they had "to critique the report of a study on the correlation between amount of brown rice consumed and incidence of gout among older men" (Amiran 1989, 17).

Socioethical Understanding. There were three parts to this section of the exam:

1. " 'History' asks students to list ten of the most important events in human record, and choosing one of those events, to name three other events that would not have occurred or would have been very different if the chosen even had not taken place."

2. " 'Exchange Student' has students answer some uncomplimentary questions about the United States asked by an otherwise friendly Western European exchange student."

3. " 'Malbavia' posits a third world kingdom undergoing modernization as a result of newly discovered mineral wealth, and asks the students, as part of a UN team, to infer societal effects and make recommendations, some of which have to do with prevailing practices of hospitality and human sacrifice" (Amiran 1989, 19–20).

WHAT HAPPENED NEXT: RESULTS

For the sake of brevity, I will only report some of the most interesting generalizations that are supported by the assessment project. Though none of us would agree that what the students wrote in the composition test was particularly well-written, it was in this area that we saw the most obvious and greatest growth. Students clearly had improved as writers. But the results on the reading test were disturbing for several reasons: First, instead of finding improvement in their reading abilities, we found little significant growth in many important areas related to reading. Second, while this might not be reason for alarm if the first-year students had shown strong reading abilities, such was not the case. Third, while most of the students accurately identified the main point of the essay they read, and many did well in identifying the author's supporting evidence, few did well in identifying the implications of the essay, in articulating the author's assumptions, or in seeing relationships between the article, their own lives, and the society in which they live. In short, after achieving success at a literal level, these readers were unable to do much more.

Unfortunately, this inability to move beyond the literal, to generalize and abstract, characterized our findings on all the other tests. Finally, the results on the reading test caused us to question the results on the writing test: if students had improved significantly as writers, one might reasonably expect similar improvement in their reading abilities. If such results did not occur, then one had to question what it was we had tested on the writing test. This confusion further increased our interest in implementing a portfolio system of some sort.

As for the other tests, let me simply present some findings quoted from the GCP Report: "In absolute terms, few students proved very adept at reflexive thinking" (Amiran 1989, 12). Most of the students "lack the problem-solving or reasoning skills that would help them think the [algebraic] problem through in an orderly way [often complaining] that they don't like math or never have been good at it." (Amiran 1979, 16). Likewise, they were very weak in recognizing the assumptions they had to make in order to solve the problems they had been given.

On the scientific reasoning, students' performance "leaves much to be desired" (Amiran 1989, 18). Their comments suggested a student belief that unless one had a course in which a specific body of information had been studied, one could not conceivably begin to solve the problem. But since the problems were not based on specific knowledge of a given area of science, this indicated to us that the students knew little about scientific reasoning, empirical scientific methodology, complexity of identifying cause-effect relationships without a clearly established control, or researcher bias.

In the area of historical understanding and presentism, students were weak both in terms of establishing a chronology of events and in terms of seeing causal relationships between or among events. And results on socioethical reasoning left us with increasing cause for concern.

The problem is not that there is no growth, but the growth is generally minimal and the level of performance is seldom particularly gratifying.

Obviously, none of us was particularly pleased with what we found. On the other hand, we were not generally too surprised. By trying to measure growth in students' thinking and languaging processes, we knew that we were trying to assess ground that is seldom addressed in schools or colleges. Most testing focuses on assessing students' mastery of discrete bits of information and/or isolated fragmented skills. And we had consciously and purposefully avoided those kinds of tests. We know that our students "know something"; we wanted to find out what they could do with what they know and what kinds of growth they might have experienced as a result of their participation in the General College Program.

If the results are dispiriting, however, they also offer rays of light insofar as they suggest several things: (1) while students did not show a high degree of metacognition, they did indicate a considerable degree of awareness of how schools were failing them and offered plenty of suggestions about what needs to be changed; and (2) the results also indicated that, if we care about our students being something more than repositories of information, if we want them to be thinkers and doers, then we need to emphasize thinking and doing across the curriculum. And we need to empower teachers at the same time.

We at Fredonia know, for example, that our faculty have been participating in highly structured workshops in writing across the curriculum over the past seven years, and this is the only area in which we found significant growth. Of course, it is not particularly revolutionary to suggest that if we want something to change, we need to help faculty make the change instead of simply carping and casting blame. But all too often one finds little support for faculty development workshops of any kind at any level. In our case, however, the dean of General Studies has organized additional workshops for faculty to help them address multiculturalism in their own classrooms and disciplines. And small cadres of mathematicians and science faculty have begun to gather to address some of the more disturbing findings. On its own initiative, the Math Department conducted workshops for the faculty members who teach the introductory mathematics courses that most of our students take to fulfill their general program requirements. These workshops focused on examining ways to help students become more proficient as problem solvers. Likewise, small committees of faculty in the sciences, social sciences, and humanities worked to develop classroom activities that would help students become more aware of their own biases and assumptions. Further, as a result of the findings, many of us involved with the assessment and other interested faculty have worked individually to change the ways in which we teach our courses in order to try to address some of the things the assessment reveals. In terms of curriculum, the English Department is in the process of implementing a three-course core in the major that will emphasize multicultural literatures and engage students in the conscious exploration of ethnocentrism as it affects the critical reader's understanding of a work. Faculty in all disciplines are trying to help students become more conscious of the approaches that characterize the reasoning processes that form the basis of a given discipline.

Have many people simple disregarded the study? Yes, of course. These are real human beings, and they act just as you might expect. In short, there has been no miracle here, but there has been some progress. Have the devastating budget cuts SUNY is presently undergoing severely interfered with the changes that the assessment suggests need to be made? Absolutely. And will the past and continuing budget cuts cause administrators to compromise the quality of the General College Program rather than improve it? Probably. It is, then, fair to say that the Fredonia assessment has not yet had the results many of us hoped it might have. In fairness, however, to all involved, small changes are occurring and a core of interested faculty and administrators remain committed to using assessment to improve programs and classroom instruction.

On the other hand, it is not unusual to find administrators who are more interested in the assessment itself than in the actions that need to be taken as a result of assessment findings. And it is even more common to find that there is more money available for assessment than there is to support the faculty and curricular development that should grow out of assessment projects. Obviously, this presents a seriously pessimistic view of the entire endeavor. Why engage in all this work if it is to come to naught because education in the United States is being devastated by a weak economy? Instead of a trickle-down effect, we seem simply to be trickled on. Why fight for local autonomy in assessment and put forth the time and energy involved in creating qualitative assessment instruments when pressures for a system of standardized national assessment surround us? Why continue to work within a superimposed system that often appears to be characterized by teacher and student bashing orchestrated by secretaries of education? Why bother at all when the destructive rhetoric that has surrounded American education over the past decade is equalled only by the continuing decline of economic support for education in this country?

Our first answer is to return to what we said earlier. If for no other reason, teachers need to be involved in order to defend themselves and their students against inappropriate assessment instruments. Second, we are professionals and must refuse to give in to ignorance or political manipulation. But beyond that, honest, well-planned assessment, carefully evaluated by those directly responsible for instruction and curriculum does offer us the possibility to do a better job. I do not think any of us needs assessment projects to tell us that schools are not teaching students as well as we might like. Thus we do not need assessment to tell us that there is a problem. Rather, we need assessment projects that might help us identify specific elements of teaching and learning that need to be changed.

The Fredonia assessment offers some ideas for the kinds of instruments faculty might create to shape their own assessment projects and suggests some very clear directions we might take to improve the quality of our students learning. Furthermore, as we intend to explain in the next few pages, portfolio assessment, carefully created and implemented, can be one of the most constructive instruments in qualitative assessment. More directly, in the face of the negatives implied above, it is essential that faculties take charge of assessment and create their own instruments *before* something is imposed on them.

Additionally, we know now that faculty development workshops can have an observable effect on instruction. We know that students can and will improve as writers if writing across the curriculum is actually implemented instead of simply being talked about. We know that our system of lecturing and testing appears to reinforce the learning of literal facts but apparently does little to help students become more powerful thinkers and doers. We know that science courses stressing large amounts of discrete facts appear to have little effect on a student's understanding of the nature of science, and that mathematics courses that stress formulaic approaches to solving problems do little to improve students' under-standing of mathematics as a discipline or to help them become more adept at solving problems. Also, even with respect to the specific contents of a given course or discipline, it appears clear that students retain very few of those facts that seemed to control the courses while they were taking them. Finally, a good assessment project may also reveal, as it did at Fredonia, that we are not nearly as successful in accomplishing some of our goals as we might wish to pretend. Anyone involved with assessment needs to be prepared to hear some news s/he may not wish to hear.

Our own major interest in the project was and is how it will affect our teaching and our students' learning. And it has. But perhaps the most significant change that has occurred so far has been a direct result of the ironic contradiction that occurs when one considers the difference between students' performance on the writing exam versus the reading exam.

Perhaps because my own major interests lie in the areas of metacognition, reading, and writing, it should be little surprise that I disliked our writing exam from the very beginning, even though I chaired the subcommittee responsible for creating it. Asking our students to engage in a significant act of writing in a fifty-minute period, and then judging that as though it represents real writing borders on a kind of lunacy. We knew from the start that the fifty-minute time limitation, the fact that students did not have time to prewrite, write, receive feedback, and revise all combined to put the students in the middle of an artificial writing activity. But even with all these problems, our results indicated that students improved in this kind of writing, suggesting that our Writing-Across-the-Curriculum efforts had some positive effect. Even so, one cannot create such an assessment tool and not also be haunted by a statement like the following. " 'I just don't get it,' said Ruby, a senior at a major state university in the Lower 48. 'In the writing classes, they tell you how important it is to do all this prewriting and revision stuff. Then they give you an exit test where you can't use any of it' " (Wauters 1991, 57).

As has already been mentioned, at the very beginning of the creation of the writing test, we had agreed that portfolios containing student writing over a period of years offered one of the best ways to go about evaluating their writing, but now we became more committed than ever to the idea because we saw that a carefully planned portfolio requirement might not only provide data useful in program assessment (Ewell 1991, 46). More importantly to many of us, such a project might help students become better writers, readers, and thinkers. Con-sequently, some of us had long ago decided to try to implement a collegewide portfolio requirement consisting of selected pieces of a student's writing over a period of three to four years: these collections of student work might best serve as the instrument for assessing their growth as writers because they would contain writing that students had an opportunity to shape and revise.

Only after the fact, however, did it occur to us that portfolios like this might be shaped in a variety of ways. Students might add critiques of their writing, looking back at what they produced over several years in order to establish a reflective, metacognitive consciousness of their thinking processes and/or the changes in these processes they might constructively undertake. If students had to maintain such portfolios in any given discipline, wherein those portfolios might be shaped in ways most appropriate to the learning demanded in the discipline, the portfolios might serve as instruments for both individual and programmatic assessment. Equally important, the portfolio idea lends itself to helping students examine their own reading, writing, and thinking processes; it gives them an opportunity to examine their own intellectual growth over a period of years; and it gives them an opportunity to see the areas in literacy and thinking in which they need further work. In short, portfolios lend themselves powerfully to outcomes-based assessment.

Having said all that, let me add that designing a portfolio requirement at any level is very complex and needs to be begun with great care. If I have learned nothing else as a teacher and as one interested in assessment and outcomes-based education it is this: never try to do everything at once; keep it simple at first; and make very sure you know what you are trying to achieve before you implement any approach. It is absolutely crucial to be " 'clear on a more-or-less campuswide basis about why assessment is being undertaken, who is to be assessed, and what educational outcomes are to be assessed. An inadequate conceptual foundation for an assessment program will produce confusion, anxiety, and more heat than light' " (Apers, et al. quoting Terenzini 1990, 476).

PORTFOLIOS AND PROGRAM ASSESSMENT

From the outset, let us be clear about the following. *First*, this discussion of portfolios is not intended to suggest that we were dissatisfied with the instruments used in the GCP assessment—quite the contrary. We are not suggesting that portfolios are the only useful instruments for assessment of student learning. We will, however, make the case that portfolios might form the center of an any ongoing system of either programmatic or individual assessment. *Second*, we are not in favor of gatekeeping devices; improve teaching and the gates will be unnecessary. *Third*, although many portfolio assessment systems presently focus primarily on assessing student improvement as writers, with the portfolios most often tied directly to first-year, required composition courses and, occasionally, some writing-intensive courses, courses in disciplines other than English—we believe their usefulness extends well beyond assessing a single skill or course. *Fourth*, we are much impressed and encouraged by a considerably different approach to portfolio assessment as exemplified by the work done by faculty at the Evergreen State College, Olympia, Washington: This brave, and apparently successful, group wanted to measure cognitive development in their students over the four-year college experience. Using portfolio collections of student self-evaluations, they used a system of ratings based on Perry's developmental scale to score the writing selections (Thompson 1991; Perry 1970).

Our excitement about projects like the one conducted by the Evergreen group is not intended to minimize the importance of the more focused efforts directed at assessing growth in "Freshman Composition, ENG 101." We simply feel that the potential for portfolios goes well beyond a focus on writing, per se: Perhaps the greatest usefulness of portfolios will occur when their contents are directly related to student performance in academic programs and majors across the curriculum and over several years. Experiments like your own (yet to come) and those of institutions like Fredonia and Evergreen should eventually help us all to understand better what, exactly, it is that we and our students are doing.

What follows, then, is a step-by-step series of suggestions that we encourage you to consider as you begin to articulate your own portfolio requirement. Unfortunately, the step-by-step journey that is outlined next bears more similarity to Dorothy's journey through Oz than it does to a clearly drawn line on a map: Lions and tigers and assessors, oh my!

FOLLOWING THE YELLOW BRICK ROAD

Getting Started

Discuss the general concept with sympathetic members in your own discipline or department, and do not try to *convert* your colleagues.

Begin small, using your own classes and those of one or two cooperative colleagues to experiment with portfolios. This step should, necessarily, involve you and some colleagues in a discussion of the kinds of writing required in given courses and additional writing activities that might be appropriate in given courses. This will help significantly when you and others begin to shape the portfolios more specifically for programmatic assessment, because it will give you some sense of the kinds of things students might include in a portfolio and the kinds of student work that might most directly contribute to program assessment.

Try to engage a standing committee in your department, a curriculum committee perhaps, to help articulate the specific goals of the major (or program) you wish to assess. In many cases, this will introduce the first major obstacle in the process. It is not at all unusual to find out that while "everyone knows the objectives of the program, and everyone agrees on the skills or proficiencies that should characterize each successful undergraduate chemistry (or sociology, or philosophy) major," no one has articulated the specifics. In many academic majors, the course contents, directions of the major, and objectives have simply grown, somewhat like Topsy. Members of the discipline at large, some anomalous group or professional association, "agree" that x, y, and z are essential to a given major. Consequently, these courses are required of all undergraduates majoring in the discipline. But then, Professor Smith, a much-published and powerful personality convinces the department that his pet courses are at least as important as x, y, and z, so these become part of the major requirements. And of course, the department rebels know that their courses, intended to deconstruct the major itself and everything the establishment believes is necessary, must also be included. Pretty soon, in desperation, the requirements are discontinued and students are encouraged to take thirty credit hours from among a broad array of wonderful courses offered by the department.

Frankly, we are not terribly dismayed by such a system. Clearly some disciplines demand core requirements and a system of sequencing, but given the arguments that often surround such curricular decisions, we wonder just how clear any of this will ever be. The point, here, is this: until the program or major is defined in terms of observable, albeit qualitative, outcomes that are central to most of the courses in the program, there can be no programmatic assessment. Why? Because in fact, there is no program. An accidental or incidental amalgamation of courses all called *psychology courses* can hardly be called a "program." Nor can it be assessed.

Problems enter rather quickly and obviously at this point. In fact, it looks like a good reason to return to standardized multiple-choice exams and focus on discrete bits of information that are emphasized in isolated courses. Even though this is a fraudulent kind of assessment, at least it's possible to do it. But as most of us know, the discrete facts and unrelated pieces of information are the things we all forgot shortly after we graduated. So assessing this kind of learning is rather silly.

Articulating Objectives

All that we've said above pretty clearly suggests that members of the department or program will necessarily have to reflect on their own courses, looking beyond specific information, to identify the kinds of thinking they are trying to teach their students: what are the thought processes, abilities, and skills that underlie the discipline and most of the courses within it? Fortunately, as problematic as this stage is, it is not impossible and may be one of the most beneficial aspects of being involved in assessment. Students already know that relationships between and among courses are not particularly clear, or at least they do not always see the interrelationships. Instructors need to learn this so that they can begin to help make the interrelationships clearer, when they exist, and create them when it is appropriate.

Of course, you may find some of your colleagues ready to explain, with care and patience, that "you can't assess critical thinking or other complex kinds of reasoning because the students don't know enough yet. First you must teach them the basic facts of the discipline, and only later (in graduate school, we guess) will they know enough to do any complex thinking or reasoning." And it should come as no surprise that this kind of statement is reflected in what students apparently believe when they say that they cannot do something because they never took a course in it. But the fact is that most disciplines genuinely share more in common than is often realized and articulated. Most disciplines and academic programs emphasize (or *believe* they emphasize) some intermixture of the following: (1) critical/analytical thinking; (2) clear reasoning (logical, mathematical, scientific, analogic, metaphoric); (3) creative thinking; and (4) the ability to speak, listen, read, and write with "reasonable" proficiency in the discipline.

More specifically, most disciplines expect students to be able to read, comprehend, and comment articulately on literature in the field. In science and mathematics, students are expected to be able to "do" science and math (but so also are they expected to "do" history, sociology, philosophy . . . if they major in one of those disciplines).

The potential difficulties involved in this step of the process are precisely why each group needs to devise its own assessment program. By identifying the objectives and desired outcomes central to a given major or program, the faculty will necessarily gain a greater sense of their own mission. Likewise, once these have been identified, instructors can begin to examine their own courses to see to what extent they try to help students achieve such objectives or be able to produce specific outcomes.

Consequently, professional self-examination must follow the identification of objectives and outcomes that one wishes to assess. After all, if the instructors teaching the courses are not actively and consciously teaching students to achieve the central objectives of the discipline, why would anyone bother to assess whether or not they are learning them? (Unless, of course, it is to find out that they can already "do" whatever it is we want them to be able to "do," which would attest to the irrelevancy of the discipline, we suppose.) But a reminder of the Fredonia experience is in order—or perhaps just a reminder to use common sense: we already know that we are not doing an adequate job of teaching students to be literate, articulate participants in many of the fields they study. Therefore we first need to more clearly identify what it is we want them to learn as a result of our teaching. And then . . .

Instructors need to identify for themselves and for their colleagues, which activities/requirements in their courses contribute to helping students achieve which objectives, and what exactly will comprise the portfolios. While this step sometimes suggests the trammelling of academic freedom, it need not and should not do so. It is absolutely essential that everyone involved keep in mind the fact that the issue is programmatic assessment; it is not an attempt to point accusatory fingers at particular courses or faculty members. In most cases, faculty will find that key courses already require assignments that will fit naturally and usefully into programmatic assessment. And the portfolio entries need not always be directly tied to course requirements. The following questions might assist in such an examination:

1. How do lab reports (or analytical/critical essays) provide evidence that the fledgling scientist (or philosopher and so on) is doing or is learning to do science (or philosophy and so on): what are the specifics that will indicate a successful report versus a weak one; what activities in the course contribute to teaching the students how to do successful reports; what student work derives from the course that might be included in a portfolio?

2. At the time they declare their desire to major in a given field, should students be asked to write "entry papers" for inclusion in the portfolios? If you wish to find out about the nature of student attitudes toward a discipline, their reasons for choosing it (as opposed to our assumptions about why they have chosen it), what they want to learn—such entry papers are essential. Aside from providing valuable information about the students we are teaching in our courses, these entry papers allow teachers to more fully understand and deal with mismatches between student expectations and program objectives. Of course, it should be obvious that the entry papers must be carefully described in terms of how they are to be used within the portfolio and as part of the program assessment. If entry papers are required, will exit papers also be required? What will they help you find out?

3. Will it be helpful for the fledgling mathematicians or scientists to write descriptions of the processes they go through in solving problems or doing experiments (as opposed to simply including a lab report or mathematical solution)? Likewise, might it be helpful to have the sociology or philosophy students write personal narratives of how they approached understanding a major concept or how they approached a research project? Note, here, that these kinds of written assignments can easily be required *in addition* to the requirements and expectations within a given course. Instructors might simply tell students that during the course of the semester they must complete at least one of these kinds of narratives for inclusion in their portfolios; a failure to do so will affect the grade in the course. Again, any decision to include such writing in the portfolios must be driven by a prior decision about how the piece will be assessed and how it contributes to assessing the objectives of the program.

4. Should instructors or students decide which work is included in the portfolios (or should they work together to make such decisions)?

5. How much should be included in the portfolio? While one might think that "more is better," it is well to remember that someone is going to have to assess these portfolios, and that almost certainly means more than simply

sitting down and reading quickly through the entries to form some generalized judgment (though holistic scoring will often be a significant part of the overall assessment of portfolios). Since most students take courses in a major over a period of about five to six semesters (using the first year or two to complete general college requirements), would it make sense to require that each portfolio contain six entries: an entry paper, papers written in at least four different courses in the major, and an exit paper?

6. Should the portfolio entries be carefully prescribed and described so that each student's portfolio will essentially contain the same amount and kinds of work that another student's portfolio contains? For programmatic assessment, it seems clear to us that this is probably necessary in order for valid, reliable judgements of portfolios to result. For example, though possibilities are endless, students might be expected to include in their portfolios an entry paper, a description of how they approached solving a problem (mastering a complex concept, developing a skill . . .); a research paper (or critical/analytical paper); an out-of-class essay exam (or, perhaps—dare we say it—a creative paper?); a paper explaining the most significant or complex aspect of the discipline they have been studying; and a self-reflective exit paper. Obviously, the contents of the portfolio will be essentially prescribed by the specific objectives/performances/outcomes that the group has decided to assess.

7. Should portfolio entries be limited to written work, or might it be appropriate in some disciplines to include photographs or videotapes of student's productions or of students actually doing something in a lab or teaching situation?

SCORING PORTFOLIOS

Now we come to the sticky question of scoring portfolios: that is, having created a system of qualitative, subjective assessment, how does one go about "objectifying" it in any sense of the term *objective*? Needless to say, it is best to start by being at home with relativism and remaining highly conscious of the purpose of the assessment. In programmatic assessment, you begin by (1) clarifying what it is you want to assess; (2) carefully constructing your instruments (in this case the portfolios and their prescribed contents); (3) defining what you consider to accurately represent weak, adequate, and strong performances for each of the pieces required in the portfolio; and (4) articulating highly specified criteria for scoring the quality of performance. Remember the importance of the grid we created for the Fredonia assessment project (See Appendix A).

Once the system for scoring has been articulated and agreed upon, it is time to teach yourselves how to score the portfolio entries, a process that will take considerable time, commitment, and the ability to compromise. Quite simply, no matter how well you have planned things up to this point, the entire project will fall apart unless this part of the process is carefully and openly addressed, so it is worth examining what is involved rather carefully.

First, remember that you are not going to score all the portfolios of all the students. Ask your local statistician to tell you what percentage of your majors you must score in order to have a statistically reliable sample. Second, do not underestimate the amount of time and energy the scoring will take. Scorers who are forced to do too much at a given sitting or over an extended period of time will score differently when they are tired (or fed up) than when they began the process. Third, create a system of subgroups. Staying with the example we have already created in which the portfolios contain six entries, it would make sense to create five to six subgroups to score each of the separate entries. Given the description we provided above, one subgroup of scorers might be responsible for comparing the entry and exit papers (unless, of course, it was more appropriate to establish criteria for scoring these two pieces separately). Each of the other subgroups would then be responsible for scoring one specific kind of entry.

Once the groups are created, the training begins. Over and over each scorer will have to be reminded that the scoring system is directly related to the criteria that have been established. It is all too easy to believe that one is scoring a piece of writing to examine the individual's expertise in problem solving when, in fact, the scorer is focusing on punctuation or syntax. Before the scoring is even begun, it is wise for each group to reexamine the criteria and discuss them. Following this discussion, each member of the group begins to score an identical set of selected portfolio entries. Next, the scores are charted, and each individual scorer *explains* his/her score.

This is "sticky wicket" time, indeed, or at least it can be. We italicized the word *explains* because the scorers must avoid defensiveness, argument, sarcasm, personal attacks, and homicide. The key element in this process is coming to a mutual understanding of what is *really* intended by the criteria that were previously established. What seemed perfectly clear before the process began suddenly becomes muddy, and it is essential that the mud be eliminated.

Consider what might occur when a group of scorers used the following criteria to score a portfolio entry focusing on problem solving in which the writer was to solve some specified problem and then produce a brief narrative explaining the steps s/he employed in the process of solving it:

A. The writer clearly articulates each step of the problem-solving process in which s/he engaged.

B. The writer articulates most of the important steps in which s/he engaged, but does not present a full explanation of the solution.

C. The writer is unable to articulately explain the problem-solving process in which s/he engaged.

After scoring an entry, using these criteria, one scorer gives the entry a grade of A, another gives it a grade of B, and a third gives it a grade of C. Believe us it happens! And at the beginning of the process it occurs more often than you might expect. But why?

The explanation is relatively simple, and very important. One scorer explains the A as follows: "This entry is exceptionally well-written; in fact the student writes better than most of the students I teach. The explanation is interesting, clear, and the student clearly arrived at the correct answer to the problem." The scorer who assigned the B says, "What you say is true, but the fact is that, even though this is well-written, the writer does not really explain the reasoning process in the step-by-step fashion demanded by the criterion. S/he states many of the steps, but not all of them." And finally the scorer who assigned a C says, "In a sense I agree with both of you, but the criteria clearly say that the student is to *explain* the process. But this writer simply *states* a few important steps and leaves the reader to figure it out." And we have not included the fourth scorer who gave the paper a score of A because "the solution suggests genuine insight into the problem-solving process, considerably more than I generally see in our students, and there is no way you can give this a low score."

What is important to note here is not which of the individuals is right or wrong—remember we began with a commitment to relativism. In a sense, each of them may be right. But in order to score portfolios, in order to assess anything, the scorers must come to full and conscious agreement on what they *really* mean by those criteria they were applying. The trick is to score the entries in direct relationship to an agreed upon definition of the criteria. And this means, at the beginning of this training process, that most of the criteria that had been originally articulated will undergo laborious reexamination. Indeed, it is not unusual, at this stage, for the individuals to find it necessary to define words that they thought were clearly agreed upon prior to the act of scoring: "What is the difference between 'stating' and 'explaining'? Since it is the writer's prerogative to decide what process s/he engaged in, how can you say that s/he did not include steps in which s/he engaged? Are you not explaining the steps in which *you* engaged?" "To what extent does it matter if the solution is right or wrong if the explanation of the steps is well done?"

In some cases, the group may decide to rewrite criteria to make them clearer or more explicit and eliminate as much confusion as possible. For example, referring to the sample criteria presented above, the group would almost certainly want to rewrite criterion C because the split infinitive "to articulately explain" creates a nonparallel structure (and different meaning) from what is probably intended by the use of the word "explain" in criteria A and B. In other cases, certain criteria may simply have to be eliminated because the scorers cannot mutually agree on their application.

While this may seem like an almost impossible morass, it is not. Even in scoring the reflective thinking exam in the Fredonia assessment, the exam that caused us the most difficulty in scoring, we eventually managed to arrive at a sense of mutual agreement about what we "meant" by the criteria. It is important to keep in mind that this kind of assessment is difficult (and even threatening) precisely because it relies on language and subjective, qualitative decisions about the exact meaning of specific words. One can hardly engage in this kind of assessment without coming to grips with the confusion and sometimes deceit that hides beneath statistical results on standardized, "objective" exams. Quite simply, if it can be this difficult for a small group of highly intelligent people to agree on the meaning of a given term as they apply it to a piece of writing, how much more difficult must it be for the students who must decipher the hidden biases and idiosyncratic meanings of the people who create "objective" reading comprehension tests, or worse yet, tests that rely on analogies? And how much harder to believe that a multiple-choice test that gives you a "critical-thinking" score is addressing relevant criteria or criteria relevant to your college's program.

It should be clear from the above that the Scoring System itself must be clearly articulated and mutually understood. For example, if the group decided to use letter grades (A, B, C, D . . .), the letters must eventually be correlated with numbers (A = 5 points . . .). Using this system, scorers must remember that the score of A is related to the stated criteria and *not* to the A that might be given for work in a course in which the criteria might very well be different. Of course, why not simply use numbers instead of letters? And you may find that this works for you. In the Fredonia Assessment, different subgroups used different systems; and by now it should be obvious that the essential element is having all the scorers of a given test understand and be comfortable with whatever system you employ.

Additionally, you must decide how many scoring differentiations you wish to make: one might argue that a scoring system ranging from 1 to 15, clearly related to fifteen carefully differentiated degrees of performance would be better than one ranging from 1 to 6. The finer the differentiations, the more statistically revealing the scores will be. Unfortunately, the finer the distinctions, the more difficult they are for the scorers to make.

And it is important to consider whether or not a *holistic* system of scoring will be helpful, in addition to the itemized scores tied to specific criteria. In the Fredonia assessment, for example, each scorer began by giving each protocol on the writing test a holistic score. In this case, each scorer was directed to read the protocol twice and immediately give it a score ranging from A to E (including pluses and minuses) based on an overall impression of the general success of the piece of writing. We later found such a system quite useful in judging the relative merit of the itemized criteria and settling disputes between scorers.

While itemized criteria can clearly be important for certain kinds of assessment, we do not mean to imply that they are always necessary. At Miami of Ohio, a university conducting a variety of interesting assessment experiments, scorers examined student writing portfolios in a global manner. As they read through the students' portfolios, the participating faculty were asked not to assess *how well* we had met the goals, but rather *where* they saw evidence of an assignment that required skills or abilities that the program faculty viewed as important; for example, assignments that gave evidence of emphasis on "critical thinking," or reflected our "quantitative reasoning across the curriculum" effort. In describing "what" we were doing, rather than "how well" we were doing, we fostered discussion that took on a less defensive tone. This permitted a level of sharing that had not occurred in any of our previous discussions of assessment. (Amiran, Schilling, and Schilling forthcoming, 12)

One might clearly apply holistic scoring to find out whether or not the academic program is asking students to write "much" or "enough," whether or not students are encouraged or assisted in any kind of revision process, and whether or not students appear to improve as writer/thinkers over a given period of time. Or scorers might assess portfolios descriptively: What kinds of thinking are evidenced in the portfolio contents? As always, the central problem of *how* any of this is done depends entirely on *what* it is you are trying to find out.

But we must still address some other issues involved in scoring: How many scorers need to score a given protocol (in the Fredonia project we agreed that two scorers would score each protocol)? And what happens when scores for a given protocol seriously conflict: that is, when one scorer scores an item as an A but another gives it a C − . Obviously, one solution would be to simply average the scores, but such a system is likely to result in most scores ending up in some sort of midrange. Several approaches to the problem suggest themselves: First, the two scorers might discuss their scores trying to determine whether or not each is genuinely committed to a score and can explain its relationship to the stated criteria. Second, in the event that this does not lead to a relatively immediate change by one of the scorers, a third reader can be used to settle the dispute: whichever of the original scores is closest to that of the third reader is averaged with that of the third reader for the official score.

Clearly, it is important to remember that we agreed to accept a relativistic world: qualitative assessment is not "objectively" perfect, but what is, really? In the Fredonia experience, we found the process of training ourselves to score to be the most gruelling part of the entire process. But once it was finished, we were ready to move beyond our self-training and begin the real scoring.

ADDITIONAL CONSIDERATIONS

So far so good? Maybe, but not quite. Here are some considerations that have yet to be confronted. For example, what about control groups?

It may appear, at first, that program assessment demands the establishment of some sort of control group against which to measure growth and improvement in a given area. Otherwise, all we will have at the end of this long, laborious process is a group of scores unrelated to a group of randomly selected portfolios.

To be able to say that a given portfolio is clearly "better" than another hardly provides the information necessary for the evaluation of a program. In the Fredonia assessment, our design included the use of a control group from another college whose student body was similar to our own (based on entrance requirements) but whose general college program was quite different. And while such a design may significantly increase the kinds of information assessments might reveal, it also creates some significant complexities.

At Fredonia we felt the need for a control group because we were not simply trying to find out if students improved in certain areas. Without a control group, we could not have found out if the General College Program, per se, was affecting student learning (as opposed to the growth one might find just because students happen to be in college). Depending on what one is trying to assess, however, control groups may be unnecessary, as Amiran, Schilling, and Schilling point out in their comparative discussion of assessment projects at Fredonia and Western College (at Miami University of Ohio):

> Fredonia began with a focus on locally constructed assessment for an internal audience but found it needed a comparative study with an external institution. Western College began with an external focus on nationally normed means of assessment, moved through its collaboration with Fredonia and on to a purely local, internally oriented descriptive approach. It is not a matter of finding what is right for each institution, but of understanding that different foci are right for the same institution at different stages in its assessment process. If Western had not begun with normed instruments it would not have appreciated its need for descriptive measures. If Fredonia had not undertaken its comparative study, it would not have been properly cautious in interpreting its local results. Comparative and local, external and internal foci, outcomes and activities, judgements by others and oneself—these alternate as figure and ground in the assessment "picture," and it may be important to retain one's ability to keep reversing them. It is also important to affirm the value of the complexity that baffles us in assessing liberal education: we cannot draw Leviathan with a hook (forthcoming, 18).

CONTROL GROUPS?

Toward the end of this chapter, we discuss methods of using the portfolios without control groups, but we believe that control groups may, in fact, be necessary to achieve certain ends: that is, especially if the assessment intends to compare one program against another, a demonstrably different one, and probably when the assessment is primarily directed at curriculum revision. To establish such a control group, you must find an institution whose student profile is similar to your own but whose program is significantly different. Second, those who teach in the program must agree to implement portfolio requirements exactly as you have defined them, which is no small task in and of itself. Third, the scorers at your institution must agree to score the portfolios that have been completed by the students at the control institution. To say that the problems of working out all the details involved here are significant is a gross understatement.

A little backtracking will be helpful here. Begin by reconsidering the purpose of the assessment project. As we have stated several times, our purpose for assessment focuses on improving teaching and learning. At present, anyone who has conducted the project as we have thus far described it would be in position of deciding that students are generally performing well, adequately, or inadequately as determined by a variety of measures used for scoring the various kinds of entries within the portfolios. But if your needs demand a control group, must you necessarily go outside your own institution?

Not necessarily. Indeed, a somewhat obvious solution immediately presents itself. For this kind of assessment, you must identify one group of students as the initial group to be assessed and another group of your own students to be the control group. And this system suggests several possible alternatives depending on the make up of your institution. In some larger institutions, for example, a given major or program may offer several distinct "tracks" for students. English Education majors might take a required sequence of courses that significantly differ from those taken by other English majors. In psychology, students heading toward clinical work in the field might take a sequence of courses significantly different from those more interested in research.

More often than not, however, this is unlikely to be the case; students in a given major or program are most likely to take courses that are either distinctly similar or have distinctly similar requirements. In these cases, we suggest that a group of students entering a program or major in a given semester be identified to comprise the control group and that a group of students entering the program or major at least two years later be identified as the experimental group whose progress will be measured against the first group. Still some very significant issues need to be resolved.

At this point, having established a control group and a second group with which to contrast scores, not much has really been accomplished. Consider this hypothetical situation. Group 1 is identified as all those entering the program in September 1994; Group 2 is composed of students entering the program in September 1996. By 1998, the assessors should be in the position of making some powerful judgements about the program, right? Wrong.

By simply establishing two different groups, one must ask what exactly is being compared? In this case, assuming that the program has remained essentially the same over the four-year period, almost no conclusions can be drawn about the program. If the program remains substantially the same, an improvement in student scores would simply indicate that the students had somehow, on their own, done better than their predecessors. If they perform poorly, one might assume that this group of students was simply not as capable as previous groups. In either case, little could be said about the program.

And this returns us to a beginning point. The whole reason for the endeavor, in the first place, is to improve instruction. The idea is to make changes in instruction and to assess whether or not the changes contribute to greater student growth and learning. Consequently, once the portfolio assessment has begun, the faculty should immediately begin the process of redesigning all elements of the program or major or courses that they feel might improve the quality of student learning. By beginning such redesigning immediately, faculty would have a two-year period to prepare to implement changes; thus the second groups of students would be exposed to a program that was significantly different in its attempt to help students improve at the kinds of skills, processes, thinking that the program intends to develop and that the portfolios are designed to measure.

In the short term, what we have described may suggest a kind of madness. The key, here, is to remember the purpose of assessment. First and foremost, it should be aimed at improving instruction rather than simply providing state agencies with "proof" that the program is an effective one through some series of short-term, deceitful assessment instruments. While the system we propose clearly involves long-term involvement and takes a considerable amount of time to complete, these qualities must be recognized as inherent in assessment projects that assess anything of importance. In fact, the system we have just described would be an ongoing one with new groups being identified every two years, or at least as often as the ongoing assessment leads to changes in instruction. We may find out, of course, that nothing changes over time and that all the instructional changes that have been implemented result in no improvements in students' performances. Obviously, this would be disturbing, but important, information. At the very least, it might suggest that the institution needed to look outside itself for help in improving the program or major. More likely, however, the ongoing system of assessment would allow those teaching the program to monitor their continued commitment to good teaching and document needs for changes in what is actually going on in courses or changes resulting from changing student populations.

No Control Groups

While control groups may be essential for certain kinds of assessment, we strongly agree with Minda Rae Amiran who so significantly assisted us in this section of the book. We paraphrase her at length, here, because her comments were so helpful to us. She points out that a portfolio being used to assess a major in a discipline like chemistry would not demand the creation of control groups: it would be clear that "any chemistry the students have learned they have learned through that department (or possibly in related internships or summer jobs). In a department with a defined curriculum, there is no reason why actual portfolios can't be compared to faculty-developed pictures of what a student should know or be able to do as a result of the program." Clearly, she goes on, if students evidence a lack of knowledge or ability deemed essential by the faculty, the department can begin to change its curriculum and/or system of instruction. And while Amiran reiterates that "curricular changes" might be best approached through the use of a control group, she suggests some ways of avoiding the "laborious steps" we itemized in the above section on establishing control groups:

> One could have students collect everything they wrote to answer questions such as [the following]: "How much and what kinds of writing are our students actually doing?" "What kinds of critical thinking are our students engaging in?" "What kinds of problems (texts, theories, authors) can our students address?" One could have students compile selective portfolios with reflections to assess the successes of the program in stimulating the making of connections and metacognition. One could specify the ingredients of portfolios to judge the general level of senior-year seminar papers or projects as compared to sophomore-year research papers. (personal letter, 1992)

Student Commitment

To paraphrase Dorothy, it really does not look much like Kansas, does it? One final qualification must yet be made, however. What good does any of this do if the students do not take it seriously, if the work in the portfolio is viewed by the students as some sort of busy work imposed on them by the institution, as an activity that has nothing to do with their own learning and growth? What if they "borrow" papers from other students in order to fulfill the portfolio requirement? And if they have had the opportunity to work with peer editors to get help from writing tutors, whose work is it that is being evaluated?

Let us take these concerns one at a time. First, we believe that if the portfolios are not directly tied to the students' growth and learning, then there is no reason to expect the students to take them seriously. Portfolio assessment that is divorced from the students' growth invites carelessness and lack of commitment from the students (at best) and plagiarism (at worst). But it has been our experience to find that when students see the contents of a portfolio to be directly tied to their own learning and growth, when the portfolios function as an important part of their discussions with their teachers and advisors, students take them very seriously. And it is for this reason that the next chapter on the role of portfolios in the learning and assessment of the individual student is particularly important to us.

Let us not forget that last question: whose paper is it, really, when the writer has received considerable editorial assistance? The manuscript for this book, for example, has gone through several drafts. We have received feedback from readers and editorial assistance from friends, spouses, and colleagues. Indeed, we quote extensively from Minda Rae Amrian's critical commentary in one of our drafts. Praeger Publishing Company assigned a professional editor to assist in the production of this book. And quite frankly, we appreciated all that help.

Nevertheless, we still think that this is our book. Does it not make more sense for us to try to teach our students to be a part of our professional world instead of locking them outside of it with demands that most of us would find ludicrous? What good is assessment of any kind if it does not contribute to students' learning?

_____

CHAPTER 4

Portfolios and the Individual Student: Assessing for Learning

By way of summary, let me begin—presumptuously perhaps—by making a point on behalf of all of us here who are faculty members... one that comes, in fact, from a letter I recently received from a faculty member from SUNY–Fredonia.... "I am concerned," Patrick Courts writes, "that assessment has become a self-regressive project concerned primarily with itself—concerned with more and better assessment but little beyond that. Personally, I have little use for it unless we allow the voices of those assessed to be heard." That's a right and timely caution (Hutchings 1990, 8).

Almost anyone interested in educational assessment these days has run across articles on the use of portfolios for assessment of student learning (Sensenbaugh 1991). Though these discussions most often address portfolios as a means of assessing student growth in writing, and often concern themselves primarily with programmatic assessment, this chapter will explore some specific ways that portfolios might be used across disciplines to assess and, more importantly, to guide student learning.

At first glance, it may appear as though there is not really much to this project. Just have the students collect their work, all of it, in a file folder and read it over from time to time to see how they are doing. Since we are not necessarily concerned, here, with reporting statistical findings that might be compared with other groups to determine whether a given approach or program works better than another, the science (fiction) of objective data need not be engaged. To some extent that is true, but it is precisely *because* individual assessment does not reduce human beings to statistics, because the goal is to directly affect the learner's growth, that the process itself is particularly slippery.

A LOOK AT THE BACKGROUND

As has been mentioned previously, even at the earliest stages of planning the large-scale assessment of SUNY–Fredonia's General College Program, it was clear to some of us that portfolios were the instrument of choice for assessing student growth in writing. While we decided that we could gather some important and instructive information about our students' writing through the single-sitting, one-hour essay, we were painfully aware that this experience barely touched on what it was we were trying to accomplish through our emphasis on Writing-Across-the-Curriculum (WAC) in the program. Likewise we knew, as anyone vaguely familiar with research in writing and discourse theory over the last thirty years knows: real writing is not generally produced in sixty minutes; most good writers go through a prewriting (prethinking) process that often involves free-writing, outlining, discussing, "aha" moments, dead ends, rough drafts, reader feedback, revision, and so on.

As we began to confront the complexities of creating a valid, reliable test of our students' reading abilities, we experienced similar, though not as many serious, problems. As we began to construct the reflexive thinking exam, how-ever, we were immediately struck by the weaknesses that were being created by test conditions over which we had no immediate control. Consequently, though we decided to go ahead with the instruments we created, and though we believe that our findings are important, we also believe that they reveal, at best, the tip of an iceberg about which we probably know very little: that is, while we may know what students are not learning, we are not at all sure we know what it is they are learning.

Thus it was that, even in the midst of creating the exams for the GCP assessment, a small group of us began planning some system of portfolio as-sessment that might address some of the problems we discovered in the other instruments. For many of us involved in the development of the GCP assessment, particularly because the assessment was not externally imposed, our major mo-tivation for such involvement derived from our expectation that the assessment might help us learn some things that might improve instruction on the campus. And even at this point, a few of us felt that portfolios, while clearly a powerful element in program instruction, were perhaps the single most direct assessment instrument that might actively affect student learning and, with a little luck, classroom instruction.

At this initial stage, we had hopes of having all students on the campus involved in portfolios, so we decided to keep things relatively simple. In this plan, the dean for Liberal and Continuing Education sends all entering first-year students a letter directing them to write "entry papers" in response to the following: "What was the experience (in school or out) from which you learned the most at some time during the last four years? How does that experience relate to your present plans (for college, for your choice of major, or for any other aspect of your life)?"

These initial essays would become part of the students' academic file and would be followed with additional entries each semester from courses the students were taking that were part of the General College Program.

The plan was almost identical to the directions for the English Education portfolio, which was eventually based on this first attempt at a broadly based system of portfolio assessment. In the original plan, students would select one piece of writing they produced in a given semester, write a brief critique explaining why they chose the piece (why it was a success/failure, did/did not contribute to their learning, was/was not difficult to write, and so on), and the paper and critique would be kept on file for the student and advisor to discuss as part of the entire advising process (See Appendix C: Information Sheet for Students).

It was our expectation that, using pretty much the same system we had used for scoring the writing test in the initial assessment, we could train a group of scorers (1) to select portfolios randomly; (2) to compare student writing performances over four years of college; (3) to interview willing students about their work and their sense of growth as writers/thinkers; and to (4) gain genuine insight into the success of our students and our program, particularly in terms of writing abilities. We also hoped that we might eventually create a system for assessing student growth in the slippery area of metacognition, but the entire project got derailed long before we entered into the complex specifics of that endeavor.

Perhaps it was naïveté or idealism or simple stupidity, but we had not expected the degree of resistance across the campus that our project encountered. We formed a small group of "portfolio ambassadors" whose job it was to move from academic department to academic department to explain the reasons for, and the nature of, the portfolio project. Though we expected pockets of resistance, we were somewhat surprised to find responses as negative and intense as they appeared to be. The kindest explanation for this resistance grows out of a belief that the faculty, having experienced a series of budget cuts over a decade, had legitimate reasons to feel that they were being overworked and undervalued and that the portfolio requirement was simply one more thing on top of an already overextended faculty. And for some faculty, this was unquestionably true.

One suspects, however, that some other, less generous explanations might exist. For one thing, such a requirement would reveal that courses that claimed to require writing did not genuinely do so or would additionally reveal that some faculty members did little real advising and did not much care to change that fact. And of course, most discussions of the portfolio project were peppered with vague comments about how the portfolios threatened academic freedom, though none of us ever really understood how academic freedom could be threatened by such a project. What was clear, however, was that misunderstandings (purposeful sometimes?) appeared to abound. Some professors worried that the grades they put on papers would come under scrutiny by another teacher when the paper became part of a portfolio. There would be back-stabbing, criticism, insult—the end of the "academy." (From an interesting discussion of the problems associated with implementing a portfolio program, especially in relationship to academic freedom, see Marcia Dickson's 1991 account of her experiences at Ohio State University at Marion.)

Most probably, however, a mix of all of the above problems, not to mention some genuine confusion about portfolios themselves and their real usefulness, worked together to stop any wholesale implementation. Even so, a partial beginning still is a beginning. And though we had not convinced the campus as a whole to implement a portfolio requirement for all students, we had described what the portfolios would contain and how they would be used in working with individual students. From this modest beginning point, we simply decided to go ahead with the project wherever we could find willing accomplices. Since three of the members of the assessment committee are members of the English Department, and the Secondary English Education Program is highly defined, we decided that we would begin the experiment there, hoping to learn as we went along.

In 1989, the English Department began requiring portfolios from all students declaring a major in English Education (See Appendix C); as of 1990 all entering students are writing the entry paper and some departments (English, History, Foreign Languages, and Education) are beginning to experiment with the portfolio requirement as a means of assessing some aspects of the General College Program and of their major. Beginning in September 1993, Fredonia's English Department will require all students declaring English Majors to begin creating portfolios (See Appendix E). In short, although our initial steps have been halting and occasionally turbulent, we have begun.

But this brief history of the beginnings of portfolios at Fredonia is not an isolated example. Although one is, perhaps, first struck by the apparent problems associated with the implementation of portfolio assessment, we should all be aware of some of the potential success stories. Miami of Ohio University is using portfolios to examine student writing/thinking activities across the curriculum. In the state of Washington, work with portfolios is being conducted on several campuses, some of them being assisted by the Educational Testing Service to do structured portfolio assessment in freshman composition. And the University of Missouri is presently working with competency-based portfolios to assess students majoring in business.

Doubtless there are other success stories, though we remain skeptical of some of the "reported successes." Indeed, as we talk with colleagues around the country who are involved in assessment, we have been struck by how few of the advertised "portfolio projects" actually occupy a place in reality. It is not unusual to find out, when one has the opportunity to discuss some of the programs with the people who are actually involved, that some institutions have "collected" student writing, called the collection a "portfolio," but have not really done anything with the portfolios. And in fairness to many of these people, this normally occurs because the assessment was mandated, but no one provided funding or staff time to do the work that is involved in assessing any kind of student writing.

In short, while the idea of portfolios has been much discussed and apparently embraced by many educators, there seem to be more problems associated with the activity than are always readily apparent. In the state of Virginia, a state committed to assessment in higher education, college faculty strongly rejected portfolios, apparently for a similar mix of reasons as at Fredonia. But having been long involved with in-service programs for teachers in both high schools and colleges, we are not particularly surprised. It sometimes seems that the most typical response to a new idea in educational circles is a detailed list of why it will not work or cannot be done. The second objection usually focuses on the question, "How can you grade something like that?" So why should portfolios meet a different fate (at least at first)? As Chris Anson and Robert Brown say in their article "Large-Scale Portfolio Assessment," in which they discuss the efforts at implementing portfolio assessment of writing at the monolithic University of Minnesota:

> No story of assessment design is benign. Historically, the development of assessment programs around the country reads like a long epic of struggle, accommodation, fear, and very occasionally, triumph. In this context, our own difficulties are not rarified or even unpredictable. Even so, it is clear that large research universities present a particularly difficult set of hurdles for reform. (1991, 257)

Thus perhaps a "first things first" list is appropriate here so that others can avoid some of the mistakes that have been made by groups trying to implement portfolio requirements on their campuses.

SOME DO'S AND DON'TS

1. Do not try to implement portfolios from the top down, relying on a mandate from a state legislature or academic vice president or dean to encourage faculty participation or support. Even if a mandate is being imposed, it does little to persuade or motivate faculty.

2. Do identify small programs or majors within the college or university in which already sympathetic faculty might design and implement their own portfolio projects in their own courses.

3. Do not envision a portfolio requirement in isolation from other elements within the institution; try to involve as many people as possible: the director of your learning center (if you have one), the individual in charge of student advisement, the director of the general education program, and any others who might be appropriate.

4. Do establish a writing across the curriculum program (for interested faculty); establish workshops to help faculty understand the nature of the writing process and ways in which they might constructively use writing

to help their students learn better in their courses; encourage faculty involved in the portfolio requirement to learn about support services on the campus (learning centers and the like) where they might send students for help with problems that make themselves evident in the portfolios.

5. Do not begin with the purpose of assessing everything in a program or major. Assessment is difficult enough without beginning with an impossible goal: carefully limit and explicitly articulate *exactly* what you propose to assess through the portfolios. It may make sense to begin with a holistic approach and let specific outcomes come into definition as you become more experienced with portfolios. (This is essentially what we are doing with the English Education Portfolio at Fredonia.)

6. Do start small, meekly. Be sure that the requirement is one that students will understand and fulfill and that it is something the faculty will be able to understand and work with. Be sure that the description of the portfolio, what it is to contain, how it is to be monitored, and so on is absolutely clear. Confusion enters like lightning in these projects and sometimes causes one to believe that the faculty members' ability to comprehend directions needs to be assessed.

7. Do not make smart-aleck remarks (like the one in the last sentence) about your colleagues; they are already threatened enough.

8. Do set up group meetings to explain the nature of the portfolios, their reasons for being, and the hoped-for results in terms of student gains and assessment. In the early stages, it is essential to establish a group of interested, sympathetic faculty, and it is equally essential to *listen* to their suggestions and seriously consider changes or modifications they might present. Dictatorially imposing anything almost certainly guarantees failure.

9. Do not assume that everyone understands what happened at the meetings just described; they did not. Remember that your audience has not been engaged in the same thought processes as you and your initial planning group. What you see as obvious may make no sense at all to others, at first.

10. Do hold brief follow-up meetings for faculty members to share their continuing confusions, iron out unforeseen problems, make necessary adjustments, and help one another.
[We like lists of ten items, but two last points are crucial. While the initial steps of creating the portfolios and of fully understanding how and why they will be used are of utmost importance, all that time and energy will be wasted if you forget the students.]

11. Do not decide that simply requiring students to submit writing for their portfolios on some regular basis is an adequate strategy.

12. Do create a plan that forces the portfolios to be the foci of an interactive

center between students and their instructors/advisors throughout the years that they are required to maintain their portfolios.

As far as the students go, everyone must work together to help them see that the portfolio is not simply some sort of busywork requirement—a sort of irrelevant gatekeeping device. Most of us would not put much energy or care into such a requirement, so why would our students be any different? We strongly suggest that small groups of faculty meet with groups of students to explain and discuss the portfolios, giving students an opportunity to understand what portfolios are, why they exist, and exactly what is expected of each student. It has been our experience that once students understand the reasons for, and the nature of, the requirement, and as soon as they have the opportunity to discuss their portfolio entries with a faculty member, they find themselves enjoying the experience. And these discussions should begin with the students' initial entries and continue through all additional entries.

PORTFOLIOS: WHAT ARE THEY FOR?

First and foremost, we need to decide what a portfolio is for, how it will be used by both learner and teacher, and how it should be constructed to facilitate such use. (For additional discussion of these issues, see Belanoff and Dickson 1991; also Arter 1990.)

While it may seem immediately obvious that individual portfolios have a clear purpose—assessment of the individual's learning/growth in a given learning experience over time—one might reasonably question why we want to do this in the first place. If the purpose is simply to assess the individual's performance (what performance?) and to assign a grade, anyone who is familiar with the work involved in portfolio assessment should quickly recognize that this is a much too time-consuming and complex activity for such a relatively unimportant act as grading (as opposed to "assessing" or "evaluating"). Indeed, the traditional notion of grading (and grade levels) has little to do with a sophisticated understanding of assessment and its purposes.

First and foremost, we believe that the best and most legitimate argument for assessment of any kind relies entirely on how well the assessment contributes to either improving the teaching process or to providing the individual learner with a metacognitive sense of his/her learning processes, in general, and of specific strengths and weaknesses in a given area of study, in particular. (For additional discussion, see Paulson and Paulson, 1990.) Only through such an understanding can teacher and learner work together to take advantage of strengths and correct weaknesses when possible.

In short, it is the Purpose of Portfolio Assessment to help the learners become integral and conscious participants in their learning processes, by having them recognize both individual responsibility and ownership within that process, and by having them become interactive partners with the teacher in shaping that learning process. Likewise, portfolios provide teachers with the possibility of examining the learning process (and performance outcomes) from the point of view of the learner (what is actually occurring) rather than from some distanced point of view that is reflected in course objectives and syllabi (what is supposed to occur or what we sometimes pretend is actually occurring).

USE OF PORTFOLIOS

An immediate distinction needs to be made in relationship to this issue because the possible uses of portfolios are, to some extent, determined by the time period over which they are created. In cases where the portfolio is part of a specific course and therefore contains work produced over a period of twelve or fifteen weeks, the uses of the portfolio for assessing and guiding student learning are somewhat limited because both learner and teacher are simultaneously working with the process of creating a portfolio and the immediate, ongoing immersion in reflective thinking and metacognition. To some extent, the immediacy and short-term nature of the process may seem contradictory to the processes of reflection and metacognition.

But if one considers the possibilities of portfolios being used throughout a specific program of study or in all appropriate courses included within a given major, then both the students and the teachers might be constructively engaged in looking at the students' work and progress as it occurs over a two-to-four-year year continuum. On the other hand, since the longest journey obviously does begin with the first step, from a purely practical point of view, it is essential that individual teachers begin the portfolio process in their individual courses. Ultimately, however, the most important aspects of this particular journey will only occur insofar as the portfolios are required across many courses and over several years, providing a map of the journey that teachers and learners might reflect on and analyze as they move forward through the learning process.

At SUNY–Fredonia, for example, all students in the Secondary English Education Program must create portfolios over a period of two-to-four years (depending on whether or not they are transfer students and when they declare a specific major). Likewise, both the Education and History departments have also instituted portfolio requirements for students electing to major in those fields. Given the fact that many faculty members on this campus initially resisted the idea of requiring student portfolios ("too much additional work on an already overworked staff"), it is fascinating to see that the idea is slowly but surely becoming a reality because individual professors began having their students keep portfolios and were able to help their colleagues see that the activity did not significantly increase workload, but, more importantly, contributed to better learning in the courses and in the majors.

PORTFOLIOS AS NEXUS: STUDENTS AND TEACHERS

Obviously individual students can look through the items in their portfolios to examine their own work over time. At the very least, a carefully ordered and indexed portfolio allows the students to see immediately what they have been doing in a given course, whether or not they have been doing all that is required, and what omissions might be important to address. More importantly, individual students can look through their portfolios to gain a sense of their own growth as learners, identifying particularly troublesome areas they experience with particular contents, concepts, and/or processes involved in the course. The more conscious students, those who already feel a sense of ownership, responsibility and active engagement in their own learning processes, can use the portfolios to identify their own strengths and weaknesses and shape their own approaches to improving their strengths and eliminating weaknesses when possible. These "ideal" students, because they are metacognitive, will also "know when they don't know," and when they need to seek help from the teacher or some other source.

Such students, however, generally comprise a relatively small minority in any given classroom, partly because such high degrees of individual engagement and metacognition are not typical of most young people (though it is entirely possible that this apparent "developmental fact" may more accurately reflect an educational system that discourages individual ownership of the learning process and that does little to foster metacognition). Whatever the case, however, most students will need assistance and direction in using their portfolios to improve their own learning experiences.

Portfolios might offer the occasion for small-group work in which groups of two or three students examine and discuss one another's portfolio entries, focusing on entries that represent particularly difficult or interesting parts of the course, and sharing their own ideas and responses about one another's entries. At the very least, such a process moves the students' work into a more public forum, creates a real audience for student writing, and allows individual learners to learn from the work of their peers as they observe and examine different approaches and responses to activities within a course (See Chapter 5 of this book for fuller discussion of methods and Writing-Across-the-Curriculum (WAC) activities; also, see Romano 1991 for an illuminating discussion of multigenre research projects and portfolio assessment).

Of course, in relationship to this small-group work, the idea might work best when directed by the teacher so that selected, small groups meet occasionally to assist one another in a formal peer review of particular entries in the portfolios in order to share strengths and, perhaps, assist with weaknesses. While such peer-review activities might be primarily oral, almost social, if you will, at some times, teachers might wish to have the students formally assess a given portfolio, selecting key entries for written analysis by peers. Likewise, it might be even more useful to have students compare/contrast their own work to that of another, trying to identify different/similar approaches to concepts or problems introduced within a course. Additionally, the portfolio should become a central element in student/teacher conferences directed at assessing the student's individual performance over a given period of time and discussing what steps might be taken to make the learning experience more constructive.

COLLABORATIVE LEARNING: STUDENT VOICES

Students in the English Education Program at Fredonia, for example, meet periodically with their academic advisors to review their portfolios, reflect on their own learning and changes in attitudes they are experiencing, and to consider areas in which they need to improve before they begin their student teaching. Likewise, though we had not originally planned to do so, the portfolios are now being used in the Senior Seminar in the Teaching of English as part of a capstone process. In this case, small groups of students meet to explore and discuss one another's portfolios as these portfolios indicate the students' growth (and confusion) as writers and thinkers, over their past several years as college students.

It is at this point that the process has the potential to become particularly valuable and exciting as it lends itself to a variety of possibilities. For example, consider the students who identify some clear-cut strengths, either in the content within a discipline or in the concepts, processes, or skills that are a part of the discipline. These students might become tutoring partners for other students in a given course or even for students in other courses who have problems in these respective areas. Again, at Fredonia, because the portfolios in English Education are reviewed by advisors who teach in the program, we are in the enviable position of telling John, for example, who is having difficulty constructing discussion questions for teaching a short story, that he ought to seek help from Mary who has indicated particular strength in this area. In other cases, depending on the nature of the problem, we can suggest that Melanie go over to a tutor at the Learning Center to further explore an idea or to receive assistance with a problem in writing (or science or math or accounting and so on).

Our own experience with peer tutoring at the Learning Center at SUNY–Fredonia clearly suggests that the tutors themselves benefit immensely from the process as they help other learners work through contents, concepts, and processes (like writing). For example, Lee Ann Symanski, a writing tutor, writes:

> Because of the [tutoring experience], I understand that *how* you approach someone's work can hurt or help a person. Before [tutoring], I never realized how direct I could be . . . leading the person down the path. . . . [Now] I find myself (almost automatically) saying, "This isn't real clear to me. How could or what could you expand on to make it more clear to me?" It may sound strange, but it amazed me

how much I could get out of someone by letting him talk, and he didn't even realize how much he explained "without even knowing it."

Another writing tutor, Molly Hanna, writes:

> I also find myself reading my writing in a different way. As I reread what I write, I step back and begin to ask myself questions about the paper I would possibly use while tutoring. I am beginning to pick out the weaker points in my own writing that never would have occurred to me before.

A math/computer-science tutor writes:

> I helped another student in Discrete Math with combinations and sets. I was really challenged. I remember that when I took Discrete, I never really questioned why things were the way they were. This student was asking "why" questions and it really made me think about what was going on. I think I ended up asking her more questions that she asked me. It helped us both to understand things that weren't clear.

Commenting on how tutoring has helped him remember some things he had previously learned in chemistry, Matt Bachman writes: "I realized that I can still pinpoint the orbital of many an individual electron about an atom even though it has been awhile. Sometimes even those basic exercises in chemistry take a little relearning though, another plus for tutoring—you just can't forget it all this way."

Reflecting on her own tutoring experiences, on students who seem to take 'forever' to learn something, and on her own learning process, computer science tutor, Tracy Specht writes:

> As a freshman, I took University Calc and I was totally blown away by the professor and the course. I more or less lived in the Learning Center that semester trying to understand the material. My notebook was full of helpful hints and guidelines that the tutors shared with me, but nothing they did or said made the material click with me. I struggled through the class and received a passing grade, but I didn't have clue as to what I learned.
>
> A year later I decided to tackle Calc I again, and again it didn't make much sense. I managed to get a passing grade, but I was still clueless.
>
> As a senior and having completed my other required classes (such as Discrete, Linear, and Statistics), I decided to try Calc I again. Finally, on the third time around I understand the course and I'm working for an A in the class. I look at my previous notebook and just laugh at the mistakes I made and concepts I couldn't understand. The hints and guidelines that once seemed like a foreign language now make perfect sense. I can't believe it took me three tries to get through the course!

And finally, one last comment from a writing tutor, Clare Thomas:

Yesterday, I had to speak to some transfer students at our open house about what I, as a student, felt about being an English major at Fredonia, as well as my opinion of the programs offered by the department and my impressions of "life as a Fredonia student," etc. So there I was with my handout about the English Department and my list of the classes I have taken that I felt were most beneficial and so on, when a mother raised her hand and told me her daughter was interested in tutoring and wanted to know about the programs on campus. I told her about the Learning Center and what we are all about, and then she asked me what I gained from my experience as a tutor. . . . I thought about it for a second and told her that the knowledge I have gained in the past semester has helped me, and influenced me more than many of my classes. That through helping other people, I have reached a better understanding of other people's needs, as well as a greater awareness of my own writing. I find myself asking questions of myself and my own writing that I ask tutees who come in for help. My writing has definitely improved since I've been a tutor.

Clearly as the tutors help the learners explore and discover for themselves the nature of their difficulties and ways of arriving at some sort of constructive solution, the tutors themselves come to understand the material or process even more fully than they did before. And what is often most stunning as one reads randomly through these tutor "reports" is this: over and over again, writer after writer indicates a growing sense of metacognition, a fuller understanding of the subject s/he is tutoring, and an awareness of the interconnections of learning over the college years. What is delightfully lacking in these reports is self-righteousness; tutors consistently mention that they, themselves, seek tutoring from other tutors in different subject areas.

It comes as no surprise to any of us that someone who is particularly strong in science or math may have difficulty in English (either as critic or writer) or in understanding philosophical concepts. Consequently, it should come as no surprise that the roles of tutors and learners would be likely to shift significantly both within and across disciplines as the philosophy student tutors the biology major in philosophy but receives tutoring from the math student in the calculus course. At this point, a portfolio system used to initiate peer tutoring, then, has the potential of changing the educational system as we know it, empowering students and engaging them in their own learning, creating a situation in which learning becomes a real process rather than an artificial ritual of simply "taking" courses and accumulating grades and credit hours until one collects enough credit to finally graduate. Instead, teaching and learning (teachers and learners) become genuinely interactive, as they are almost everywhere else in society except in schools. Differing radically from the isolated, competitive system presently in place, such a change encourages collaborative learning and a sense of scholarly community.

Of course, some students may simply need to read, think, and write more about a given set of ideas in a discipline. These students may find that others in the course are experiencing similar difficulties with some concept or skill, and they might create self-help, study groups working either on their own or under the direction of the teacher, solving problems on their own, when possible, and seeking the teacher's assistance when appropriate. Again, in the English Education program, it is not at all unusual to find that one student is particularly strong at organizing a series of lesson plans on a novel or short story, but is stymied when it comes to poetry. Or that a student who is particularly strong at creating discussion questions has difficulty creating and implementing small-group, dramatic activities.

These are, of course, important outcomes that students are expected to be able to perform as they leave the program. And the portfolios, along with the coursework, allow teacher and student to recognize the strengths and weaknesses and pair up with other students who might help or whom they might help. And because of the genuinely reciprocal nature of collaborative learning, both learners benefit. In this particular example, it should be obvious that, since these students are about to enter the teaching profession, the opportunity to teach one another is particularly productive and appropriate. But regardless of the students' majors, the process of teaching someone else almost always results in a much fuller "knowing" of the material.

SOME RESULTS

Finally, it has been our experience that portfolios and the conferences based on portfolios often reveal some facts that typically stay well hidden from many teachers. It is not at all unusual to find that a concept the teacher thought most of the students understood is almost universally confused among the students in a class. In normal circumstances, a test sometimes reveals the group's confusion, but often no one, neither teacher nor learner, fully realizes the failure to understand some central concept or the nature of the misunderstanding because no one recognizes that s/he doesn't know. Certainly one of the most revealing facts in Fredonia's assessment project is the finding that we often seriously overestimate how much and what our students are learning. In short, it has been long convenient to assume that receiving passing grades on ("objective") multiple-choice tests indicates mastery or learning in a given area when, in fact, they reveal only that students can pass multiple-choice tests.

Again using the English Education program as an example, we often find that students who, in the Composition for Teachers course, appeared to understand the nature of the writing process and ways of teaching students to write seem suddenly to have forgotten all of this when, in the Senior Seminar for Teachers of English, they see no connections between teaching a short story and incorporating the writing process. While we might argue that the learners simply "forgot" what had been learned in an earlier course, it is much more likely that, like many students, they see courses as isolated entities. They have not so much forgotten to make connections among courses; they never thought of making them in the first place, and the educational system, as it presently exists, does little to encourage such connection making. Regardless of the cause, however, the accumulated writing in the portfolio, in addition to the teachers' knowledge of the sequenced elements in the program, allow students and teachers to work together to make the necessary connections. And this is a key point here—one of the most important things that portfolios are about—making connections over time.

More directly, portfolios have the potential to encourage and facilitate a psychological/intellectual interaction among students *and* teachers that schools, in the past, have almost seemed purposely to avoid. In this system, being able to know and do what one could not previously know and do becomes central to the educational process. Knowing about knowing and knowing how to know replace passivity.

Equally important, however, teachers begin to become aware of what is (or is not) occurring in other courses. In a system that has traditionally allowed (encouraged?) teachers to operate in a kind of self-induced isolation, characterized by an overt lack of interaction among teachers about why and what they do in their separate classrooms, portfolios invite overt examination of interrelationships across courses and disciplines. Again, using Fredonia's English Education portfolios as an example, portfolios provide us with windows that allow us to see beyond our own classrooms.

A FEW EXAMPLES

Recently, for example, while discussing Marilyn K.'s portfolio entries with her, her critique of a particularly successful paper she had written led to a discussion of what she perceived to be seriously different, though personally confusing, contradictions she experienced when writing for professors in the hard sciences and social sciences versus the humanities (especially English). Using this particular paper on the economic issues surrounding the institution of slavery in the United States, and comparing this paper with another she had written as a subjective response to *The Scarlet Letter*, she pointed out that her use of the first-person pronoun *I* was encouraged in the response paper and frowned upon in the research paper on slavery. This in turn led us into a discussion of point of view and caused us to examine this question: to what extent does the embracing of a third-person point of view lead to a more "objective" discussion of a topic. Her point—quite legitimate and insightful, I think—was that the use of the third-person pronouns created the "appearance" of objectivity but in many ways was less honest than the use of the first-person pronoun. She also revealed that she had been told by the history professor that she "wrote too much like an English major," which was considered "inappropriate" in the social sciences. When asked what this meant to her, she said that the history teacher was bothered by what he called "flowery" writing. And though she was still not sure what he meant by this because he had not been able to present her with a clear explanation, Marilyn suspected that he was bothered by her use of extended metaphor and analogies based in her own personal experience that she used to identify with some of the issues she was exploring in the paper.

While we are not presently concerned here with a central issue of what is "appropriate" in "scholarly" writing, this example fascinated us because it brought to light so many important elements of what students experience as they bounce around among our various academic biases across disciplines: first, though Marilyn felt herself somewhat entrapped by the different demands made on her by professors in different disciplines, she also found the problem relatively easy to solve. She is a strong writer and almost intuitively was able to meet the demands of each audience. One wonders, however, what happens to the students who are not facile writers—they must feel helpless as they try to figure out what it is that "the teacher wants." Second, these issues led us into a fruitful, interesting discussion on the nature of *truth and objectivity* in the sciences and social sciences as opposed to the possibility of truth and objectivity in the arts and humanities. Third, this led us into a discussion of the human "subject" who is observer, experimenter, and writer and the relationship of this authorial role to issues she had studied in a literary criticism course and a course in philosophy—issues focusing on postmodern philosophical positions and the nature of self.

Again, we came to no concrete conclusions in this discussion. What mattered, however, was her growing ability to make connections across disciplines. She was moving well-beyond simple, objective facts into the different ways in which disciplines characterize, examine, and discuss reality. Next, the discussion caused Pat Courts, who had taught several of the history professors in the WAC Workshops, to ask those teachers how they perceived the issue. Again, nothing clear-cut was resolved, but the history professors agreed to raise the issue with their colleagues in hopes that, at the very least, they might more clearly explain the rhetorical demands made on the students in these courses. And finally, Courts was able to use the paper and issues it presented with the writing tutors in the Learning Center so that they might explore the same issues and be ready to help students who came to them confused about such demands.

Clearly, then, portfolios have the potential to work powerfully as part of the teaching-learning process as they reveal confusions and encourage explorations of experiences that students have across courses and disciplines. And regardless of assessment, if this was all they did, it would present a powerful argument for their use. Beyond this example of how the portfolio affected the learning of an individual student and teacher, the portfolios additionally allowed us to gain a fuller sense of what so often remains hidden in education and something that should be at the very heart of any emphasis on systems of assessment: instead of simply assessing whether or not students are learning what (we think) we are teaching, they provide us with a window on what students are actually learning, something that we may know much less about than we like to pretend.

Thus it is that, in concert with other elements in the program, portfolios allow us to see that what Pat Courts, for example, is sure everyone learned in the seminar or the course that examines the nature of the reading process, is suddenly curiously absent in many of the learners five weeks later, as evidenced by their work in another course or in student teaching. This kind of discovery should and does lead to the teachers involved in the program gathering together to examine and try to address the problem, in order to eliminate or at least moderate it. Consequently, what begins as an emphasis on the individual students' learning and growth leads directly to programmatic assessment and programmatic changes when appropriate.

In the abstract, all this sounds pretty good. Students create their portfolios, learn and benefit from the process; teachers read and discuss the portfolios, learning more about adjustments they must consider in order to make the courses more successful. Both students and teacher gain valuable insight into the teaching learning process. A happy world, this!

In reality, of course, the happy world of generalization often becomes particularly complicated by real students and teachers. The following example grows out of an experience that occurred shortly after we had begun the portfolio requirement in the English Education program. Because the requirement was new, both teacher and student had only two semesters' work to examine as they formed certain judgements. And it is particularly important to note that the brief time span covered by the portfolio significantly contribute to some of the problems that occurred in this specific case.

In the Senior Seminar for Teachers of English, Marty A. felt that he had recognized some weakness on which he needed further work, but generally felt that he had evidenced real strength in the areas of preparing and organizing lesson plans and units. From his point of view, his written work in this course, including a detailed personal essay exploring his own philosophy of teaching and an extensive unit on teaching *Macbeth*, which was filled with highly detailed, daily lesson plans characterized by well-planned discussion questions, writing activities, and small-group work, all contributed to his expectation of clear sailing in student teaching: his philosophical, whole-language base and his growing ability in organizing and planning lessons suggested to him that he would be a good teacher. Likewise, other additions to his portfolio—poetry, short stories, and critical essays—indicated a reasonably solid understanding of the discipline. Unfortunately, about halfway into the student-teaching experience, everyone involved (except Marty) agreed that things were going very badly and he was removed from student teaching.

This may seem like a rather curious example, certainly not much of an argument for the success of portfolios as indicators of anything. But, keeping in mind that this incident occurred at the very beginning of the portfolio requirement, it is useful to examine the rest of this particular student's story. Of course, Marty was devastated at first, as anyone would be. Initially directing his anger at his cooperating and supervising teachers, his uncooperative students, and "the system," he began by projecting his own problems on any and all available screens. But once things quieted down and he began to confront the experience, he stopped in to see his advisor and sort through all that had happened. In preparation for the conference Marty had, on his own initiative, reviewed his portfolio entries, the journal he had kept during the seminar and student teaching, and the written plans he had used in student teaching.

This self-directed reflection on his own writing and experiences led him to some surprising self-discoveries, and, at least as important, the process led him to a peaceful and constructive plan for future action. In reviewing his written journal, he realized that he had several entries in which he defensively rejected counsel offered by two separate teachers who had suggested that he might find himself very unhappy as a classroom teacher because his critical views, though well-articulated, were rigid and left little room for dissension or discussion. He noted that the teacher who had commented on the personal essay he had written narrating his philosophy of education had suggested that his ideas were in need of considerable elaboration and exemplification because they were vague and overgeneralized. More specifically, the teacher had said that "until the personal philosophy was more fully and specifically articulated, you will have difficulty creating and implementing your lesson plans." And Marty remembered that the written feedback on his unit and lesson plans suggested that he needed to "work much more on creating questions about literary works that would engage students in interactive discussions which actively solicited their ideas. While your present discussion questions are thorough from a New Critical point of view, you do not at present include questions that encourage personal response from the student or that move beyond the specific work to the lives of the students and the world in which they live." And though it was not directly part of the portfolio, he remembered that two teachers directly involved in the English Education program had expressed genuine concern that he had not fully embraced the difficulties inherent in teaching: they had explicitly asked him to reevaluate his decision to teach, telling him that they felt he might find himself unsuited to the demands of the profession.

Perhaps the example is getting "curiouser." Thus far the portfolio appears to have accomplished little to head off a problem, and, in retrospect, the portfolio appears to have done little more than exemplify a series of qualified negatives about Marty's performance prior to student teaching. For Marty himself, however, the self-reflection and lengthy discussions with his supervising teacher from the college and with his advisor allowed him to recognize that he really did not like teaching very much at all. The lack of energy and planning that had characterized his student teaching occurred because he did not want to spend every evening doing that kind of work. And this reluctance had caused him to employ a self-imposed deafness to all that had been said about his prior performances, a fact that he came to recognize as one of the most powerful parts of this learning experience. [We note that egocentrism is clearly not a phase that suddenly disappears at some early developmental stage.] His irritation at the high school–

students' inability to see *his* point of view caused him to feel hostile toward them. He had not rethought his philosophy of education nor revised the unit and lesson plans because he simply did not feel like doing so and did not really see any reason for such revision.

Thus far, it still looks like a considerable amount of bad news, but the good news is extremely important here. Of course, all of us would have preferred to have been able to spare him (and the cooperating teacher and the supervising teacher and the high school students) the entire unpleasant experience. And yet, as was said earlier, the result of all of this was Marty's sense of personal peace and direction. His self-reflection and review of his portfolio and related journal writing allowed him to see that his real love for English was centered in a love for writing, particularly creative writing. Through his own personal strengths and the help of his teachers, he genuinely came to view the entire experience as an important part of his learning. And he decided that he would work for awhile (he already had a job lined up), save some money, continue to write on his own, and eventually enter a Masters of Fine Arts Program that would allow him to further develop his writing skills.

As far as teaching was concerned, he had not entirely given up the idea. Indeed, he felt that he had learned enough about himself and his own strengths that he had some hopes of teaching creative writing at the college level. And even this decision was supported by his portfolio and student-teaching experience because his major successes with his students had all been in the area of teaching writing.

Obviously, this is not a neat, packaged example; it is however a true one. And while it serves to highlight the complexities involved in the teaching-learning process and the perhaps obvious fact that portfolios will not solve all problems, it was the initial purpose of the example to suggest how the activity might help us, as teachers, rethink and revise our own practices. Thus it came about, as a result of this particular case, that the teachers directly responsible for the English Education program decided to review student portfolios before the students' senior year, discuss the students' progress as shown by the portfolio and the students' performance in relevant courses, and conduct interviews with individual students in order to share observations and identify areas of concern and/or weakness. Likewise, the faculty agreed that students would include in their portfolios at least one and preferably two videotapes of themselves giving class presentations, microteaching, and/or teaching a mini-unit to high school students prior to student teaching.

Again, although we are presently discussing the role of portfolios in individual assessment, it should be obvious that, in this case, the process was integrally tied to programmatic assessment and change. Additionally, it should be obvious that portfolios, especially insofar as they contribute to the individual student's learning and growth, must not exist in isolation. They must be viewed within the context of the program and courses within which the entries are generated. And any given entry should be examined and discussed in relationship to the other entries. Furthermore, it should be clear that this kind of integration demands that the teachers who will review the portfolios with the individual students must have more than a passing acquaintance with goals, objectives, and activities that comprise programs and courses within programs. It is in this context that even portfolios that focus on the individual student lend themselves to program improvement, as instructors discuss one another's courses and student performances within the courses.

A note of thanks and qualification is appropriate here. Several years ago, when I was beginning to write about the Fredonia GCP assessment, focusing on comments that students had made about the entire process, I sent a lengthy draft of this work to Pat Hutchings, then director of the Assessment Forum sponsored by the American Association of Higher Education. After kindly reading the work, she wrote back suggesting that what was implicit in the article needed to be made explicit: based on the comments made by these students, teachers in general appeared to be grossly overestimating what their students were learning. In the past, because methods of assessment were so intensely focused on data derived from "objective" instruments (read multiple-choice tests), the student voices had been eliminated and ignored. But qualitative assessment, assessment instruments that made students active partners in the process and that recognized the need for them to speak in their own voices, possessed the potential to provide all of us with long hidden and very significant information.

Though many of these student voices have already been presented in Chapter 2, a little reminder of those voices may help us see our students:

> Most GCP courses are an exercise at listening. All's they ever are, are lecture classes. —upperclass student

> I believe that what we term learning is not learning at all. Learning is a process that involves relationships between facts. Most learning, or what we call learning is the memorization of disjointed facts. In real life we see and feel the flow of how things go together. In the class that flow is disrupted and made disjointed. Most of the school structuring I find useless. Most courses teach facts and don't stress putting the facts together. Most courses teach in hunks and sections. The flow of ideas from one section to another is lost or loose. The problem most students have with courses is not the content but trying to understand why they are getting all those disjointed facts. I don't know a better way, but there has to be one.

> What is least helpful about the school learning experience is that teachers are generally too concerned with covering a curriculum and not concerned enough with making sure that students really gain new understanding from coursework.

PORTFOLIOS: SOME DESCRIPTIONS

Pluralizing the word *portfolio* suggests not only that there will be more than one portfolio, but that there may be more than one kind of portfolio, depending on the purpose.

The Nonselective Portfolio

In this kind of portfolio, all of the student's work in a given course would be collected, chronologically dated, and clearly labeled in terms of its relationship to a given assignment. In the case of essay tests, for example, both the questions and the students' written responses would be included. In science courses, copies of lab reports and a personal narrative describing the specific experiment would be included. [We note our own experiences, here, regarding undergraduate lab courses: although our experiments almost never worked the way they were supposed to, we "pretended" they did and created our lab reports accordingly. It would have helped significantly if someone had explained that our *experience* with the experiment and our understanding of that experience were more important than "right answers."] In math courses, problems and written solutions would be included. In courses that require "readers' notes" and/or "annotated bibliographies," these would be included (Courts 1991, 147–54). In art courses, paintings, photographs, and so on would be included. In short, all of the concrete evidence the students can collect to indicate their involvement in a course would be a part of these portfolios (accompanied, of course, with written explanations of the importance of an item included in the portfolio).

Advantages. The major advantage of a nonselective, all inclusive portfolio is probably quite obvious. The teacher has access to all of the student's work and therefore has the opportunity to gain a complete perspective on the kind of work and growth that appears to be occurring. If there are particular sections of the course in which the students' work appears to be weaker than in others, the teacher will know that either the student was not fully engaged at that point or that the student did not fully understand the concepts or processes that were being studied. By looking over the entire portfolio and reflecting on the student's day-to-day classroom performance, the teacher should be able to gain a relatively complete sense of the student's general progress, identifying both weak and strong areas of performance.

A further advantage of such portfolios is that the students have an opportunity to look at and reflect on everything that they have been doing. In the face of such a collection, one can hardly say, "I've been doing my best and working as hard as I can and really understand everything we've been studying" if glaring gaps or weak performances characterize the work in the portfolio. On the more positive side, students can determine for themselves which areas, processes, or concepts suggest a need for individual help or further study and thought.

From the point of view of programmatic assessment, one would be able to see immediately what kinds of and how much writing is being required in the program, how well students perform, and whether or not they improve.

Finally, and no small point here, consider the potential advantage graduates would gain if they could present a prospective employer or graduate admissions staff with selections from their portfolios indicating the amount, kinds, and quality of writing they had been doing. Next consider the possibility of these applicants being able to talk about their strengths (and weaknesses) as writers/thinkers using concrete examples from their portfolios in order to illustrate their abilities.

Disadvantages. Aside from the "bulk" involved here, the additional disadvantages of such portfolios may be equally obvious. First, by virtue of being all inclusive, everything in the portfolio becomes equal and potentially indeterminate. Most of us know that, in terms of visual perception, if one tries to see "everything at once," one becomes blind, unable to see anything at all. The more one concentrates on *all* the details, the more likely one is to see a confused blur. For example, look at a page of print and try to see each individual letter: you will either see little more than a gray blur, or you will go so slowly from letter to letter that the words and concepts represented by the print will be unintelligible. In short, the "complete picture" may be no picture at all, just a confused conglomeration of stuff.

This is not so much an argument against this kind of portfolio as it is a suggestion that the Nonselective, all-inclusive portfolio will be most constructive when both teacher and learner together have determined the priorities of the most significant activities in the courses and their interrelationships ahead of time. Such a process not only makes assessment much more direct and possible, but it also provides the learner with a sense of ownership and understanding about his/her participation in the course.

A second disadvantage arises because this kind of portfolio creates a heavy demand on the teacher's time and energy. While one might reasonably argue that a holistic review of the portfolio might reveal a reasonable assessment of the students' overall performance, it would hardly reveal the most important information: where, specifically, is the student experiencing difficulty and what is the nature of the difficulties? And without such information, the teacher will be unable to do much for the individual student beyond some generalized assessment. ("Well, yes. Your writing does seem to be getting better.")

But if the teacher engages in a careful review of each entry in the portfolio, literally analyzing and critiquing each piece of the whole, s/he will be engaged in a task that makes Sisyphus look as though he is acting constructively as he forever rolls his rock up the hill only to watch it roll down again creating the necessity that he roll it up again. While we may need to admit the existential absurdity (the potential hubris, perhaps?) involved in the process of assessing another human being, we do not need to purposely engage in such a process.

Selective Portfolios

First, remember that selective portfolios, intended for individual and/or programmatic assessment, should not preclude encouraging individual students to keep portfolios of all the significant work they produce in their courses. Aside from the obvious fact that a "selective portfolio" assumes that a body of work exists from which something might be selected, it is often helpful and interesting for students to be able to look back on what they have produced in courses over several years. But in terms of the practicalities of assessment and teaching, some system of selectivity appears almost essential.

A broad variety of possibilities present themselves when one considers the make up of a system of selective portfolios. First and foremost, of course, the purpose must be clearly identified. In the case of the portfolio requirement in the English Education Program at Fredonia (see Appendix C), we began with a reasonably clear purpose that appears, at present, to be in the process of relatively consistent modification as we find things that need to be added or changed.

A *Singular Example.* As should be obvious from the directions in Appendix C, both the requirements and uses of these portfolios are presently modest and practical. In short, we took our own advice and started "small." At present, our purpose is almost entirely pedagogical in nature, focusing on the individual student's work as included in the portfolio. Assessment is highly individualized, qualitative, and subjective. Because students are not directed to include particular kinds of papers from particular courses that are a part of the English Education program, we make no pretense of comparing one student's growth with that of another or one group with another as was done in the large-scale evaluation of the General College Program.

In part, our reasons for such a decision should be relatively obvious. Even if we created a system of required inclusions in the portfolios, mandating that specific kinds of papers be required in specific courses so that scoring criteria might be created for rating the student work and comparing the contents of one portfolio with another, we would have no outside control group with which to compare the improvement or lack thereof. Our primary purposes are met by the present design, and they are as follows.

1. To provide students with the opportunity to reflect on their own performance in a given course or on a given assignment in an attempt to increase their metacognitive awareness both in the moment and over time.

2. To empower individual students by encouraging them to choose for themselves what is or is not important in their performance on given assignments and courses. (Note: Although students select single papers they have written, the discussion of a portfolio almost always moves beyond the specific paper or set of papers to a discussion of what happened in the course in general and how it compares with students' other significant learning experiences.)

3. To help students see that learning is not supposed to be disconnected across disciplines nor isolated within a given course—to encourage them to make connections among and across their own learning experiences

(which is the reason that their selections need not be limited to work produced in a course, but may be work they produced on their own for their own reasons).

4. To provide a concrete basis for open, learner-centered discussion between advisor and learner: That is, instead of prescribing what *should be learned,* we hope to explore with the learner what *is being learned* and find out what and why our students value particular learning experiences. This is no small point because it is directly related to Dr. Hutchings' remarks (1990) mentioned earlier: rather than presuming that we know exactly what is or should be happening with our students—though we obviously have our own objectives—we are using the portfolios, first, to find out what they deem important. Before we over- or underestimate student learning as we create assessment criteria from a distanced perspective, we need to learn who and what it is we are estimating. We believe that this may be one of the single, most important *initial* assessment objectives of portfolios.

5. To identify areas of strength and weakness in the students' performances, as evidenced in the portfolios and through the discussions, so that advisor and learner might work together to identify ways of exploiting strengths and eliminating particularly problematic weaknesses.

6. To provide students with a concrete, conscious sense of their accomplishments and growth over the two-to-four years covered in the portfolio.

7. To help students become conscious of the constructive role that various modes of writing play in their own psychological-intellectual development.

8. To help students recognize that learning is a cumulative process that has barely begun as they end their undergraduate years, a process they are fully capable of continuing on their own in the future.

9. To help advisors identify gaps or problems in the students' undergraduate preparation that might be specifically addressed in the courses students take as part of the English Education major. Since English majors must take a core of courses that are part of the major, this kind of information affects the "program" well beyond the Education component of the program.

At this point, it should be obvious that we are not particularly interested in providing data to some overseeing group to "prove" the value of the program and statistically document improvement in student performance. Indeed, the most revealing element of these portfolios lies not so much in what papers the students decide to include in them as it does in their reasons for including a given paper. The most important element of a given entry is not the paper itself, but the written critique the student produces explaining why an entry is significant.

Of course, it is unquestionable that portfolios might be used to meet the assessment demands of some political or educational overseeing group. And the English Education Portfolio at Fredonia is unquestionably still in an evolutionary process (and probably will remain in an evolutionary state for quite some time). But as Chapter 1 suggested, we are more than a little skeptical of the reasons that overseers impose such objectives. First, the imposition itself invites deception and fraudulence: "If you force us (especially under threat of losing funding for the institution or program), one way or another, true or not, we will prove that students are learning better (than what? whom?) as a result of this program." Second, one is hard put to find many cases where assessment has led to an overseeing group increasing funds to support an institution or program. Third, let us say you proved that your students are learning "more": Can they continue to do so? Each new group? That the much discussed implementation of a national system of assessment of learning at all educational levels will almost certainly fall into this trap, at major expense to taxpayers and learners and teachers, seems blatantly obvious. When, one wonders, does someone assess those who impose the assessments?

Likewise, as we envision student portfolios, they do not operate as a "gate-keeping" device: (1) they are not graded; (2) grades on papers included in the portfolio are not a focal point for discussion; and (3) the system is not devised to second-guess or criticize another professor's grading practices. While some might argue that using the portfolios as gatekeeping devices would increase their importance to the students and cause the students to take their writing more seriously, we would argue that, under such conditions, the portfolios cease to facilitate student learning, cause students to view them in much the same way they view multiple-choice exams (Do what you have to do, get it over with, and forget it!) and invite plagiarism. More directly, the very need or desire for gate-keeping devices should lead to an assessment of what is going on in the courses these students are taking over their four years in college rather than leading to an additional hurdle over which students must jump. If, as we have emphatically suggested, the portfolios represent an interactive center among students and instructors/advisors, then students may be helped to acquire necessary skills and/or advised to consider academic or career paths that more clearly fit their strengths.

The fact remains, however, that we all have to be accountable in one way or another, regardless of whether or not the demand for accountability is mandated or self-imposed. And an argument against simplistic (and often harmful) gate-keeping devices is not an argument against accountability. Likewise, we cannot simply cry out in anger against the demands of the overseers. Again we quote the insightful editorial comments offered us by our colleague, Minda Rae Amiran, on these matters:

The real question is how to get legislators to accept portfolio-type evidence (or other kinds of performance assessment). Possibly one might argue that, say, 80 percent of our students reach level 4 [that is, some previously established level of expertise] in the writing of research papers, defining level 4 and providing a few examples . . . from the portfolios.

What are some other ways one could use evidence from portfolios to satisfy legislators? "We have documentation to show that 90 percent of our students perform successful original laboratory research"? "We have evidence to show that 85 percent of our students can critique their own writing and improve it"? "Our students use their portfolios to help them land jobs, and here is an employer-satisfaction report"? (personal letter, 1992)

FINAL WORDS

We do not mean to insult the intelligence of our readers by stating the obvious: clearly the above portfolio requirement might be adapted and modified in a variety of ways. But perhaps a brief discussion of some of the factors that might influence modifications and a few specific suggestions might save some time and energy for those who are just embarking on the creation and implementation of portfolios in their own classrooms and programs.

First and foremost, it is important to note that widespread, broadly envisioned uses of portfolios in colleges has, for the most part, focused on student writing and on the assessment of student performance in that area. Indeed, the focus is often limited to an assessment of student growth in the first year of college, directly related to required writing courses, often serving as gatekeeping devices of one sort or another. Although we clearly oppose this use of portfolios, readers may wish to read Part I of Belanoff and Dickson's *Portfolios* (1–98). For a discussion of a portfolio system that might be used to assess student growth in writing and metacognition, see the article "Metacognition and the Use of Portfolios" by Minda Rae Amiran and Karen Mills-Courts (also in Belanoff and Dickson, 101–12).

Whatever modifications one considers, however, they must always derive from a clear, prior statement of purpose by those creating and implementing the plan. Consequently, what follows is necessarily generalized.

For those who wish to compare students' progress within a program, students would almost necessarily be required to include portfolio entries as identified by the instructors running the program or major. This would additionally demand agreement among those teaching courses in the program or major to require certain kinds and amounts of writing in given courses. For example, entry-level courses in a program or major might require personal essays in which students explore and narrate their reasons for choosing a given major or program. Other courses might require that students write analytical essays focusing on concepts of particular significance in the field; still other courses might require argumentative essays focusing on controversies in the discipline or on research papers related to the specific subject matter or on lab reports or observation reports when appropriate within a discipline. Others might wish to require students to write annotated bibliographies or reader-response notes focusing on readings in the course.

In cases such as these, it would even be possible for instructors in given courses to indicate to students which given assignment is to become a part of their portfolios. While we feel committed to the value of empowering students and of having them choose what they include in the portfolio, clearly one might legitimately implement a more rigid, directive system. And the choice need not necessarily be black and white. For us, the central emphasis focuses less on what is included in the portfolio than on what is eventually done with the portfolio. If portfolios are simply repositories of accumulated student work, selective or not, they will mean nothing to students. If they are primarily used as gatekeeping devices, they will be important to students in the ways that tests and grades are presently important to them—a fact that will militate against the portfolios functioning as tools for learning.

In terms of the constructive value of portfolios for the growth and learning of individual students, what will matter most is the nature of the discussion that instructors and learner have about what is included in the portfolios. It is for this reason that, regardless of the system of selection, we urge that students be required to write about why a given entry does or does not matter to them and about how it did or did not function in their growth and learning.

And this leads us to the next chapter, which engages the issues of classroom methodology and writing across the curriculum. After all, if the students are not writing across a broad variety of courses and disciplines, what will they have to put in their portfolios?

Making Sense: Teaching and Classroom Assessment

THE CENTRALITY OF LANGUAGE PROCESSES IN LEARNING

> "Get inside this house," they would say. "get y'all tail in here. That dust from the plant fenna fall." And the silver came just as the women said it would. To some children it looked like glitter, to some it looked like snow, and to some it looked like it was raining pieces from the bottom of the sky.
> —Connie Porter (1991, 23)

The "pieces from the bottom of the sky" were the metal filings, detritus of the manufacturing process, spewed forth daily and without constraint, from Bethlehem Steel into the air of Lackawanna, the steel town just south of Buffalo. My father had worked in the coke ovens until he got too old to stand up to the heat. The neighborhood children breathed in, danced under, and played with the filings and other discharges, donations from the largest employer in that town whose sulphurous air could be seen in Canada. These children were my first teachers. I was a Head Start volunteer—a high school girl who, on weekends and after school, worked in the dusty African Methodist Episcopal Church basement to teach three eight-year-old girls to read.

The first thing these girls taught me was that they were not about to do any "schoolwork" until they learned to trust me. We played a lot of games and told a lot of stories about ourselves. They also taught me that the best way to shut down their energy and enthusiasm was to pull out the SRA (Scholastic Reading Associates) cards—staple curriculum in the program. Each time I set out a new "tan" card or moved them up to "forest green," their lowered eyelids and gloomy silence telegraphed my betrayal of them. I poked around in dark closets and found an old typewriter in reasonable working order; we packed away the SRA kits and began to work on writing stories, plays, and skip-rope rhymes. The girls learned how to compose, to spell, to revise. They took their stories home to their families and shared them with the other Head Start kids. I learned about the power of narrative in naming and authoring one's self and experiences and the world—a dimension that seemed to be pointedly missing from the "individualized" reading kits.

The girls obtained library cards and the Bookmobile began to stop at the church. Years before I ever heard of an educational theory called *whole language*, the girls taught me that there is, as Gerard Manley Hopkins wrote, a "juice and joy" in language, in creating meaning, and in personal growth through language, in a climate of trust and high expectations. I saw the synergy that accrues from collaborative learning and reciprocal teaching before I ever read about those terms in a textbook.

The girls taught me something else—that not everyone loved them as much as I had come to, nor did everyone recognize their talents and potential. One child was African American, one Chicana, and one Anglo. All were from families who lived in poverty. I remember our final field trip to Niagara Falls. As I swung the girls around on a grassy hill by the Horseshoe Falls, and slipped my way, reluctantly, through the Cave of the Winds with the girls pulling me toward the thunderous opening upon the Falls, I heard the remarks of tourists about "my" girls. I saw the expressions of disdain and dis-ease—parents holding their well-heeled children away from us as we came near to share the view. My young charges were not seen as gifts, or achievers, but unsanitary effluence leaking out from the southern edge of town and the still mill—the bottom of the sky. I learned and began to understand how *difference* has consequences.

Through these teachers, these girls, I learned about the importance of a nurturing and responsive learning climate, about the nature of learning and literacy, about the dynamics of cultural beliefs and their effects on society's dispossessed. Clearly, the girls gave me good lessons on the importance of listening closely to learners, working alongside them rather than from above, and learning from them as they developed their understanding of literacy and school tasks. I went on to study and teach literacy, and the principles I came to understand in the church basement have been affirmed, refined, and amplified.

From the findings of the Bristol study, Gordon Wells asserts:

> It is not possible, simply by telling, to cause students to come to have the knowledge that is in the mind of the teacher. Knowledge cannot be transmitted. It has to be constructed afresh by each individual knower on the basis of what is already known and by means of strategies developed over the whole of that individual's life, both outside and inside the classroom. (1986, 218)

Writing and speaking assist in this construction; they are powerful tools for learning, self-reflection, personal growth, and increased participation and empowerment in the world. Literacies are personally as well as culturally shaped, and while there are different literacies, semiotics, and ways of making sense of the world through language, these do not exist on a hierarchical scale of bad to good or deficient to proficient. Literacies are diverse and embedded in, and shaped by, differing contexts, beliefs, and social practices. Language learning is not imitative, but creative; growth in language is engendered through purposeful, meaningful, and challenging uses and tasks. Language learning is developmental, and students need to learn how to use language to reflect upon and direct that process. Learning is constructive; learners must be allowed to be active participants in the making of meaning; a teacher must allow for the negotiation of meaning as well as the learner's integration of the personal woven together with "rational" epistemologies—true learning, according to Mary Field Belenky, is the "reconstruction of self," the process of becoming a "connected knower." And learners have much to teach their teachers. These are the assumptions about language and learning guiding this chapter, assumptions that have correspondence to literacies in all disciplines and to developing literacy in all disciplines through language.

These assumptions also tend to complicate teaching rather than simplify. Bill Hendricks writes:

> As an American academic, a member of a professional guild one of whose characteristics is to continually discover, as all professional guilds must, that its schemes and routines are not *only* schemes and routines, that they do more than blindly reproduce themselves, I daily experience prods and promptings to sustain a belief that . . . knowledge ought not to come cheap, that it wants work, and that its great value is confirmed, paradoxically, by its always being just out of reach, deferred, in perpetual need of further elaboration. (1992, 41)

Teaching, too, must be continually reinvented, responsive, reflective. The more closely I look at and with learners, and research about learning, the more complex and intriguing teaching becomes—and the further I am from the self-assured curricula, instruction, and evaluation of SRA skill-building or E. D. Hirsch Jr.'s Core Knowledge Foundation or Graduate Record Examinations. There is a compelling richness to teaching students as well as teaching a subject. Friere writes: "A pedagogy is that much more critical and radical the more investigative and less certain of certainties it is. The more unquiet a pedagogy, the more critical it becomes" (Freire and Macedo 1987, 54).

In this chapter, we will look at how the goals of conscientious assessment and the goals of good teaching, or an "unquiet pedagogy," cohere and articulate. We will discuss teaching and learning as active and interactive, and how we might work *with* students, not apart from them, with the underlying belief that what we all do, finally, can transform our lives and purposes in school and, with luck, beyond. We will look at smaller and younger learners as well as at college students. We believe that a knowledge of the school experiences that students bring with them is important and that our own theoretical understandings, as teachers at all levels of learning, should be shared and interactive, not isolated by grade level, building, or title. The assessment conversation has been occurring for some time in elementary schools, and we in college have much to learn from the thoughtful assessments devised by good elementary, middle, and high school teachers. The approaches and practices we present here are vitalized by the spirit of possibility—not with answers fitting all problems—but with ways of framing inquiry into "practicing theory" and "theorizing practice" in teaching.

ASSESSMENT AND INSTRUCTION

> An alternative to formal tests is the use of a bachelor's paper as the assessment tool . . . such a paper is an appropriate means of assessment for the individual sociology student and for the program as a whole.
> —David Hartmann (1992, 125)

Perhaps it is conceivable to have a departmental portfolio with a single paper in it, but we would not recommend this practice. So far, we have been advocating assessment approaches having multiple dimensions, accounting for learning in many contexts and students as active constructionists of their knowing. And we would be hard-pressed to defend using one paper as the sole assessment tool for measuring individual as well as programmatic success. While a departmentally required senior paper is a worthy and important component of an assessment program and reflects a good move away from formal tests and toward faculty developed performance evaluation, it is only one part of a larger view. We see assessment as integrally tied to a conception of instruction that operates daily and centrally in classroom practice, not simply in the senior seminar or as represented by the scope of a writing assignment. We need to explore and clarify instructional approaches that are germane to an institutional commitment to assess learning—ways that teachers go about engendering learning in introductory courses as well as senior capstone classes. And, indeed, the current phase in assessment discussions reflects a concern not so much for "how to get started and how to win over faculty" but "how to use assessment to improve education" (Wright, in Blumenstyk and Magner 1990). We begin with the vital relationship of literacy and oracy to learning.

LANGUAGE AND LEARNING

Language, clearly, is central to learning, growth, and change. Language theorists, teachers, writers, and researchers have described the fundamental role of language in learning, and the call for writing throughout the disciplines began over two decades ago (Vygotsky 1962; Martin et al. 1976; Langer and Applebee 1987). Writing is central to learning because of

(1) the permanence of the written word, allowing the writer to rethink and revise over an extended period; (2) the explicitness required in writing, if meaning is to remain constant beyond the context in which it was originally written; (3) the resources provided by the conventional forms of discourse for organizing and thinking through new relationships among ideas; and (4) the active nature of writing, providing a medium for exploring implications entailed within otherwise unexamined assumptions. (Langer and Applebee 1987, 5)

Judith Langer and Arthur Applebee's research provides powerful documentation of the correlation between writing and learning: "Across the studies, there is clear evidence that activities involving writing (*any* of the many sorts of writing we studied) lead to better learning than activities involving reading and studying only" (1987, 135). Language activities, writing in particular, are not simply a product or reflection of good thinking, but they assist and shape cognition. Language enables us to codify, explore, recall, discover, create, and imagine. While thinking, or "inner speech," according to Lev Vygotsky, tends to be elliptical and only privately intelligible, the process of committing thought to writing requires and prompts us to elaborate and to begin to understand what it is we mean. Vygotsky described a model of the relationship of thought and language as we move between inner speech and public discourse:

Inner speech is condensed, abbreviated speech. Written speech is deployed to its fullest extent, more complete than oral speech. Inner speech is almost entirely predicated because the situation, the subject of thought, is always known to the thinker. Written speech, on the contrary, must explain the situation fully in order to be intelligible. The change from maximally compact inner speech to maximally detailed written speech requires what might be called deliberate semantics—deliberate structuring of the web of meaning. (1962, 182)

Further, said Vygotsky, thought and language interanimate: "The relation between thought and word is a living process; thought is born through words. A word devoid of thought is a dead thing, and a thought unembodied in words is a shadow." (1962, 153). Without the mediation of language, then, particularly extensive language production as in writing, the thinking we ask of students in school may be insubstantial.

Writing and other language-based problem-posing activities are, then, epistemic and find their home at the heart of good instruction, not simply in the form of term papers. But this requires a radical reconception of writing—one that perhaps contrasts sharply with your own writing experiences in school. As a high school student, I did not write very much. The notorious New York State Regents Exam reigned in the curriculum, and there was little time to write or even talk about the concepts we were furiously memorizing for the "Regents." My writing experiences mirrored what Applebee discovered about writing instruction in the schools: 97 percent of all writing is less than a paragraph in length—filling-in-the-blanks or worksheet-like in nature (1981, 58). When I did write, it was usually to display how accurately I could hunt down symbols in close readings of literary texts—writing for teacher-as-examiner, the audience for most writing in high school (Applebee 1984).

This pattern continued, for the most part, in my college education. In the few courses requiring writing, the teacher would assign paper topics and we would go home and write what we thought the teacher wanted to hear. Those of us who could "do school" well would usually be able to figure out the teacher's favorite themes, and we would focus on those. Grades, after all, were at stake— and we were not, as Shor says, "educational virgins" (1987, 28). We would turn in final drafts, often written the night before, and be evaluated. Teacher response was usually comprised of two-word terminal phrases: "Interesting analysis" or "Superb job." While I liked the good grades, my problem was that I had no idea *what* exactly had been interesting or superb, or *why*, but I had finished another "job."

Writing, by default, was a mysterious and private activity; writing papers was usually an exercise of intuition (second-guessing the teacher's notion of an ideal paper) and drudgery (good typing). Exploratory writing or dialogue with teachers or peers about drafts in process was not even imagined. We seemed to get by on the finely turned phrase and the lack of typos. As a graduate assistant, I learned that meaningful writing was less important than error-free writing. Once a week, a few first-year students would drop by the office I shared with another teaching assistant. These students were on their way to submit their weekly essays to another teacher. We did not know them, but I guess the students thought we must be friendly, helpful folks—they would ask us to proofread their papers. At first we refused, but then it was clear that the students were really worried; they had been told that their papers would be failed if there were any errors. We helped the students proofread, tried to teach them ways of proofreading for themselves, and also responded to the content and style of their work. But these issues were our issues, not the students'. They just knew that the best papers were error-free. We saw, as the weeks passed, the subjects of their papers became more trivial, the "ideas" flatten and disappear, the sentence structures more simplistic, and the vocabulary dwindle to only the shortest and easiest-to-spell words.

Such notions of literacy linger. Recently, leaving an all-day workshop on writing-across-the-curriculum, I heard a foreign language professor say, "This has helped me a lot. I'm really going to crack down on grammar from now on." This statement echoes the philosophy of Warriner's composition textbooks, the ubiquitous English handbooks most of us worked through in high school (a text still found in many districts). The writing process is defined, according to Warriner's, in this way:

> A good writer puts words together in correct, smooth sentences, according to the
> rules of standard usage. He puts sentences together to make paragraphs that are

clear and effective, unified and well-developed. Finally, he puts paragraphs together into larger forms of writing—essays, letters, stories, research papers.

A writer begins with a general plan and ends with details of wording, sentence structure, and grammar. First, he chooses the *subject* of his composition. Second, he tackles the *preparation* of his material, from rough ideas to formal outline. Third, he undertakes the writing itself, once again beginning with a rough form (the first draft) and ending with a finished form (the final draft) that is as nearly as perfect as he can make it. (Warriner, Morsand, and Griffith 1958, 379–80)

This idealized (and unrecognizable) Warriner's writer haunts many of us, however. Our students confess with embarrassment that they never wrote the outline until after the paper was done; and, of course, this is true and sensible, because if we are to learn from writing, why bother writing what we already know? However, if school assignments ask us to attend only, or mostly, to formal rather than communicative and epistemic functions of writing, then writing is an empty, mechanical routine. Peter Elbow calls this brand of school writing "backwards"; that to define the writer's task as thinking very well first and then transcribing that thinking into correct texts is like teaching people to touch their toes by putting their hands to the sky (1973, 13–15). And, to focus on written products, solely for evaluation and never for exploration is a falsely constricted notion ignoring the powerful and central role of language in facilitating learning. In an essay, Patrick Courts writes:

Literacy is always more than mere propriety and good usage, matters that are more imitative than liberating—important as most matters of propriety, but no more important. The ability to manipulate, to "use," and to know in and through written (and spoken) language is the basic requirement of the creation and communication of knowledge. Learning to speak, to write, and to compose is the means by which a person creates, discovers, and externalizes what s/he knows. It is coextensive with the knowing process (in Tchudi 1986, 91).

Writing is a generative activity, prompting us to record, reflect, move forward, and return in more connected and elaborated ways. Of course, this idea seems to make sense—that to write in elaborated and purposeful ways about concepts would prompt better comprehension and more meaningful recall than memorization. Indeed, I retained the names of all the bones of the Australopithecus in Physical Anthropology by singing and rhyming them—at least long enough. But my tenuous understanding of relativity from Astronomy class was deepened and clarified when I wrote a letter attempting to explain what I was learning about relativity to my dad.

George Newell's 1984 study of the effects of writing on learning in social studies and science classes provides compelling evidence for the power of writing as an important instructional strategy. Newell examined the effects of three kinds of writing (taking notes, answering study guide questions, and writing analytical essays) on recall and comprehension of content. Students in the protocol who were asked to write essays scored significantly higher in knowledge gains than those who wrote notes or completed study guides. The key task demand that distinguished the effects of the different types of writing (mechanical, or filling-in as opposed to composing) was

> the production of coherent rather than fragmentary text . . . while a great deal of information is generated [in completing study guides], it never gets integrated into a coherent text and . . . into the students' own thinking. Essay writing, on the other hand, requires that writers, in the course of examining evidence and marshalling ideas, integrate elements of the prose passages into their knowledge of the topic rather than leaving the information in isolated bits. (1984, 282)

Newell also found that in note-taking, the least effective strategy for text comprehension, students focused on simply recodifying truncated information into written bits rather than coherent, explicit texts. This strategy, as well as answering study guides, did not require the students to study or understand globally nor to consider the social/rhetorical dimensions of writing (such as an interested reader).

In a 1992 study of the effects of writing on learning in young students, Charles Hyser found that third graders who wrote their own summaries of social studies passages had better long-term memory of material in a year-end test than those who did not do so. Also, the quality of the students' written essays on unit tests was better, as was the students' ability to generate written expository response to texts. While typical study assignments in elementary school are comprised of filling-in information, or answering end-of-chapter questions, this study reaffirms the positive influence of extended writing activities on cognitive measures. Another interesting finding in this study involved the influence of the types of writing probes on the students' fluency in response. Imaginative as well as summary probes produced, overall, the longest written responses. Certain types of writing, definition in particular, can be challenging cognitive operations for younger children, perhaps accounting for the differential success of various modes of writing. However, it might also be suggested that teachers note what types of writing tasks elicit more extensive responses.

Composing, whether it constitutes producing a senior thesis, writing to study for a test, or keeping a journal during a year of foreign study, is also clearly a social activity occurring within particular speech communities. Literacy practices are embedded in, and influenced by, the multiple contexts in community, school, and individual classrooms (Heath 1983; Hymes 1974; Bazerman 1981; McCarthy 1987). Indeed, in Lucille McCarthy's case study of a college student's interpretation of writing assignments, the student perceived similar writing tasks in each class as "totally different from each other and totally different from anything he had ever done before" (1987, 245). This suggests that a term of English 101, or even twelve years of previous schooling, will not equip students with all the practice and knowledge they will ever need to approach and engage in writing/learning in other classes; writing to learn and learning to write require frequent practice and explicit instructional supports.

The social nature of writing also encompasses, fundamentally, the dimension of personal engagement and meaningfulness. When the student in McCarthy's study was asked about a literature paper written just six weeks earlier, he could remember almost nothing about it. He explained this by saying "I guess it's because I have no need to remember it" (1987, 254). On the other hand, in a class where writing was frequently talked about and shared, where he "communicated personal positions and insights to his friends," he and the other class members could easily recall the writing and responses from that class a year-and-a-half later (1987, 255).

Writing (plus reading and learning), in real life, counters the stereotypical image of the prematurely wizened and isolated scholar hunched over a text. While the act of writing itself may occur at a keyboard or on a yellow pad, what precedes and follows is a lot of mumbling to oneself, running up big telephone bills, enlisting others to hear ideas, submitting drafts to peers, soliciting response from anyone willing to read your loose, exploratory writing as well as third, fourth, and fifth drafts, and caring a great deal about being understood. Imagining an audience, as Newell found, requires us to clarify, shift our stance, and decenter. In academic publishing, most spouses are apparently indispensable, accomplished readers and responders, essential to the completion of their partners' books, if acknowledgments pages are to be believed. Real writers need careful and thoughtful response to their works and thinking in progress, and students deserve no less. Without a social context and climate fostering purposeful writing, the task becomes a dummy run—students will recognize it as such and respond appropriately.

Writing-to-learn also bears parallel concerns and motivations with instructional models advocated in other disciplines. Inquiry-based learning in science and mathematics classrooms has been a subject of research and instruction for some time: "There is a natural affinity between such emphases and the goals of process-oriented writing tasks" (Langer and Applebee 1987, 7). Also, across the disciplines, collaborative learning has been suggested and implemented as a more inclusive classroom approach that better mirrors modes of interaction outside school and can assist both less experienced and better experienced learners in devising methods of inquiry into content (Bruffee 1984; Golub et al. 1988; Stuckey 1990). At this time in the academy, when we are most interested in promoting active and collaborative learning practices and in engaging students as partners in the learning process, in all disciplines, and at all levels of education, writing-across the curriculum has a powerful model to offer.

Writing also offers us a way to make learning more personally meaningful with the idea that to begin to comprehend or evaluate, we must first connect new information with the known—our individual experiences, expectations, and beliefs. Schema theory reveals how our comprehension of texts and "scripts" is shaped by our prior knowledge. Writing and other language activities can offer the bridge that helps students to explore and make explicit their beliefs as well as procedural knowledge of tasks so that new information is better and more fully comprehended, in all the realms of personal/analytical/critical understanding. Writing that incorporates personal exploration and narrative in investigating the students' relationship to his/her own learning recognizes and values both cognitive and affective learning.

Teachers incorporating frequent and varied writing in their classes gain a window onto what Vygotsky called the "zone of proximal development," the teachable moment. Attending to students' written and spoken discourse gives us a way to assess individuals as they encounter new concepts and allows further instructional scaffolding or support. Conventional tests yield discrete numbers or letter grades, but dialogue, written and oral, among teacher and students affords a qualitative vision of learners' work and allows for facilitation from the instructor, tutor, or peer group.

Writing, collected over time, provides us with a record of learning that counters the "gas-and-go" model of college that may resemble, in students' minds, a kaleidoscopic collection of courses, ideas, and experiences, that, once in a while, accidentally touch each other, but quickly shift into another elusive pattern. In reviewing her writing and learning in a first-year sequence, a student wrote:

> When I first signed up for these classes, I had no idea how sociology, music, and English could go together. But writing and studying about the themes in all my classes showed me that language, society, and the appreciation of music have a lot in common. I understood each of the courses better because of the way the classes interacted and the papers I wrote connecting them.

You may have already reenvisioned your teaching to include writing and other language processes as modes of enhancing learning. If, at your college, you have a vigorous writing-across-the-curriculum program, then many of the pedagogical issues of assessing learning are integrated currently into classroom practice. If the writing-across-the-curriculum policies have languished at your college, then it is time to reconsider and reinvigorate them. If there has been no discussion of writing, speaking, and reading throughout the curriculum, then consult with the chair of the English Department, the director of the composition program, and/or the director of the writing/reading/learning center. These people have expertise and great interest in the relationship of literacy to learning.

PRACTICING THEORY

How, then, can instruction be improved through using literacy-to-learn tasks and strategies, and, in particular, what kinds of writing and reading tasks can be articulated with portfolio assessment? We turn first to some teaching strategies that can be found in many disciplines, and then focus our attention on more specific assignments and activities that address the more particular concerns of certain fields of scholarship.

Instructional approaches encouraging more active and conscientious learning through writing are not necessarily burdensome, as some would imagine. Writing-to-learn tasks are often quick and require only brief teacher response, if any. And these strategies promote enhanced learning by casting the student in the role of an active participant, a participant in what Gordon Wells calls the "guided reinvention of knowledge" (1986, 218). Stephen Tchudi names these kinds of frequent classroom writing activities "workaday writing" (1986, 18). Tchudi notes the concern for developing more participatory models of teaching in many disciplines:

> Workaday writing works best when it promotes inquiry rather than mastery of fixed concepts. . . . This focus of inquiry is consistent with approaches being advocated in a great many disciplines. . . . the movement away from atomism toward holism, from rote learning to integrative and synthetic learning, comfortably meshes with current views of rhetoric, writing, and knowing. . . . Through the simple vehicle of introducing more workaday writing in the course, the content teacher can help students develop the kind of vision they need to know their discipline in the truest, most liberal sense. (1986, 28)

WRITING FOR LEARNING

Journals

Keeping class journals provides students with the opportunity to explore their interactions with new knowledge and ways of knowing through expressive, personal, and ungraded writing. Writing to oneself as well as to teacher and peers as trusted others (Britton 1970) works against the restricting notion that writing in school is only to inform and perform, and that reading and learning are only information-retrieval activities; journal writing requires a student to move beyond literal level memorization for the test into more qualitative and sophisticated ways of knowing. Journal keeping also resists the model that knowing is only rational and objective; to narrate one's experiences with and in relation to coursework provides a more meaningful basis for comprehension, synthesis, and evaluation and an integration of cognitive and affective learning.

Journal keeping can also be used to frame reasons and motivations for learning new content; "I'm enrolled in this course because it's required" or "because my parents/my advisor told me to" are frail (but too often true) incitements for studying in a discipline. Purposeful and open learning is predicated on students' creating an understanding of the value of knowing a subject. Students can begin their work in a course by exploratory writing in journals and in read-around groups with the questions and prior understandings they bring with them to a discipline or a topic (e.g., "Sociology is really just common sense" or "I've avoided math whenever possible") and then return to those initial writing "warm-ups" to contrast and to observe and to connect as their questions about, their perceptions of, and their stances toward a discipline unfold and extend. Such summary pieces naturally lend themselves to inclusion in a portfolio.

These reflections also offer teachers a way of gauging students' growth over time. Such entries can be read quickly and responded to briefly, responding as a co-investigator of knowledge and a mentor, one who joins in with genuine questions and interested responses. And reading journals is simply a lot more fun than much of the other student writing we read: the burden of reading to grade disappears, and students' voices, personalities, queries, puzzles, and objections develop a presence that is often more reticent in the classroom. In a course evaluation, a student wrote: "At first, the journal was kind of a pain, but then writing in it made me realize that I had something to say. It forced me to think about the topics we were learning instead of just memorizing. It was good to get your comments, too. They take a lot of time, but *keep requiring journals.*"

There are cautions with assigning journals. The first is that teachers also keep one; it is valuable for all the reasons above, reasons that are fitting for third graders as well as professors. The most important purpose for keeping a journal yourself, however, is to "learn how it works firsthand" (Fulwiler 1984, 119). It is then possible to understand better the peculiar rhythms, energy, and recursiveness of expressive writing. If you can, model and motivate journal keeping by sharing your own journal with classes; a colleague of mine periodically reads from and makes his journal available to students by putting it on reserve in the library. His students read this with much interest and talk of a greater willingness to describe challenges in their learning when they see their teacher volunteering to do so. The journals become another text for the class—responses to entries and issues begin to generate further dialogue not possible in the time constraints of class periods or office hours. Computer networks offer new ways of housing and communicating through journals.

There are many other ways of writing in journals or learning logs—they can be adapted to fit the structures and perspectives of any course or discipline. Briefly, here is a list of kinds of writing that might be included in journals or simply undertaken as writing activities in class.

Classroom Writing

At the Beginning of Class. Summaries of or questions about the readings assigned, the previous class discussion, current events that relate to the topic at hand can all be effectively undertaken. Such strategies vitalize classes and address the remarks of an undergraduate:

> In my lecture classes I am very quiet and don't ask questions. This isn't because I'm shy but because I don't have anything to ask or comment on. Outside of class I work very hard to keep caught up and understand what is going on. . . . But this

. . . brings up an interesting question about how much I really need classes. Could I just read and still get an "A"? I think in some classes this is possible. It's too bad, too. . . . I think the instructor should teach more than just what the book says—explain more, go into more depth—to make class more meaningful (Anderson et al. 1990, 25).

During Class. Vigorous discussions may best be stopped, briefly, and continued in the journal. It might seem counterproductive to interrupt a good, 100 percent participation discussion; however, writing, at this point, gives everyone an opportunity to elaborate on/discover their responses without having to wait for a pause. Students might write for five minutes trying to articulate the central point, confusion, or exciting new idea that is provoking the discussion. This helps avoid a later sense of "that was a great discussion, but I don't really remember what happened." A writing interlude during discussions also allows students to address class process, if that is a concern.

At the End of Class. During the last five minutes, assign everyone to summarize the lecture, discussion, to discuss an important concept, or activity, anticipate the subject of the next class, or analyze the most confusing or clarifying moment in the lecture/discussion. Ask one person to read his/her writing before ending class. This keeps all students on their toes and also prompts students to look for the continuity and connections in the course—a framework that is very clear to you but often unavailable to students. Toby Fulwiler writes:

These issues can be handled orally, of course . . . but forcing loose thoughts onto paper often generates tighter thinking. Too often instructors lecture right up to the bell, still trying to make one last point. Better, perhaps to cover less territory and . . . the final act of writing/thinking helps students synthesize material for themselves, and so increases its value. (1984, 19)

Before a Test. An antidote to the silence that can follow "Are there any questions?" is to require students to anticipate test questions in their journals or to discuss the information they feel least confident about. These can be shared in class. If students are uncomfortable sharing their uncertainties, have them remove journal pages with the test-related writings and give them to other students to read for them. Anonymity can prompt more candor. Ask students to construct essay questions they believe should be on the tests, emphasizing questions to which there are no easy (regurgitative) answers.

After a Test. "Write about something you really hoped I would have asked on the test." No test can be complete, and material simply not included on a test because of time constraints sometimes jilt students out of discussing learning that has been important to them. Teachers can augment their assessment of student progress in this way. Also, asking students to describe how they studied for a test and to evaluate what was successful and what was not lets both the instructor and the students identify successful teaching/learning strategies.

Working with individuals in the Reading/Writing Center, I have often asked students how they prepared for a test, and the common answer is "I studied." With further probing, it becomes clear that "to study" means to "optimistically read over the chapters, hoping it all sticks." By assessing and sharing ways of learning material, learners can develop more sophisticated and successful strategies. Also, too often, tests end up in the trash instead of being used as a learning tool. Entries can be devoted to analyzing errors as well as material learned well.

Additional Writing-to-Learn Activities for All Disciplines

Questions Prior to Class Discussion. Ask students to be responsible for preparing questions from assigned readings to bring to class. This shifts the ownership of whose questions structure class, circumvents pseudodiscussions, and encourages purposeful reading of texts.

Assessment of Students' Prior Knowledge. Ask students to "freewrite" on key terms from the subject at hand (e.g., political economy, class consciousness, surplus value). Students can then evaluate each other's freewriting, saving you time as well as providing information as to how familiar this material is to students and how challenging the readings will be for them. Using measures derived from reading research (Langer 1980; 1984; Newell 1984), ask each student to assess a peer's freewriting using the following three-part ranking system:

3—Highly Organized: [contains] superordinate concepts, definitions, analogies, linkings;

2—Partially Organized: examples, attributes, defining characteristics; and

1—Diffusely Organized: associations . . . no apparent prior knowledge (Newell 1984, 269).

To simplify this procedure, while retaining its spirit, I ask students to rate freewritings, using the 1-to-3 scale, according to two dimensions: (1) rank *quantity* 1-to-3 (how fluently has someone written about this topic in two or three minutes?); and (2) rank *quality* 1-to-3 (how organized and developed is the writing?). If you were to incorporate this procedure frequently to obtain a rough measure of students' knowledge, perhaps prior to the introduction of new topics as well as after, you might want to familiarize them with the task; simply have half of the class write about dorm food and the other half write about an esoteric topic such as innovations in peptide chain research. This dramatically demonstrates how existing knowledge interacts with one's ability to write fluently and coherently about a topic. This assessment procedure also offers another instructional benefit as well: By asking students to explore prior knowledge, teachers activate such associations, and thus, more purposeful and meaningful learning of the topic at hand.

The Recursive Nature of Reading and Writing Activities

The results of *The Reading Report Card*, conducted by the National Assessment of Educational Progress, suggest that while students are able to comprehend text at literal levels, their abilities to read critically and interpret are limited (Applebee, Langer, and Mullis 1985), as was found in the Fredonia study. Too often the reading histories of our students reveal that, for them, reading is defined as a painful (or soporific) and narrowly defined routine of memorizing "important" facts for tests. Indeed, the emphasis on a model of reading as information retrieval appears to dominate in schools. As one of my students said, "Reading in high school was just training for the questions the teacher would ask." Frederick Smith and Karen Feathers found that middle school and high school students reported the following perceptions of their social studies teachers' expectations for reading:

> The teacher is after facts more than ideas.
>
> The teacher is after facts. We have to remember them and
>   what goes with what.
>
> He teaches us about the language and culture of China—facts,
>   traditions.
>
> He likes dates and stuff.
>
> We have to learn about the presidents, information about when
>   they were born, died, served in office. (1983, 351)

Interesting political observations aside, these students' comments describe an impoverished set of purposes for reading. Furthermore, it seems clear that students coming to college may be inexperienced readers, and therefore bamboozled by our expectations for reading loads. In the same study, students were asked to estimate the reading requirements as well as the importance of the readings. Bear in mind that the classes observed were social studies classes—typically including a heavier reading load than many other subjects. The amount of reading was estimated to be only six-to-ten pages per week (while in one class, researchers observed the number to be five pages per week), and the students perceived the text not to be the primary source of information. Observations in the classroom yielded the following approaches to the required reading:

> When given time in class to do worksheets, most students use the text, but many students read superficially, only to find the answer to worksheet questions. Often, reading the text is avoided entirely by students who copy answers from others or

fill in the sheet as the teacher reviews it in class. Once worksheets are reviewed, we saw little evidence that text information was referred to again by either teacher or students except in review sessions.

Students in my classes echo these meager notions of literacy, alienated from what is the primary artifact of the academy:

To tell the truth, I have not read a whole book in three years.

From this class, I am hoping to enjoy reading and not just because I have to, but because I really just want to enjoy a good book.

In fact, my problem is that I have absolutely no desire to read a book or even article that may be interesting.

When I entered school . . . I started to get a bad attitude towards reading. It was a real struggle for me to learn the new words and pronunciations. Reading became a real discouragement.

Reading and Studying Activities. Given these patterns of previous experiences with reading, we need to enlarge our students' repertoire of approaches to, and interactions with, text. The next group of activities, specifically the use of reader's notes or responses, addresses the difficulties students face with both the quality and quantity of college reading assignments. Reader's notes can amplify and reinforce the notion that reading assignments require active and thoughtful interpretation and response, not cognitive photocopying. Reader's notes can be required for every assigned reading, affirming the expectation that responsible reading is valued and necessary. Notes can take the form of questions, personal responses, connections to other classes, imaginative writing, letters to the author, memoranda to other students, critiques, summaries, comparisons with other readings, notes on process (problems/successes reading the material), or queries to the teacher. Reader's notes should *not* be tiny polished essays produced at the end of a reading (although they may become that eventually); students are used to being tested through writing, and their initial temptation, in my experience, is to perform for me with three-to-five paragraphs of empty "school writing" rather than writing during *and* after reading (and rereading) to learn for themselves. Nor should reader's notes be outlines or selective copying from the text. Although outlining might be useful at times with especially complicated text, outlining and copying do not afford elaboration or interpretation, nor do they invite response.

In one class where we read widely, including literature, anthropology, history, and biology, the students often struggled to make connections among the books, although there were many themes in common. Hoping that the class would find their own ways of making sense of the texts and the perspectives of the disciplines represented (rather than my simply telling them *my* way, that is, the "right" way), I began to model my own associations in the reader's notes I brought to class. I maintained a genuine stance of inquiry in the notes and began classes by reading them aloud. The students, happy to find that the teacher seemed fuzzy on a few points, started to talk back, help me out, in their reader's notes and they also began to pose problems for themselves. They saw that reader's notes were a place to think through "talking on paper." These students were also unused to finding multiple and competing meanings; they held a firm belief in a single, correct response to a reading and a strategy of making premature judgements rather than using the wait time and tentative hypotheses used by more sophisticated readers. In helping them move beyond these constricting and unproductive ways of reading, the reader's notes served not only to mediate and assist reading but also to make the readers more conscious of the activities they were engaged in as they read. Such metacognitive acts not only reveal to the students how meaning shifts during reading and through discussion, but they also turn up the volume on the reader-speaking-to-author and author-speaking-to-reader relationship in a way that precludes the passive reception of "just the facts." Critical, reflective, dialogic, and creative reading become integral and necessary stances for readers composing reader's notes.

The reader's notes were used as a basis for class discussions: the class participated firsthand in becoming a discourse community negotiating and collaborating meaning. The notes also became the seedbed for more polished and reflective compositions. Essay-test-questions were also generated from reader's notes: the students were required to collaborate on and construct the kinds of evaluation used in the course. The classes devoted to composing essay questions were some of the most interesting; the students moved quickly from literal summary and comparison/contrast questions, rejecting these as too easy and uninteresting to write, to constructing evaluative and creative questions. Clearly, the students began to see the essays less as onerous performance measures but as opportunities to explore and clarify in writing the issues raised by the readings. In the end, they asked if they could read each other's essay exams. There was, I felt, an integrity and a democracy to the class requirements (as well as an incredible amount of learning in that 1:00 class section), and these began with the reader's notes.

Maps/Graphic Organizers. Students can create images that represent material from lectures, laboratory work, or readings. For example, a student in an introduction to psychology course drew a miniature golf course, with appropriate traps, to assist her comprehension and recall of a chapter on abnormal psychology, organizing all the concepts to be learned around the holes. Not only was it inventive and interesting, qualities that assist memory and comprehension, but the task required the student to subordinate and connect information in a more elaborate and structured way than an outline would have. Also, because the assignment allowed for individual creativity and active learning, it invited more investment from, and connection to, the learner.

Class Notes. Students can use the double-entry journal described by Ann

Berthoff. On the left side of the notebook, students keep their class notes. Students can then use the right side to pose questions, speculate, make connections, voice befuddlement, generate topics for papers, reflect, and set up a dialogue with themselves. Too often, students dutifully record notes in class without processing what they hear: they hear but they do not listen, and promise themselves that they will return to their notes later and sort it all out. But making sense later is difficult because of the limits of aural memory. Faced with incomprehensible notes, students may then fail to ever reinvestigate their lecture notes until the night before an exam. Of course, at that point, particularly when notes may cover four- to fifteen-week periods, reconstructing the meaning of the information is trying. Using class time, student conferences, or tutorials to discuss concepts, questions, or connections generated in double-entry notebooks fosters continuity and cohesiveness in students' understanding of a subject.

Double-entry notebooks can also be used for reader's notes. Here, the right side of the page would be used for glossing, quotations, lists. Students use the left side of the page for response to and elaboration of the right side to "conduct that 'continuing audit of meaning' that is at the heart of learning to read and write critically. The facing pages are in dialogue with each other" (Berthoff 1981, 46).

Tests and Writing. In addition to preparing for tests through extensive writing, tests requiring written responses provide greater opportunities for learning. As portfolios suggest a certain conception of learning discussed throughout his text, so do classroom tests. And for the same reasons: learning, writing, and reading theory and research direct us toward more democratic, integrated, and language-based pedagogies. But, of course, college teachers frequently teach four or more sections of classes with as many as seventy (or more) students in each class; time is always a challenge. Toby Fulwiler and Robert Jones give the example of a teacher who admitted she wrote essay questions when "she didn't have time to compose a good objective test" (1982, 47). Constructing an objective test takes a good deal of time; so does evaluating essay answers. But the authors note that choosing an evaluation method is more than a matter of time management:

> In objective tests, the teacher does most of the conceptual work, thinking through how to best create choices and how to word those choices. In the essay test, the situation is reversed, with the student being asked to make choices and to choose the words. To *compose* something is a more demanding task—coordinating knowledge with both logic and rhetoric—for the student than simply deciding (or guessing at) something. (1982, 48)

Further, the types of questions asked imply the kinds of learning a teacher expects. Producing simple dates asks for recall; elucidating causes asks for analysis; discussing relationships asks for synthesis; and taking a position asks for judgment and evaluation, note Fulwiler and Jones. "These four different test objectives . . . suggest in concrete terms the manner in which the teacher's question determines the kind of thinking students must do" (1982, 48). If we want students to interact critically and in ways that are meaningful beyond school, it seems clear that classroom testing is an issue for faculty development. And, if a goal of assessment is to occasion and document thoughtfulness and growth in learning, classroom tests requiring extended written response are certainly more fertile artifacts for portfolio construction than scantron sheets.

LONGER PIECES: POLISHED PAPERS

The Research Paper (my first-year students always capitalize this, as if a research paper were a genre unto itself, existing apart from any disciplinary context), according to student belief, is boring, hard, and useless busywork. While in real life things can be boring and often are hard, that students consider researched writing "useless" is an expectation we ought to address in shaping our writing assignments. Purposeful writing assignments will authentically reflect the work of the discipline, cast students as participants in the work of the discipline to assist them in adopting the "spectacles" of the particular academic community, and require that the writer say something meaningful to an interested audience. To assign a paper topic or offer a few paper topics, give a due date, and then grade the papers is to ruin your weekends; you will be disappointed in the students and the papers, the "topics" will have been abused, and most of the students will have learned almost nothing about the subject or writing. There are multiple alternatives to The Research Paper. Shorter, more frequent papers with real purposes and audiences can accomplish the same goals as The Research Paper and help to circumvent the typical problems associated with traditional research papers (plagiarism, procrastination, and canned writing). Shorter assignments need not look like small versions of The Research Paper nor must they (if that is not your purpose) mimic the discourse conventions of your discipline.

In interdisciplinary courses or sequences that are cotaught, writing to connect and explore disciplinary perspectives also teaches students to interpret discourse conventions—not as discursive muffin tins (biologists write in this way and literary theorists write in that way) but as meaningful constructs. Moore and Peterson write of their Writing Across the Curriculum (WAC) program at Yale, a program that gives prominence to convention: "Presenting students with a core of conventions for any particular discipline . . . was less important to us than showing students how the presentation of material within a discipline was controlled by the expectations of a scholarly community" (1986, 475). Further, the interdisciplinary writing served to show students that writing for a particular discipline is not limited to its polished products, the imperative always to "sound" like a computer scientist or a philosopher, or to separate fallaciously imaginative and expository writing:

> For many students, expository writing means, in practical terms, writing about "facts." Yet most students assume that all facts are equal: fact in art history is

granted the same status as fact in biology. We countered this assumption by suggesting that conventions determine what kinds of evidence is deemed legitimate and, more importantly control the ways in which evidence is presented. . . . Facts are shaped creatively by rhetorical strategies. . . . Effective and imaginative writing can occur within the academic essay when students discover why a discipline imposes limitations on itself and when they learn to work creatively within those limitations. Students usually learn . . . to work within those limitations, but the discovery is often negative; they inadvertently break a convention, for example, by offering a personal opinion in the "material and methods" section of a biology essay. If students were to learn, however, both the conventions imposed by a discipline and the reasons why scholars have agreed on these . . . instances in which they break convention would no longer be such *faux pas*, but might become for them what they are for many professionals: calculated choices to alter or transcend the dialogue between members of the community. (1986, 475)

There are many successful WAC courses and programs, as in the Yale model above. Although there are no recipes for creating writing assignments that will "work" for your students, your discipline, and you, the most important rule of thumb is to clarify, at the outset, what you want a writing assignment to do for your students and work from there. Shaping assignments is a lengthy discussion beyond the scope of this chapter, and much information is already available on assignment-shaping across the college (see Tchudi 1986; Jolliffe 1988; Walvoord 1982; Fulwiler 1984). Collaborating, reading, writing, and experimenting with students and colleagues—within your department, other departments, or a writing center—in teaching groups will offer the most fertile and energizing place to begin.

Some suggestions for the kinds of writing assignments that can replace The Research Paper and promote learning include letters, interviews, and newsletters.

LETTERS

Students can broaden their writing audience and add purposefulness to their learning by writing letters of inquiry or argument to elected officials, school administrators, the college community, favorite authors, researchers, real estate developers, or others. A student in an urban geography class might counter a city council's plan to erect a floodwall. Students in a history or anthropology class might write letters to convince speakers to come to campus and address the effects of Columbus's "discovery" of the Americas. Bahamian women in a college preparatory English class ended their semester with an eloquent and cogent "Open Letter to Bahamian Men" concerning the physical and psychological violence endured by women in Bahamian family relations (Fiore and Elsasser 1987).

While we tend to think of letter writing as outside of, and less challenging than, traditional academic discourse, these writing tasks can present more complex rhetorical and cognitive challenges than a term paper, and students tend to take published writing more seriously—they must save face, after all, in front of a "real" audience. Such tasks also wed complementary theories of language and education. Fiore and Elsasser wrote:

> Focusing on the learner's environment, Freire discusses the social and political aspects of writing. . . . [He] maintains that the goal of a literacy program is to help students become critically conscious of the connection between their own lives and the larger society and to empower them to use literacy as a means of changing their own environment. Like Vygotsky, Freire believes the transformation of thought to text requires the conscientious consideration of one's social context. . . . Vygotsky's theory of inner speech would enable students to understand the writing process. Freire's pedagogy would encourage them to bring their culture and personal knowledge into the classroom, help them understand the connections between their own lives and society, and empower them to use writing to control their environment. (1987, 128)

INTERVIEWS

Interviews require students to focus, initiate, and actively direct a written project largely of their own making. Interviews grant authority to students, and such assignments also signify that research is more than assembling a meaningless pastiche of quotations from library books. Interviews can be amplified with library research as well as other students' interviews.

Assignments to better induct students into disciplinary discourses and concerns could include first-year students interviewing upperclass majors. First-year students in psychology, for example, might not fully understand that real psychologists do something beyond the cartoon version of practicing clinicians ("and how do you feel about that?"). Students might interview upperclass psychology majors who hope to go on to graduate school in experimental work, industrial psychology, teaching, or pediatric therapy.

Interviewing professionals is another assignment useful to both first-year students and majors in a field. I have had students interview foresters, physical therapists, local politicians, accountants, musicians, FBI agents, professors, day care directors, and writers. Students can gain a wider and more concrete understanding of the subject they are studying by composing the questions they plan to ask, conducting the interview, and writing the results of the interview. Students can work in interest groups or committees to brainstorm questions for the interviews. In writing the interview, the easiest but least challenging organizational strategy to use is question-answer. It is better to ask students to synthesize the information by writing an essay that includes selected quotations.

NEWSLETTERS

Require each student to write a page (typed and single-spaced) on a "burning issue" related to the course on a specified day each week. Each student should provide enough copies for everyone else in the class (or enough copies for members of a stable reading group, if the class is too large for effective whole-class interaction). The first fifteen or twenty minutes of class on publishing day can be devoted to reading and talking about these newsletters, or the newsletters can be read outside of class and responded to in the next newsletter—there are many ways the logistics can be handled (the toughest part is getting everything handed out to everyone). Almost certainly, students will have no experience writing newsletters, although the form is most like an extended, scrubbed-up academic journal entry; their inexperience with the form is the strength of this assignment—students find no pat structures to lean on and find they have to discover and decide for themselves what constitutes a pressing issue in the course material and why they care about it.

Newsletters require everyone to speak *and* to find a voice. Newsletters are public, and because students are even more sensitive to the written bluff, I believe, than we are, there is pressure to say something sincere and worth their peers' time. Newsletters invite students into the "literacy club," as language theorist Frank Smith says, or the biology club, or the history club to become practicing members of the community, discussing substantive issues, rather than just peeping in the door. Newsletters are particularly appropriate to studies that include field work, such as geography students surveying residents of public housing projects, international students attending their first U.S. political rally, or teachers-in-training observing and working in local day-care centers.

Initial newsletters will be awkward and fairly brief; students need time to trust each other as well as you, and they need opportunities to test what they are thinking against the rest of the class and to negotiate the shape, scope, and content of newsletters. These will provide fertile material for discussions and they also constitute discussions, much like letters of reply and rebuttal in the academic journals. In the evolution of class newsletter and in discussions growing from it, we see students begin to synthesize all aspects of their learning—from texts, class material, writing, field experiences, and personal histories. Moreover, the students begin to adopt and internalize the various perspectives in the discipline as their own, "trying them on," for texture and fit. Pat Courts writes:

> The class begins to change. The discussions take on a youthful professionalism. Yes, sometimes it looks like . . . self-righteousness as they easily dismiss a perfectly good idea because it does not mesh with their own, but that is what the classroom is for. It is here we can quietly deflate some of the pomposity (including our own) and attempt to arrive at reasonable conclusions. (1991, 153)

Professional Writing

Where the goal is to ask students to write scholarly pieces following particular discourse conventions, in senior seminars and as preparation for graduate school, it is important to provide considerable instructional scaffolding. Reflect on the support you received (or should have) in writing a thesis and then a dissertation, and remember that your undergraduates are facing similar tasks and apprehensions in their writing. Three useful kinds of support, out of many, are modeling, journal keeping, and annotated bibliographies.

Modeling. Show students professional writing, including yours—polished as well as in process. Bring to class a rough draft of a paper you are currently working on and have the students assist you in moving toward an improved draft. Show them a letter from a journal editor who rejected your work as well as acceptance letters with editorial suggestions. Students need to see yours and others' work as it evolves, with its false starts and its epiphanies. All too often, scholarly writing, because it is judged by its authority rather than its humility, is privatized. Howard Becker notes:

> No one connected with schools, neither teachers or administrators, tells students how the writing they read . . . actually gets done . . . The separation of scholarly work from teaching in almost all schools, hides the process from students (just as, according to Kuhn, histories of science hide all the false turns and mistakes in the research processes that produced the success they celebrate). Students' don't know, never seeing their teacher, let alone textbook authors, at work, that all these people do things more than once . . . that journal editors routinely send things back for revision, that publishers hire editors to improve the prose of books to be published. They don't know that revising and editing happen to everyone, and are not emergency procedures undertaken only in cases of scandalously unprofessional incompetence. (1986, 45)

Annotated Bibliographies. These provide extensive opportunities to read and write about (whether analysis, personal response, or précis activities) the discipline. The production of scholarly writing requires, of course, considerable contextualization and time (in all reality, a lifetime, given the radical fashion shifts in academia). Students in a senior thesis class need to be given opportunities to rehearse for lengthy papers, to find pieces of research they particularly admire as well as flawed works, and discover their voices within disciplinary stances. Lucille McCarthy notes that "teachers . . . 'native speakers' who may have used the language . . . for so long that it is partially invisible to them . . . must make explicit the interpretive and linguistic conventions in their community, stressing that theirs is one way of looking at reality and not reality itself" (1987, 262).

Journal Keeping. We all know the experience of having an amazing idea for something we are writing or thinking about writing, and how these ideas often spring forth when we are away from the work at hand (and perhaps doing something unrelated to writing—I know I am not the only one who tries to drive and write at the same time). Too often, these good ideas are then interrupted by everyday life before we can capture them on paper. Students working through complex and dauntingly long papers can forget their good ideas as well. Keeping a journal matches the recursivity of writing, reading, and thinking, thereby assisting in discovery, provides a useful repository that shores up memory, and helps students to "keep it together" through the paper. Rather than thinking "I have to write a forty-page paper," which can lead to great anxiety and procrastination, students are able to see their processes and progress, as well as set reasonable goals for themselves, through the journal.

Responding to Writing

Frequent teacher and peer response to writing is especially important to sustain the multiple tasks of a professional piece as well as to write authentically as well as correctly in the more effaced style of much conventional scholarship. But all writing to an audience requires response.

If it is our job to create writing assignments that require writers to say something significant to someone, it is also our job, as facilitators/mentors to say something significant and constructive about what it is they have written. A central question in the teaching of writing has been, and continues to be, what can a teacher say to help the writer improve as a writer/thinker/learner? The kind of response made by a teacher (or peer) is dependent, of course, on both the instructional goals for and the writer's intent in the assignment. Briefly, there are three basic approaches to giving feedback—the use of questions, narratives, or directive feedback.

Questioning. "Why?" is a useful question to solicit elaboration and more critical thinking from students. It directs them to refer to the text they have produced thus far and read it as a blueprint, one that leads the writers to reconsider, clarify, and discover more. "Why?" also prevents us from filling in gaps that may be painfully obvious (to us) and asks a student to see the writing from a reader's perspective. Sometimes, writing that seems clear to the writer will be mystifyingly elliptical to us, and questioning helps the writer to understand this. Other kinds of questions may be evoked as we read through a draft—genuine questions that any interested reader might have.

Narratives. These kinds of responses are evoked when we see ourselves in written dialogue with students, for example, "This happened to me too . . ." or "I have been reading a study about this and. . . . " This kind of dialogue affirms that we are reading the writing as meaningful, not just as evidence of a correct performance, which, in turn, tells the student that what is being written matters.

Directive Feedback. When it is appropriate to intervene in the writing or the writing process directively, teachers need to be as specific as possible. Brief, evaluative comments may not be enough to explain the problems or possibilities you see. Here, as with all responses, individual conferences may be more effective, at times, than written commentary.

These kinds of responses are useful and important to discuss and model in class for peer review as well. Students may be unaccustomed to seeing multiple ways of reading and talking about each other's writing, and their tendencies are to fall back on simplistic extremes (e.g., proofreading, "search-and-destroy" reviews, or saying "That's nice!"), none of which is very helpful to the writer. Richard Beach and James Marshall offer the following as components of response appropriate for both students and teachers:

1. **praising:** providing positive reinforcement for students;
2. **describing:** providing "reader-based" feedback about one's own reactions and perceptions of the students' responses that imply judgements of those responses;
3. **diagnosing:** determining the students' own unique knowledge, attitudes, abilities, and needs;
4. **judging:** evaluating the sufficiency, level, depth, completeness, validity, and insightfulness of a student's responses;
5. **predicting and reviewing growth:** predicting potential directions for improving students' responses according to specific criteria and reviewing progress from previous responses;
6. **record keeping:** keeping a record in order to chart changes across time in students' performance; and
7. **recognizing/praising growth:** giving students recognition and praise for demonstrating growth. (1991, 211–12)

Responses to student work should be made when the writing is in progress, mostly, and at the end, some. The research on terminal comments is convincing; students play little attention to what we carefully and painstakingly append to their final drafts. As do all writers, students need response as writing evolves, not when it is too late.

Finally, a geographer friend of mine says, "But we do all that. We have tons of office hours at all times for these students; we go through how to write in the style of physical geographers, cultural geographers, geologists; we give the students over a year to prepare for research, to research, and to write, but still some of them won't come in." Procrastination and refusal to commit to the assignment, despite doing all the "right things"—and they are very "right things"—may plague and undermine some students, preventing them from producing the quality of scholarship of which they are capable. I think that it is most important to remember that a collegewide commitment to, and climate for, responsible and responsive pedagogy, including assessment, is, finally, necessary to making any real dent in the way students perceive and enact school tasks. If, most of the time, students are not invited to write, speak, learn, act in self-directed, critical, and responsible ways, then those occasions when they are asked to do so will be perceived as anomalies, not significant enough to interrupt business as usual. Ongoing dialogue about pedagogical theory and practice must occur with catholicity, within and among the contexts of classrooms, faculty meetings, and administrative discussions.

SCIENCE, MATHEMATICS, AND WRITING: WHERE TRUTH AND MUSH MEET

One dazzling September morning, I headed off toward an unfamiliar part of campus to find the room I had been assigned for a college writing class. The biology secretary directed me toward the basement, into the pungent atmosphere of laboratories. I found twenty students, equipped with new pens, notebooks, and the required anthology of essays, poised affably over sinks. I was almost willing to experiment with this, wondering if balancing our writing on a thin edge of porcelain would shake us out of clichés, five-paragraph essays, and worn stances toward writing, inducing us to observe together and hypothesize about each consuming piece of writing as it evolved, emerged, and took form; however, we capitulated and asked for a classroom with desks. After a few weeks of our meeting in the new room (and my forgetting about furniture etiquette), my chair received a note from the chairman of the Biology Department, requesting that I be reminded to return the seats to straight rows at the end of class. The note was wonderful and funny, mostly addressing the nature of learning and truth in the hard sciences requiring the arrangement prized by real scholars, while the "touchy-feely" kinds of classes (English) might gleefully wallow in relativism and other kinds of softness. I resisted the temptation of asking the biology teacher who preceded me to be sure to arrange the desks in a circle before s/he left.

Now I feel as if I am here trying to destabilize the furniture again—a teacher of literacy, a person of circles, addressing pedagogical issues in the world of straight lines. Yet teaching issues in both worlds share similar concerns as well as models of learning, and writing to enhance both scientific and mathematical thinking has developed over the past two decades to become more common practice (Ford 1990; Havens 1989). The cross-disciplinary discussions have been challenging.

Toby Fulwiler tells the story of one well-intentioned mathematics professor at Michigan Technological University who participated in a writing across the curriculum workshop. The teacher "stated later that the only thing he could think to do, practically, was to send all his 150 calculus students to tour the writing lab—under penalty of failing the course" (1984, 117). This seems to raise questions more of personal habits of mind than disciplinary constraints that operate in approaches to teaching. Scientists and mathematicians know that the ability to verbalize and explain through writing one's problem-solving procedures is a powerful way of understanding, representing, and extending one's knowledge.

Aaron Hayes, a senior math major at Augustana College investigating literacy and mathematics teaching, wrote:

> This past fall, I took a math course here at Augustana called Differential Equations. It was a difficult math course, with some of the concepts hard to understand. One class period, Dr. Bengston said we had to write a paper for class due the following Wednesday. I groaned silently to myself. Why do we have to write a paper explaining the advantages and disadvantages of using differential equations, I thought. It's pointless.
>
> The following week, I started on the paper.... As I was typing the words into the computer, the concepts started to click, the clouds started to clear from my brain. I could see the reasons behind why we used a different method of solving equations under differing circumstances. I never realized what Dr. Bengston's goal of that paper was until I started thinking about this paper. Writing could be used as a tool for better understanding in mathematics... I wish I could do more in my current classes. I'm sure it would help. Writing forced me to think about the concepts I was writing about, clarifying them in my mind. (1992)

Having examined this subject through research, personal connection, and writing, Hayes hopes to, in turn, use writing as a way of learning mathematics when he begins teaching. He writes that problems with math and students' relationship to mathematical learning need an "outlet" in journals, pointing to the ways in which students have been alienated from the discipline. Joan Countryman, a mathematics teacher at Germantown Friends School in Philadelphia, says:

> For many years, I've been asking my students to write about mathematics as they learned it, with predictably wonderful results. Writing seems to free them of the idea that math is a collection of right answers owned by the teacher—a body of knowledge owned by the teacher that she will dispense in chunks and that they have to swallow and digest. That's how most nonmathematicians perceive it. But what makes mathematics interesting is not the right answer but where it came from and where it leads. (quoted in Zinsser 1988, 149)

Further, Countryman maintains, a language-based pedagogy in mathematics encourages students to think beyond the textbook and the problem at hand to make connections with other disciplines, upending the idea that math is an isolated study of abstract X's and Y's:

> If your only notion of a math problem is . . . about those two trains going in opposite directions, that's a very limited notion of the kinds of things that mathematics does. But if you encourage students to write their own questions, there's no limit to where they can go. . . . I co-teach an introductory course with the woman who's the head of our classics department. One thing I did was to read Euclid with the

class. . . . It was very useful . . . because Euclid's style, which was to make propositions and derive theorems from them, was adopted by many later philosophers, like Spinoza. (1988, 163)

Writing is central to students' learning of mathematics, Countryman maintains. If writing had not been a part of her pedagogy, most students in her classes would have been untouched:

> Two or three kids with an aptitude for numbers would probably have come up with a fairly quick answer . . . but even then they wouldn't have thought about what they were doing as thoroughly as they did when they wrote . . . and the rest of the kids wouldn't have been forced to think about it at all; they would have just waited for someone else to come up with the answer. Real writing gets everybody involved (1988, 167).

Barbara King (1982) offers a variety of teaching strategies informed by James Britton's model of writing, a model that defines writing by function: transactional (writing to get things done—e.g., to explain, to persuade), expressive (exploratory, personal), and poetic. King suggests that both transactional and expressive writing can and ought to be incorporated into mathematics teaching "to help students . . . think interactively about mathematics concepts, problems, and their interrelationships . . . to focus on an assignment, to analyze and synthesize new information, to consider alternate solutions, to confront math anxiety, and to record their thought processes (1982, 44). She suggests transactional writing in the form of questions, explanations, definitions, word problems, and reports. Expressive writing, or writing to one's self or trusted other (the teacher and/or peers) can also find good fit with mathematical thinking by providing students with a nonthreatening (ungraded) opportunity to discover, explore, and reflect upon their mathematical thinking, their process and progress, uncertainties, and associations (1982, 40–44).

A colleague told of his fifteen-year-old son's difficulties with algebra homework. The father, a professor of math, knowing that the problems at hand built upon previously learned procedures, attempted to assist his son by prompting him to articulate what had been learned in previous work in the class. The son, however, kept insisting that he needed to know how to do the work in chapter 7, not talk about chapters 5 and 6. The boy's universe for math was neatly divided by chapter titles, each world a new one, with no connection among them. Of course, work in school is often fragmented by a kind of curricular amnesia ("This is European history; we can't talk about the Gulf War here"). But writing-to-learn activities—journals, in particular, come to mind with this example—provide a different stance for both learners and teachers, allowing for a richer and more global view of material, both new and from the last chapter, and maybe even beyond.

Marilyn Frankenstein argues that mathematics and statistics teaching need to address students' critical knowledge of the world and beliefs and practices that reify and perpetuate cultural mythologies about who may not be mathematically apt, for example, women or lower-class students and who may not be capable of analyzing technical information (anyone who is not an "expert") (1987, 194). Frankenstein argues that mathematics teaching must incorporate the critical analysis of practical applications.

Language-rich classrooms offer the possibility for students to analyze and confront ways in which the manipulation of numbers can serve to obscure and confound—the knowledge they gain, in class as well as class process, writes Frankenstein, authorizes them to read mathematics critically (1987, 199–200).

Writing-to-learn activities in mathematics share much with those in science. But one particular challenge of science is students' notion that science is mostly, if not only, a huge list of things to memorize. Science textbooks are characterized by densely packed, incomprehensible prose, physical heaviness, and incredible cost. "Oh no," groaned one of my first-year advisees. "I'm not taking any science classes—ever again."

Imagine an eight-year-old boy; one who has not been doing too well in school, writing lab notes on his observations of mealworms:

> Mealworms live in the grain. They crol in the grain. Mealworms have six legs. They wiggle with the back and crol with the front. Their legs are in the front of the body. Wen they walk their legs arnt stif. You can see the mouth in the front. You can't see the eyes very well because they are little. Most of them have 12 or 13 jonts. It has jonts on the front and back to. (Newman 1985, 149–150)

J.P., the little boy who was having trouble in school, had found, with the help of his teacher, a way to wed literacy learning and science learning. He was participating in real scientific work, engrossed, in discovering as much as he could about mealworms. He initiated and experimented with different tools for observation (magnifying lenses and microscopes), conducted experiments (tapping the glass to see if mealworms could go backwards), and published his findings in the class book. J.P. was working in, reinventing, the tradition of great scientists of whom he has not yet learned.

Using literacy to learn in science is found here, embedded in the practice of learning science by doing science. We have long argued that college teachers (and all teachers) need to pay more attention to how younger students learn. We need to examine the underlying theoretical sense that informs the classroom methods of good elementary school teachers. Maybe college students and professors are just bigger and not so different from those younger learners.

In college, writing science is often found in upper-level classes, but, clearly, writing-to-learn science can enhance scientific knowledge at all levels. Sandra Boatman, a biochemist at Hollins College, says:

> Most of them [students] have been unwilling . . . to volunteer, to risk anything but a safe, memorized answer. The use of several short papers . . . seems to be a more

effective way to encourage students to engage the material actively and really use it. A good test of student's understanding of a subject is how effectively she can explain it to another. Having her do this in writing requires her to process thoroughly and integrate the information she has heard in lecture and discussion, read in text and literature, observed in the laboratory. (Quoted in Faery, 1987, 207)

Rebecca Blevins Faery, in discussing writing across the curriculum, notes that Sandra Boatman's pedagogical practice "recognizes the political implications of the classroom scene and the student-teacher interaction. . . . [Students] are actively initiated into the scientific community through adopting its discourse and . . . are encouraged to see themselves and other women as legitimate members of that community" (Faery 1987, 206).

Boatman recognizes that these writing and speaking assignments—empowering modes of learning—are particularly risk-laden, but crucial, for women students, in a field dominated by men:

> All of these writing experiences combine more or less to force the student to be a scientist and do more than simply memorize facts. In the laboratory and in class, she must actively participate; she cannot simply observe the work of others. If we provide our students with opportunities to act, think, write, and speak as scientists, they should develop the confidence to compete with anyone for jobs or positions in graduate or professional schools. . . . Perhaps, if we provide our young women who are interested in science with every opportunity to affirm themselves as scientists at the undergraduate level, they will gain the skills and self-confidence needed to overcome whatever barriers they face (Quoted in Faery 1987, 207).

J. Elspeth Stuckey and Kenneth Alston describe a cross-age tutoring program involving literacy and chemistry that was instructive for sophomore tutors, ninth-grade students, and two college professors:

> Negotiation is the form that experimentation takes. . . . The older students tend to know the arcane terminology; they explain it. The younger students tend to gather materials and learn the terminology. . . . Knowing the experiment involves keeping notes of the progress made. Experiments succeed, experiments fail, and figuring out why is what matters.
>
> The students explain the experiments in letters to the advisor. The advisor is an English teacher, not a scientist. The advisor is often confused. . . . What is teaching, what is learning? The scientific experiment is an example of the negotiation between the two—an example of the continuum of learning and teaching—which is an example of the authentic practice of literacy as well. The science professor writes the English advisor: "You missed the point in the last write-up. The students were right." The English advisor responds, "Okay, so what am I to do, pretend I understand?" The science professor writes, "Come to the next lab."
>
> The ninth-grade students in the project . . . learn to learn. They complete an experiment, arrive at an answer. The college sophomores . . . learn to teach, which is to learn. (1990, 252)

Peer and cross-age tutoring are powerful modes of understanding literacy, learning, and, in this case, chemistry. Tutoring programs can link our interest in enhancing literacies across the disciplines with another concern in the academy—to provide and to require community service of our students.

Increasing our students' literacy in science through their active, personal, and meaningful relationship with it echoes the goals of scientific inquiry for Barbara McClintock, nobel laureate geneticist. Helen Fox Keller writes: "To McClintock, science has a different goal; not prediction, per se, but understanding; not the power to manipulate, but empowerment—the kind of power that results from an understanding of the world around us, that simultaneously reflects and affirms our connection to the world" (1985, 166).

WRITING IN THE SOCIAL SCIENCES

"Suppression of Adult Copulatory Behaviors Mediated by Conditioned Social Aversions Elicited in Juvenile Male Rats."
—Paul Koch and Ronald H. Peters

We all, in one way or another, have to write within specific disciplinary discourse constraints; however, not only are we immersed in (and the students baffled by) such language patterns as shown in this title, our intimacy with the language may compromise our patience for, and understanding of, the kind of messiness and imprecision that typifies "writer-based" exploratory writing-to-learn. Scholarly writing in psychology, history, political science, economics, and sociology involves specialized discourses, but each carries its own rhetoric and conventions. As sociologist Howard Becker (1986, 1) admits, "Everyone knows that sociologists write very badly, so that literary types can make jokes about bad writing just by saying 'sociology', the way vaudeville comedians used to get a good laugh by saying 'Peoria' or 'Cucamonga'."

The social sciences, being younger and "softer" than the "true" sciences, have suffered a disciplinary insecurity, leading, some argue, to a writing style both obscure and befuddling—evincing the prestige of "specialized knowledge." "Classy" or obfuscatory styles of writing, says Becker, attempt to infuse authority in the persona; he quotes C. Wright Mills, who argued that

lack of ready intelligibility [in scholarly writing], I believe, usually has little or nothing to do with the complexity of the subject matter, and nothing at all with the profundity of thought. It has to do almost entirely with certain confusions of the academic writer about his own status. . . . In large part sociological habits of style stem from the time when sociologists had little status even with other academic men. Desire for status is one reason why academic men slip so easily into unintelligibility. (Mills, quoted in Becker 1986, 31)

John Kenneth Galbraith writes: "Complexity and obscurity . . . keep down the competition, preserve the image of a privileged or priestly class. The man who makes things clear is a scab" (1984, 27). All jargons, of course, function to keep insiders cohesive and outsiders confused. Any fourteen-year-old knows that she employs a certain linguistic code to distance herself from authority figures; adolescent vernacular shores up the tenuous boundaries of self-concept—being other than one's parents and teachers. Anyone visiting a bad physician knows that jargon, slung injudiciously or deliberately, serves to maintain unequal status and power differentials in the doctor-patient relationship.

The pedagogical issue here for students of the social sciences is that the discourse conventions may obstruct rather than invite learning. One particular pitfall of learning in the social sciences is that novices tend to focus on the surface features of texts, written and oral ("I have to memorize all these weird terms" or "when presidents were born, died, and served in office") rather than learn to see the world through the lenses and perspectives of these disciplines.

Using language to learn a discipline, however, can mediate that sometimes cavernous distance between the learner and the content. Entering into disciplinary thinking requires the acquisition and translation of concepts, not rote memorization. Young children overgeneralize linguistic conventions in language learning (my three-year-old says "the girls's bathroom," revealing her understanding of rules of pluralizing as well as possession—an indication of language development, not error). So too will students approximate the language of a field in eccentric ways as they begin to appropriate it—a sign of growth, not sloppy thinking.

Reading journals, reader's notes, five-minute responses, and other writing-to-learn pieces will allow the teacher to recognize and observe these signs of intellectual development. Writings to assist learning also demand that students make more resonant connections with the material. The ability to recognize and recall information for a true-false test question is a rather skimpy kind of comprehension. But analyzing role strain, marginality, and occupational status through the journal writing of a nontraditional aged female mother student not only makes learning these concepts compelling and meaningful, it can be a transformative experience. Patricia Bizzell argues that it is "the interaction of the professor's and the students' cultural resources" that promotes literacy across the disciplines (1988, 150).

Creating writing assignments that require personal and active engagement with concepts, whether analyzing the social stratification and belief systems of fraternities on campus, the usefulness of initiating a peer counseling program in the counseling center, interpreting the cultural signification of campus architecture as it evolved, or creating alternative budgetary solutions for the fiscal problems at one's college, students can be involved in real ways in the work of these disciplines. "Covering" all the material, of course, in addition to incorporating writing-to-learn will present challenges, but the central issue raised here requires examining and determining the quality and kinds of learning one hopes to engender.

One professor, tired of the glumly minimal student discussion of assigned chapters in introductory sociology, began to assign students short (1-2 page) writings about the topics in the text. For example, one week the students were to write an informal analysis of the groups to which they belonged; another time they described themselves in relation to a test of gender characteristics identification; one assignment asked the students to perform a legal and innocuous act of deviance (such as facing the other people in the elevator instead of facing the door) and analyzing the definitions and consequences of deviance. The professor was pleased with the results for class discussions (students read and responded to the writings in class) as well as on test performance. And her time investment in this project was minimal; she read the writings and assigned a check-plus to those done well, a check to those done sufficiently, and a check-minus to those writings failing to incorporate any real data or analysis. The writing, informal narrative and analysis, were not evaluated for "goodness" of writing, although written grace and clarity was praised and writing problems were responded to. The teacher also learned that the label she chose for the assignments was important: one student, upon learning she had to write eight papers in a ten-week term, tearfully called her father who promptly ordered her to drop the course. After that the teacher learned to call these assignments "writings" or "responses"—but never "papers."

I have worked with many students in an introductory psychology course who have great difficulty passing the weekly multiple-choice quizzes. Although frequent testing has been shown to facilitate learning (Light 1990, 90), it seems that the format of the testing, challenging questions requiring evaluative, synthetic, and applicative thinking, may reward test-taking skills over knowledge of the material. While the students can explain and elaborate on the material in conversation, many of the same will earn dismal grades on the quizzes. Then, in makeup exams, where students write essay responses, the students improve their grades sufficiently. Some might argue that the initial poor scores lead students to study harder, or that people grade essay exams with a greater portion of generosity. I would argue that it would make a lot more sense, if one is determined to retain the multiple-choice tests, to explore essay writing—or many other kinds of writing—in class (with discussion groups, peer review, task forces) as a way of summarizing information, enhancing comprehension, and preparing for the quizzes.

ENGLISH AND ELSEWHERE

Learning in other fields of scholarship can incorporate writing-to-learn, and some, possibly, with more facility than the subjects discussed above. Many

English teachers, as teachers in other fields, have radically revised their pedagogical approaches, although the following discussion certainly does not characterize all teachers of English.

In many literature classrooms, teaching, following theoretical shifts, is no
longer an enterprise of memorizing biography or ignoring biography and reading
closely for privileged meanings in canonical texts. Learning and "doing" literature (as learning many other disciplines) have become more diverse, displaying
various principles of phenomenology, reader response theory, new historicism,
gender studies, non-Western criticism, post-structuralism, and (other) political
frameworks (sometimes all in one semester for an English major). The texts in
the literature classroom have become less insulated, meaning more open to
negotiation, and the process of making meaning more transparent and central.
Using literacy to learn is more seamless in a class that gives prominence to
interpretive moves; personal narrative and collaboration become more germane
with pedagogies assembling learners as interpretive communities. Using language
to make meaning is centered in these classes: journals, inventive essay exams,
discussion groups, student-chosen paper topics, narrative responses, letters, student publications—all these are employed in most English classes.

Yet, Jane Tompkins argues, in English and in other departments, even where
literacy-to-learn is a central notion, we may continue to be stymied in our
teaching because of a model into which we have been firmly acculturated since
graduate school—a performance model (1990, 654). Tompkins writes reflectively
and personally, in "Pedagogy of the Distressed," of graduate school as "boot
camp," a coercive model, "destructive of creativity and self-motivated learning
(1990, 654)," and that, finally, this is our classroom legacy: "This . . . more than
anything else, is what we teach our students: how to perform within an institutional setting in such a way that they will be thought highly of by their
colleagues and instructors" (1990, 654).

Tompkins defines teaching and learning in particular ways that transcend
disciplinary borders and resonate with a shared construct of what college teaching
is: something like sex, she argues, "something you weren't supposed to talk about
or focus on in any way but that you were supposed to be able to do properly
when the time came" (1990, 655). Pedagogical concerns have typically been
muted in college. We do not groom our favored students to become teachers,
but to be historians and anthropologists. Teaching is something done to younger
and shorter people; education departments, in the folk belief of the academy,
are a "natural repository for the unsmart, people who scored in the 50th percentile
on their tests and couldn't make it into the higher realms (Tompkins 1990,
655)." To be overly concerned with teaching seems to distract us from and dilute
our "real" work.

Tompkins notes one aspect of classroom life, however, that is a current topic
of college conversations—the political (or apolitical) dimensions of our subjects—
that we can and must engender critical and thoughtful understanding of, and
response to, events in the world, resisting unexamined beliefs and prejudices.

Yet, she notes, in the tradition of critical pedagogy, the classroom is also a site of social change; our teaching should create and reflect those notions. Tompkins writes: "The classroom is . . . the chance we have to practice whatever ideals we may cherish. The kind of classroom situation one creates is the acid test of what one really stands for. And I wonder, in the case of college professors, if performing their competence in front of other people is all that that amounts to in the end" (1990, 656).

Tompkins outlines the transformation of a humanities class, one in which the students became the teachers, responsible for preparing classes, presenting material, making assignments, facilitating classroom interactions and learning. The class was "the most amazing class I've never taught," she says, although there is guilt that accompanies giving away one's usual role and duties:

> Still, there is the question of whether, in shifting the burden of performance onto the students I'm not doing the work I'm too lazy to do myself, sending them off on a journey with inadequate supplies, telling them to go fishing without a rod or bait, demanding they play the Kreutzer sonata before they can do a scale. It's true that in some classes the students don't deal with the material as well as I could, but that is exactly why they need to do it. It's not important for me to polish my skills, but they do need to develop theirs and to find a voice. (1990, 657)

The linguistic space in this classroom has been yielded to students, and the notion of teacher as performer upended to promote active learning. The centrality of language, "finding voice," "free to talk," "plenty of written feedback," permeating classroom practice here affirms the notion that using language to create and assist learning becomes essential, not just as a minor addition to the syllabus, but for revising and transforming the ways we conceive of teaching and learning and our assessments of those processes.

A prescriptive set of procedures for guaranteeing that students will articulate, compose, reflect, critique, and collaborate does not exist; there are no hard and fast rules, nor should there be. The approaches in this chapter suggest ways of thinking about the structures and goals of classroom practice and a pedagogical stance of inquiry and experimentation. Of course, we all long for the term when we finally "get it right," when the students, the books, the assignments, and we all click to make the perfect and repeatable course. And, as always, each class in each term presents multiple new challenges as students, information, institutions, and we ourselves change—we unravel the "perfect" course only to begin revising it again.

Yet this artistry is the strength of the "reflective practitioner," as described by David Schön, in his study of the nature and the construction of professional knowledge. The reflection-in-action stance involves demystifying the role of "expert" as an autonomous authority who is certain to be one who "recognizes that his technical expertise is embedded in a context of meanings. He attributes to his clients, as well as to himself, a capacity to mean, know, and plan. He recognizes that his actions may have different meanings for his client than he intends them to have, and he gives himself the task of discovering what these are" (1983, 295). The relationship between the professional and, here, the student, is not adversarial, but one in which the practitioner listens and reveals his uncertainties and discoveries: "When a practitioner becomes a researcher into his own practice, he engages in a continuing process of self-education" (Schön 1983, 299). Reciprocal reflection-in-action, between teachers and students, creates a climate grounded in thoughtful and responsive learning.

This model seems particularly important as we attempt to respond to the teacher's role in assessment. While a reflective pedagogical stance seems unfamiliar—"the professional . . . gives up the rewards of unquestioned authority, the freedom to practice without challenge to his competence, the comfort of relative invulnerability"—new competencies and satisfactions emerge (Schön 1983, 299). Indeed, an organizational investment in defining authority may paradoxically constrain it: if the professional "works within an institution whose knowledge structure reinforces his image of expertise, he tends to see himself as accountable for nothing more than the delivery of his stock techniques according to the measures of performance imposed upon him (Schön 1983, 345–46)." The bureaucratic nature of educational institutions affects teachers in that they "learn to optimize the measure of control on *their* performance, striving to meet the letter of the standards imposed on them without worrying very much whether, or how, their students are learning" (Schön 1983, 332). Students, too, as in the narratives opening Chapter 2, "discover how to pass tests, get grades, and move through the levels of the system, without thinking very much about the knowledge they are supposed to be acquiring" (Schön 1983, 332).

Reflective practice affects the nature of assessment as well as pedagogy. There is a dissonance between bureaucratized notions of measuring learning and reflective teaching/learning. In the model of technical expertise, "quantitative measures of proficiency and progress which are independent of individual judgement . . . are much preferred to qualitative, narrative accounts of the experience of teaching or learning. Quantitative measures permit the system of control . . . to take on an appearance of consistency, uniformity, precision, and detachment" (Schön 1983, 331). But a move to reflective practice would value those messier, but richer, measures—ones that account for human beings and the contextualized nature of learning, incorporating a "shift from the search for centrally administered, objective measures of student progress, toward independent, qualitative judgements, and narrative accounts of experience and performance" (Schön 1983, 333–34). Reflective assessment, then, is not easily nor authentically calibrated by highly bureaucratized and standardized organizational structures.

CODA: ASSESSING THE ASSESSORS

Teachers who explore reflective practice and recompose their pedagogy with the kinds of classroom assessments and language-to-learn discussed in this chapter will also change the climate for teaching and learning. Language across the disciplines "promotes fruitful, invigorating exchange of perspectives and methods among teachers who all too often have been strangers across curricular walls" (Thaiss 1990, 36). Students, too, will enter into a different relationship with learning and their instructors. When asked to do peer editing or discussion facilitation in a class, for example, students have resisted: "I'm not the teacher. You are." Integrating more democratic practice invites some chaos, purposeful chaos, but chaos all the same, into the classroom routine; student-led discussions or presentations or small-group tasks may make you feel as if you are not working hard enough as a teacher. "Giving away" some, most, or all ownership of learning to students contradicts what they may have come to expect from teachers (who are supposed to have all the answers). Inviting personal writing may strain the traditional relational borders between and among teachers and learners. Journals may contain information calling for a personal kind of response not usually associated with college professors.

Transforming our pedagogies to embrace more reflective, critical, student-centered, and literacy-based approaches will change teaching structurally and profoundly so. It is important to question how these shifts will operate within the larger structures of the academy. What purchase, really, does pedagogy hold? And how do we evaluate ourselves? If our assessments and instructional practices are going to change, then it is clearly important to address conventional teacher evaluation as well. Do traditional methods of evaluating teachers correspond to the experiences, values, and goals of a pedagogy predicated in language and literacies for intellectual and personal empowerment? Does becoming more "uncertain" undermine our students' beliefs about authority and expertise? And, if we are to create richer and more contextualized assessments of learners, are we to remain comfortable with "off-the-shelf" teacher evaluations? According to Schön, a "reflective institution must place a high priority on flexible procedures, differentiated responses, qualitative appreciation of complex processes (Schön 1983, 338). Teaching and learning are complex processes, not easily or conscientiously reduced to Likert scales and scantron sheets. If we agree that rich, qualitative, and functional assessments of student performance—as in portfolio assessment—are the most meaningful, then it is important to extend the assessment conversation to transform our evaluations of teaching as well.

CHAPTER 6

Final Words: Look Out Below

A FABLE

Once, on a faraway college campus, there was a teacher who was having little success teaching his students to write. They had been practicing writing introductory paragraphs, paragraphs developing what was said in the introductory paragraphs, and concluding paragraphs repeating what had already been said. The teacher said their writing was dull, lifeless and devoid of real thought.

Seeking help with his problem, the teacher braved the long trek down the corridor, moving stealthily past hostile students from his classes, and humbly entered the room wherein resided the teaching wizard, Grayjeans. The smell of studentcenteredness and smallgroupwork hung heavily in the air, almost smothering the timid seeker.

He approached Grayjeans and said, "I am told you can help me teach my students to write successfully. What should I do?"

Grayjeans smiled, invited the guest to sit, and kept him spellbound with stories of collaborative, communal approaches to learning wherein students wrote freely of their own ideas and experiences, shared and critiqued their writing, created their own research quests, and even used the first-person-singular pronoun, *I*. The adventurer shivered in response and left.

After he had returned to the safety of his own room, surrounded with the warm and welcome comfort of handbooks and well-worn treatises containing great model essays from earlier times when all was well in the Academy, the teacher puzzled over what the wizard Grayjeans had told him. Deep in his heart he still doubted. His students were not capable of original thought. They did not know enough to critique one another's work. Surely this would fail if he tried it.

But try it he would.

Girding himself with carefully writ plans for weeks of freewriting, peer-editing, classroom workshops, and various wonders the wizard had described, the teacher approached the sullen mob of freshpersons. "You probably won't like what we are going to do," he said, "and it probably won't work because I'm not at all sure that you can even handle it. But we are going to do some freewriting and stuff like that. So I want you to all write what you *really* think about something, then break into pairs and edit each other's work, and then rewrite for tomorrow."

Not a sound was heard. Not a pen moved. The freshpersons stared in puzzlement. The teacher waited thirty minutes before he ran from the room screaming, "I knew it wouldn't work! This is the same kind of crap the high school–wizards use to screw up these kids in the first place. Someone ought to get rid of all these damn wizards!"

Grayjeans, looking out his door, shook his head sadly, and then returned to conferencing with the three freshpersons about the essays they had recently written about their sense of personal alienation in the university.

Now fables being what they are, you must obviously think this one through for yourselves. For our part, we wish to identify neither with Grayjeans nor with the devastated teacher. Our "conclusion" to this book grows directly out of a question that Kathleen McInerney asked at the end of one of our writing conferences over earlier chapters. The theoretical Chapter 2 was almost fully revised, the two portfolio chapters were finished, and we had brainstormed the fifth chapter on teaching approaches, when McInerney said, "Okay, but what do I do about my concern for teachers who have never tried what we are suggesting— things dependent on a belief in, and understanding of, collaborative learning? What happens if our readers think that you can just plug this stuff in and expect it to work automatically? What happens when they try peer-editing and, as has happened to us, it does not work? Will they just quit and condemn the whole approach? Our concern has been to promote better teaching and learning, but it could backfire."

In an attempt to respond to the concerns McInerney articulated, our conclusion is a cautionary one that promises no magic methods or wizardry. Of course, we hope the book in its entirety provides considerably more information and support than Grayjeans provided his visitor. If wizards there are, and we have met none, we all would deserve better from them.

We end, then, with a series of reminders related both to the use of portfolios for assessment (any qualitative assessment, for that matter) and to the implementation of methods and approaches outlined in the last chapter.

Points to Remember

1. Experiments are called experiments because they sometimes fail. If we are sure something will work, we can hardly call it an experiment and we know of no teaching method that always works. For us, then, teaching is always experimental. **Experiments in teaching and in assessment will contain moments of success and failure, especially at first, and that is exactly why we must all engage in experimenting.** We know of no set of directions that will guarantee success. In short, for those of you who are new to writing-across-the-curriculum (WAC) and assessment of student learning, be prepared for problems along the way.

Part of the constructive fun in trying new approaches to teaching and in engaging in genuine assessment is to find out things you did not know before; so do not underestimate the complexity of what you are engaging in.

2. **Demand support, and create your own support systems whenever you can.** If we are to respond constructively to demands for assessment and if the demands are made in good faith, we have a right to expect the financial support necessary to carry out authentic assessment projects. Quite simply, if an assessment project is imposed *in addition to* the already significant demands made on most teaching faculty, especially if it is a programmatic assessment, it is likely to fail. The Fredonia project was supported through funding from Fund for the Improvement of Postsecondary Education, and those conducting the assessment received small stipends. Most of us agreed, however, that, though a little extra money was nice, what we really needed was more time—we needed to be relieved from some of our other duties in order to find time to do the work involved in qualitative assessment.

Likewise, if your administration believes that writing-across-the-curriculum (WAC) is an important activity, then workshops should be provided for those teachers who are willing to experiment with writing activities in their class-rooms—and we mean genuine professional workshops, not just a few brownbag lunches. On the other hand, once workshops are in place, casual lunch or evening meetings for those who are implementing WAC activities are essential: They provide an opportunity to discuss successes and failures; they become brainstorming, collaborative learning sessions through which teachers can help one another. Having taught WAC workshops and participated in a series of follow-up discussions over the years, we are struck by a singular comment that pops up with almost every group new to the process. Inevitably someone says, "You know, I've been teaching for ten years and I've never really discussed how and what I teach with another colleague. It never occurred to me that chemistry and math teachers experience some of the same problems in the classroom that we experience in sociology."

In short, if you believe that it is important to establish a learning community in your own classrooms, then you should recognize the importance of estab-lishing one for yourselves. We believe it helps significantly to know that other committed, intelligent, good teachers experience difficulties in the classroom. And though it will not improve your weekend, sometimes it helps to know what others on your campus are spending the better part of Saturday and Sunday commenting on drafts of student writing.

3. Collaborative learning, small-group activities, peer-editing—none of these approaches "work" all of the time. If you are reasonably well-prepared and willing to experiment a little, you are unlikely to experience often what the teacher in the fable experienced. But you may have that experience sometimes. The fable's teacher believed the problem was caused by high school wizards who used collaborative learning techniques with the students, but often the case is just the opposite. It is a mistake to assume that your students come to you ready

and able to participate in such activities. Often they have been schooled in a "sit straight, stay quiet, and identify the correct answer" atmosphere and have not the slightest idea why you are putting them into groups. Often they believe that they have nothing important to say and cannot help one another in any significant ways. Understand that what looks like recalcitrance may simply be confusion and fear. **If you think that some of these collaborative learning activities are new to you, remember that they may be very new to your students.**

4. **If you genuinely believe an activity will not work, do not try it.** If students think that you have no faith in an idea, why should they? On the other hand, it has been our experience that most students are genuinely delighted to work collaboratively and interactively. All the student examples and comments that we have offered in this book and in Appendix A indicate that students are looking for a change. They simply need to be helped to understand the ways in which they can constructively engage in these new learning situations. But again, if you genuinely believe a teaching approach will not work—as did the professor in the fable—it probably will not.

5. If portfolios and WAC activities are limited to a few English courses, students will decide, as they have for decades, that this "writing stuff" is just something that English teachers make people do. **If the writing for the portfolios is divorced from learning experiences in courses across disciplines, if it is simply something done for assessment, the writing is likely to be artificial and formulaic.** Writers do not write in order to be assessed: they write in order to know and to communicate with *self* and *other*.

6. Portfolios are likely to raise more questions than they initially appear to answer; real assessment projects are likely to reveal that many of our assumptions about student learning are based in our private and collective fictions. If nothing else, the Fredonia assessment caused us to seriously question just how much change *can* occur in students in four years of college? We wonder if there are developmental/maturational "ceilings" that characterize learners between the ages of 17 and 22? In fact, some of us ended "wondering about" a great many things. Indeed, if you do not like wondering, stay away from assessment. But we believe that this is some of the most important "wondering" any of us might engage in. **Authentic assessment projects such as portfolios may provide the window we need to see some things more clearly.**

7. But number 6 immediately above is really the whole point of assessment. **Any honest attempt at qualitative assessment of student learning at any level is going to demand considerable energy and time from those involved.** But a system of portfolio assessment may offer tremendous rewards, especially when it is tied to writing/learning-across-the-curriculum, and especially when it involves faculty interaction about teaching/learning processes of the students. The "sense of wonder and wonderment" suggested in item number six offers the possibility for professional renewal.

My participation in WAC workshops and the Fredonia assessment provided me with some of the most significant insights and moments of professional growth that I have experienced in my twenty-five years in teaching. Perhaps because of an exaggerated and still present egocentrism, I thought I knew my students and colleagues well. I thought I had a strong sense of what students in my own courses were learning and developing as thinkers and writers. I was fairly sure I knew what went on in "other" courses. But my recent experiences have helped me understand the students better (and I know that this process of understanding will continue as long as I teach). The workshops have also shown me that my colleagues have much to offer me. At a more practical, concrete level, I find myself more open to classroom experimentation, changes in curriculum, and risk-taking in the classroom. I find myself rethinking my syllabi from the students' point of view. (Of course, I thought I did this before, but I have learned that I did not really know how.)

Perhaps most important, I find myself teaching as one among a community of learners. No longer self-righteously isolated in my own office (or mind or classroom), I am constantly engaged in discussions of teaching with various colleagues whose concerns are similar to my own.

8. **Assessment, like any educational reform movement, does not grow out of a wizard's spell, nor can it be constructively imposed from the top down.** For assessment to produce positive results, the assessment instruments must be created by the teachers who design the programs and teach the students to be assessed.

9. **Any assessment project that focuses on the tools of assessment prior to engaging in a careful examination of the learners and curricula to be assessed is likely to produce irrelevant (and probably misleading) data.**

10. **Try some of the teaching and assessment approaches we have suggested.** We hope and expect that you and your students will find the enterprise to be as rewarding as we have found it to be. (And, of course, good luck!)

Grid for Reading

Item Being Measured	No. of Related Test Item
Ability to identify central point(s)	#1
Ability to identify X amount of supporting details, arguments, etc.	#2
Ability to identify underlying assumptions	#3
Ability to make/explain judgement of article's sense, truth value, quality	#4
Ability to identify implications	#5
Ability to identify relationship of central points to personal experience	#6
Ability to recognize and comment on author's technique, organizing principle, or style	#7

TEST ITEMS TO WHICH STUDENTS WERE ASKED TO RESPOND

#1. Using your own words and/or quoting directly from the article, explain what you think are the author's major points: why is the author telling us about "saints and roughnecks"?

#2. Based on whatever you have identified as the major points of the article in number 1 above, present two or three of the major reasons *the author* provides to support his central point and explain why you find this supporting evidence to be particularly significant.

#3. All of us operate from certain assumptions and we can never state all of them when we write. Referring to page *x* of the article, and/or any other parts of the article you find particularly relevant, present 2 or 3 of the author's *unstated* assumptions (that is, do you see any biases or beliefs that seem to be behind what he is saying?).

#4. Explain which of the author's major points you most strongly agree and/ or disagree with. Be sure to explain why you feel this way.

#5. Explain what this article suggests or implies about the ways different kinds of groups are treated in our society.

#6. Provide one or two examples from your own experience that illustrate or contradict the central points of the article; be sure to develop the examples fully so the relationship between them and the article is clear.

#7. Write a paragraph explaining the style or system of organization the author appears to use in this article. How does it contribute to or detract from your ability to understand his central points?

Sample of Scoring Criteria Based on Item #6 on Reading Test

(including rationale for the given item and directions to scorers): "Provide one or two examples from your own experience that illustrate or contradict the central points of the article; be sure to develop the examples fully so the relationship between them and the article is clear."

A. *Rationale for the Item.* Students should be able to see the relationship between what they read and their own experience. (Or they should be able to articulate their reasons for asserting that there is no relationship, though that would be difficult to imagine dealing with this article.)

B. *Scoring Criteria.* Grade of A: "Clear statement of relationship to personal experience with explanatory detail: personal experience is genuinely related to the reading." The answer must assert more than a general acceptance of what the article says. There must be a specific application of what the article says either to the students' own experiences or the experiences of others that they have witnessed. Sample Answer: "I agree with the main thrust of this article because I have seen how money, power, or social status can change peoples opinions. I babysit for a very predominant social figure. This man is a member of the NFL and very well known. He is African American, married to a white woman with mulatto children. The kids look very black, and are terrific kids. However, there is another black family living in my all white, suburban neighborhood also. The little boys of the football player have lots of friends and are never called "nigger," . . . the other black children have significantly fewer friends in the neighborhood (due to other people's parents) and have been called names." This student provides a specific experience and then explains how that experience is related to the article.

Grade of *B*: "Assertion of relationships to personal experience but lacking any elaboration or specification; or personal experience is only vaguely related to the reading." This is closer to a general acceptance of the article's points without specific detail to explain the relationship between that acceptance and the students' experience. Sample answer: "My father is well known in the state of Illinois. Many policemen of our community have let me go on speeding, while my friends who are going slower received speeding tickets." The student has some awareness of the relationship between this experience and the article, but the student does not articulate the relationship.

Grade of *C*: "Fails to provide an example or gives and example that misses the point, or sees no relationship." Answers receiving this grade either miss the point of the article or of the question. Sample answer: "High school privileges middle-class kids over lower-class kids. This is tracking. Also I'm in college; most lower-class kids are not—that's because America is fascist." The answer is very general and does not really relate to the article.

NOTE

This entire section on scoring is directly from *A Test of Reading*–Scoring Manual, General College Program Assessment Committee, State University of New York College at Fredonia, August 1989, 8–9.

APPENDIX B

GCP Assessment Project
Outcomes and Findings

General Education Outcomes

I. CRITICAL THINKING
  A. LOGICAL/RHETORICAL
    1. Identify/state central point or supporting arguments
- satisfactory level
- satisfactory growth in writing and reading, not in scientific reasoning

    2. Identify assumptions
- little improvement on any measure   *Priority*
    3. Identify contradictory or irrelevant information
- satisfactory for reading, not for problem solving

  B. DIALECTICAL
    4. Recognize or state relationships
- satisfactory growth except in reflective reasoning
    5. Relate process & context
- improvement in ethical judgement

  C. REFLEXIVE
    6. Explain one's own thinking
- little improvement   *Priority*
    7. Identify significant elements
- satisfactory level
    8. Abstract & generalize
- little improvement   *Priority*

II. READING
    9. Read charts and graphs
{not tested in final instruments}
    10. Recognize author's methods
- satisfactory growth

III. WRITING
    11. Establish voice/stance
{not tested in final instruments}
    12. Develop argument fully
- satisfactory growth
    13. Employ standard usage
- satisfactory level

IV. PROBLEM SOLVING
    14. Understand requirements
- inadequate   *Priority*
    15. Judge reasonableness of answer
- inadequate   *Priority*
    16. Confidence to try problems
- inadequate   *Priority*

V. CULTURAL AWARENESS
    17. Knowledge of history
- inadequate   *Priority*
    18. Identify mainstream US values
- inadequate   *Priority*
    19. See relations among values and other causes/effects
- inadequate   *Priority*
    20. See other values as viable
- growth on one measure only   *Priority*
    21. Use considered personal values in judgements
- satisfactory growth

Appendix C

Information Sheet for Students

PORTFOLIO REQUIREMENT

In order to improve advisement, and in order to help you improve as readers, writers, and thinkers, the English Department is requiring that you begin a PORTFOLIO that will be a partial record of your growth over the next few years. While you will not find the requirements for this PORTFOLIO particularly taxing in terms of the amount of work you must do in order to fulfill this requirement, you will find that the more thought you give it, the more you will learn from it. Quite simply, the PORTFOLIO will contain samples of your writing and thinking that you select from some of your English courses and that represent particularly important learning experiences for you. A more specific description follows below.

Requirements

A *completed Portfolio* will contain the following:

a. an Entry Paper;
b. four papers written over a period of at least two years (two papers from Part I of the Major, and two from Part II);
c. brief (approximately one page) critiques of each of the four papers;
d. an Exit paper;
e. a Checksheet including dates on which entries were handed in, comments on critiques and conferences with the students about the entries, and signed by the advisor attesting to the completion of the project.

Assessment in Higher Education

Description of Requirements

A. *Entry Paper*. Each student will write a paper of no-less-than-one or more-than-three page(s) exploring one or more of the following questions:

1. Why have you chosen to be an English major and what do you personally hope to accomplish through your work in the Major?
2. In what ways is the study of English particularly important to your own goals and desires?
3. What do you see to be your major strengths and/or weaknesses as an English major?
4. In what areas would you most like to improve?

B. *Four Papers*. Each semester the declared Major takes a course in either Part I or II of the English Major, s/he will select a paper from the course(s) that somehow represent his/her most significant work of the semester. While one might expect that these papers will be among the "best" a given student has written, students should be encouraged to choose papers that represent new, difficult, and perhaps unsurmounted challenges. The point here is that the portfolio need not be comprised of "showcase essays"; students should be encouraged to select papers that indicate the creative/intellectual challenges they are experiencing in their studies. For example, papers might be selected according to criteria like the following:

1. the paper that caused the writer particular difficulty or anguish;
2. a paper representing the individual's best work in the semester;
3. a paper that represents the individual's greatest progress as a reader/thinker/viewer;
4. a paper representing continued confusion; or
5. a paper the student found to be particularly rewarding or interesting to produce.

C. *Critique*. Each student will write a 1-to-2-page critique/explanation for each paper explaining why s/he chose the paper for the portfolio and how it represents his/her best (or most complex or most troublesome) paper of the semester—why does this paper matter to you?

D. *Exit Paper*. After reviewing the contents of their portfolios, students will produce a 1-to-2-page paper addressing one or more of the following:

1. In what specific ways have you changed or improved as a reader/writer/viewer/thinker?

2. To what extent has the English Major here at Fredonia met your needs as a student? To what extent have you met the demands of the English Major?

3. Describe the one or two most beneficial/significant learning experiences or assignments you have had as an English Major and explain why this was particularly important.

4. Write whatever you would like regarding your own learning and progress as an English Major.

E. Checksheet. Each advisor should keep a checksheet recording the title of each paper included in the portfolio, date submitted, and noting that the critique is completed for each paper, along with comments on the critiques and brief notes on conferences with the writer.

Information Sheet for Advisors

ENGLISH DEPARTMENT: PORTFOLIO/ ADVISEMENT PLAN

Timeline

Students will begin their portfolios at the time that they declare an English Major *and* begin to take courses as part of that major. The portfolio must be completed prior to graduation.

Requirements

A *completed Portfolio* will contain the following:

a. an Entry Paper;

b. four papers written over a period of at least two years; (two papers from Part I of the Major, and two from Part II);

c. brief (approximately one-page) critiques of each of the four papers;

d. an Exit paper;

e. a Checksheet signed by the advisor attesting to the completion of the project.

Description of Requirements

A. *Entry Paper*. Each student will write a paper of no-less-than-one or more-than-three page(s) exploring one or more of the following questions:

1. Why have you chosen to be an English major and what do you personally hope to accomplish through your work in the Major?

2. In what ways is the study of English particularly important to your own goals and desires?

3. What do you see to be your major strengths and/or weaknesses as an English major?

4. In what areas would you most like to improve?

B. Four Papers. Each semester the declared Major takes a course in either Part I or II of the English Major, s/he will select a paper from the course(s) that somehow represent his/her most significant work of the semester. While one might expect that these papers will be among the "best" a given student has written, students should be encouraged to choose papers that represent new, difficult, and perhaps unsurmounted challenges. The point here is that the portfolio need not be comprised of "showcase essays"; students should be encouraged to select papers that indicate the creative/intellectual challenges they are experiencing in their studies. For example, papers might be selected according to criteria like the following:

1. the paper that caused the writer particular difficulty or anguish;

2. a paper representing the individual's best work in the semester;

3. a paper that represents the individual's greatest progress as a reader/thinker/viewer;

4. a paper representing continued confusion; or

5. a paper the student found to be particularly rewarding or interesting to produce.

C. Critique. Each student will write a one-page critique/explanation for each paper explaining why s/he chose the paper for the portfolio and how it represents his/her best (or most complex or most troublesome) paper of the semester. More directly, why does this paper matter to you?

D. Exit Paper. After reviewing the contents of their portfolios, students will produce a 1-to-2-page paper addressing one or more of the following:

1. In what specific ways have you changed or improved as a reader/writer/viewer/thinker.

2. To what extent has the English Major here at Fredonia met your needs as a student? To what extent have you met the demands of the English Major?

3. Describe the one or two most beneficial/significant learning experiences or assignments you have had as an English Major and explain why this was particularly important.

4. Write whatever you would like regarding your own learning and progress as an English Major.

E. *Checksheet.* Each advisor should keep a checksheet recording the title of each paper included in the portfolio, date submitted, and noting that the critique is completed for each paper. Students are expected to meet with their advisors each semester for brief discussion of the portfolio entries.

Advisor's Role

In addition to assuring that students are completing the requirements of the Portfolio Plan, advisors will also meet at least once each semester with each student to discuss the paper(s) submitted and the students' comments on the critiques. While these meetings need not last more than twenty minutes or so, they are crucial to the "sense" of the entire project insofar as they may be, for some students, the only way to help them see that the process has something to do with their learning. But regardless of whether the portfolios are simply part of a given course or an organized requirement within a program of study, both students and teacher can benefit.

Portfolio Handout for English Majors (Fall 1993)

All English majors are expected to keep a portfolio. The portfolio requirements for English Education majors are set forth on a separate sheet. This sheet describes the portfolio for majors in the general track.

PURPOSE OF THE PORTFOLIO

Research has shown that the exercise of examining one's own learning is a powerful tool for expanding and deepening that learning, and for taking charge of one's own mental development. The English Department believes you can engage in this exercise by keeping a file, or portfolio, of reflections on your learning, and by discussing each semester's entry with your adviser. As you will see from the description of its contents, the portfolio is not a diary or journal, nor does it involve your personal life. Instead, it is a means of reflecting on yourself as an English major. Although the Department requires you to keep this portfolio, and hopes you will see how important it can be for you, nobody will grade it. The short papers you write for it you are writing to yourself, explaining to yourself where you are as an English major, where you have come from and where you are going. You are also writing to your adviser, both to help him or her understand your development and to give him or her some insight into the way the English major works for the students involved in its courses.

This being the case, there is no need to think of the portfolio as a record of nothing but successes. On the contrary, it is often the difficult experience, the assignment not done as well as you wished, which stimulates growth and increases understanding. Reflections on a struggle with such an experience or assignment can provide rich insights into your own learning which, in turn, you can direct toward new growth.

CONTENTS OF THE PORTFOLIO

1. An "entry paper" one or two pages long in which you explain your reasons for wanting to study English and your expectations from the program.

2. A short paper you write at the end of each semester, describing the intellectual and aesthetic experience that most influenced your development as an English major during that semester. The experience might have taken place in a class, or in connection with writing a paper, or during a debate, concert, or play you attended or took part in, on in some other venue. Your paper would briefly describe the experience and explain its effect on your perception of yourself as a writer, or on your understanding of your purpose as a student of English, or on your interpretation of literature, or whatever. You should write such a paper for every semester from the time you declare the English major until you take the required writing course in your senior year.

3. Four papers you choose among those you have written for English courses over the years you are in the program. (Transfer students may have to choose fewer than four.) For each paper, you will write a one-page statement explaining why you chose that paper to put in your portfolio. (Possibly, some of these papers would be the subject of your essays in #2 above.) At least one of these papers should analyze a literary work (or film), and at least one should be a paper in which you use secondary sources to support a thesis or analysis of some kind.

4. An "exit paper" in which you review your portfolio and focus on your sense of your intellectual growth over the time you have been studying English. You will write the exit paper in connection with work in the senior writing course.

THE MECHANICS

When you first declare an English major, you should write your entry paper and give it to your adviser, who will read it and discuss it with you.

Thereafter, during the first week of every semester, you will give your adviser your entry for the preceding semester. This entry will always be your short reflective paper, and sometimes will also involve a paper you have written for some English course and chosen for your portfolio, with an explanation of your choice. You and your adviser will then set a time to meet and discuss what you have written for the portfolio.

Entry to the required senior writing course will depend on your portfolio's being complete to that point.

Bibliography

"A Back to School Concern: The Warning in '91 SAT Scores." *Buffalo News* Editorial (September 1, 1991): F8.

America 2000. Education Goals Panel. Washington, D.C.: Superintendent of Documents, GPO, 1991.

Amiran, Minda Rae, Karen Schilling, and Karl Schilling. "Interpreting Liberal Education Assessment Results: Interrelated Stories from Two Schools." In *Are We Making a Difference?* edited by Trudy Banta. Forthcoming.

Amiran, Minda Rae, and Karen Mills-Courts. "Metacognition and the Use of Portfolios." In *Portfolios: Process and Product,* edited by Pat Belanoff and Marcia Dickson. Portsmouth, N.H.: Boynton/Cook, 1991. 101–12.

Amiran, Minda Rae, with The General College Program Assessment Committee. *The GCP and Student Learning: A Report to the Campus.* Fredonia, N.Y.: State University College of New York at Fredonia, 1989.

Anderson, Worth, Cynthia Best, Alycia Black, John Hurst, Brandt Miller, and Susan Miller. "Cross-Curricular Underlife: A Collaborative Report on Ways with Academic Words." *College Composition and Communication* 41 (1990): 11–36.

Annas, Pamela J. "Silences: Feminist Language Research and the Teaching of Writing." In *Teaching Writing: Pedagogy, Gender, and Equity,* edited by Cynthia L. Caywood and Gillian R. Overing. Albany: State University of New York Press, 1987. 3–18.

Anson, Chris M., and Robert L. Brown, Jr. "Large-Scale Portfolio Assessment: Ideological Sensitivity and Institutional Change." In *Portfolios,* edited by Pat Belanoff and Marcia Dickson. 248–69.

Aper, Jeffery P., Steven M. Cuver, and Dennis E. Hinkle. "Coming to Terms with the Accountability Versus Improvement Debate in Assessment." *Higher Education* 20 (1990): 471–83.

Applebee, Arthur N. *Writing in the Secondary School: English and the Content Areas.* Urbana, Ill.: National Council of Teachers of English (NCTE), 1981.

———. *Contexts for Learning to Write: Studies of Secondary School Instruction.* Norwood, N.J.: Ablex, 1984.

Applebee, Arthur, Judith Langer, and I.V.S. Mullis. *The Reading Report Card: Progress Toward Excellence in Our Schools*. National Assessment of Educational Progress. Princeton, N.J.: Educational Testing Service, 1985.

Aronowitz, Stanley, and Henry A. Giroux. *Postmodern Education: Politics, Culture, and Social Criticism*. Minneapolis, Minn.: University of Minnesota Press, 1991.

Arter, Judith. *Using Portfolios in Instruction and Assessment*. Portland, Ore.: Northwest Regional Educational Laboratory Test Center, 1990.

Au, Katherine. "Participation Structures in a Reading Lesson with Hawaiian Children: Analysis of a Culturally Appropriate Instructional Event." *Anthropology and Education Quarterly* 11 (1980): 91–115.

Ballard, Leslie. "Portfolios and Self-Assessment." *English Journal* (February 1992): 46–48.

Bartoli, Jill Sunday. "Is It English for Everyone?" *Language Arts* 63 (1986): 12–22.

Bazerman, Charles. "What Written Knowledge Does: Three Examples of Academic Discourse." *Philosophy of the Social Sciences* 11 (1981): 361–87.

Beach, Richard, and James Marshall. *Teaching Literature in the Secondary School*. San Diego: Harcourt Brace Jovanovitch, 1991.

Becker, Howard. *Writing for Social Scientists: How to Start and Finish Your Thesis, Book, or Article*. Chicago: University of Chicago Press, 1986.

Beckwith, J. B. "Approaches to Learning, Their Context and Relationship to Assessment Performance." *Higher Education* 22 (1991): 17–30.

Belanoff, Pat, and Marcia Dickson, eds. *Portfolios: Process and Product*. Portsmouth, N.H.: Boynton/Cook, 1991.

Belenky, Mary Field, Blythe McVicker Clinchy, Nancy Rule Goldberger, and Jill Mattuck Tarule. *Women's Ways of Knowing*. New York: Basic Books, 1986.

Bell, Shirley H. "Portfolio Evaluation and Paulo Freire's Pedagogy of the Oppressed: A Descriptive Analysis." *Teaching English in the Two-Year College* (May 1992): 95–96.

Bennett, William J. "To Reclaim A Legacy: A Report on the Humanities and Higher Education." Washington, D.C.: National Endowment for the Humanities, 1984.

Berthoff, Anne. *The Making of Meaning: Metaphors, Models, and Maxims for Writing Teachers*. Portsmouth, N.H.: Boynton/Cook, 1981.

Bizzell, Patricia. "Arguing About Literacy." *College English* 50 (1988): 141–53.

Blumenstyk, Goldie, and Denise Magner. "As Assessment Draws New Converts, Backers Gather to Ask 'What Works?' " *Chronicle of Higher Education* (July 11, 1990): A11.

Britton, James. *Language and Learning*. London: Penguin Books, 1970.

Brown, Rexford G. *Schools of Thought: How the Politics of Literacy Shape Thinking in the Classroom*. San Francisco: Jossey-Bass, 1991.

Bruffee, Kenneth. "Collaboration and the Conversation of Mankind." *College English* 46 (1984): 635–52.

Bunda, Mary Anne. "Capturing the Richness of Student Outcomes with Qualitative Techniques." *New Directions for Institutional Research* (Winter 1991): 35–47.

Castellano, Olivia. "Canto, Locura y Poesia." In *Race, Class, and Gender: An Anthology*, edited by Margaret Anderson and Patricia Hill Collins. Belmont, Cal.: Wadsworth, 1992. 376–85.

Cazden, Courtney B. *Classroom Discourse: The Language of Teaching and Learning*. Portsmouth, N.H.: Heinemann, 1988.

Cohen, Muriel. "Decline in Top Student Scores." *Buffalo News* (September 4, 1991): A3.

Committee C on College and University Teaching, Research, and Publication. "Mandated Assessment of Educational Outcomes: A Report of Committee C on College and University Teaching, Research, and Publication" adopted by the Council of the American Association of University Professors in June 1991. *Academe* (July-August 1991): 49–56.

Composition Chronicle, "Florida Composition Teachers Protest Workload," April 1991, 7.

"Company Contracts for Educational Tests." *Quad City Times* (August 1, 1992): A10.

Connor, Katherine, and Ellen J. Vargyas. "The Legal Implications of Gender Bias in Standardized Testing." *Berkeley Women's Law Journal* 7 (1992): 13.

Cook-Gumperz, Jenny. *The Social Construction of Literacy.* London: Cambridge University Press, 1986.

Courts, Patrick L. *Literacy and Empowerment: The Meaning Makers.* Westport, Conn.: Bergin and Garvey, 1991.

Crouse, James and Dale Trusheim. *The Case Against the SAT.* Chicago: University of Chicago Press, 1988.

Cummins, Jim. "Empowering Minority Students: A Framework for Intervention." *Harvard Education Review* 56 (1986): 18–36.

Curry, Wade, and Elizabeth Hager. "Assessing General Education: Trenton State College." In *Student Outcomes Assessment: What Institutions Stand to Gain*, edited by Diane Halpern. San Francisco: Jossey-Bass, 1987. 57–65.

Darling-Hammond, Liz, and Ann Lieberman. "The Shortcomings of Standardized Tests." *Chronicle of Higher Education* (January 29, 1992): B1–B2.

Dickson, Marcia. "The WPA, The Portfolios System, and Academic Freedom: A Cautionary Tale with an Optimistic Ending." In *Portfolios*, edited by Belanoff and Dickson. 270–78.

DiPardo, Anne. "Acquiring a Kind of Passport: The Teaching and Learning of Academic Discourse in Basic Writing Tutorials." Ph.D. diss. University of California–Berkeley, 1991.

D'Souza, Dinesh. "Standardized Tests Are Imperfect But Necessary." *Buffalo News* (August 28, 1991): B3.

Edgerton, Russ. "National Standards Are Coming! . . . National Standards Are Coming!" *AAHE Bulletin* (December 1991): 8–12.

Elbow, Peter. *Writing Without Teachers.* London: Oxford University Press, 1973.

Elbow, Peter, and Pat Belanoff. "State University of New York at Stony Brook Portfolio-Based Evaluation Program." In *Portfolios*, edited by Belanoff and Dickson. 17–36.

Ellis, David. *Becoming a Master Student.* Rapid City, S.D.: College Survival, 1985.

Elshtain, Jean. *Public Man, Private Woman: Women in Social and Political Thought.* Princeton, N.J.: Princeton University Press, 1981.

Ewell, Peter T. "Assessment and TQM: In Search of Convergence." *New Directions for Institutional Research* 71 (Fall 1991): 39–52.

———. "Back to the Future." *Change* (November/December 1991): 12–17.

———. "Establishing a Campus-Based Assessment Program." In *Student Outcomes Assessment*, edited by Halpern. 9–24.

Faery, Rebecca Blevins. "Women and Writing Across the Curriculum: Learning and

Liberation." In *Teaching Writing: Pedagogy, Gender, and Equity*, edited by Cynthia C. Caywood and Gillian R. Overing. Albany, N.Y.: State University of New York Press, 1987. 201–14.

Fiore, Kyle, and Nan Elsasser. " 'Strangers No More': A Liberatory Literacy Curriculum." In *Freire for the Classroom: A Sourcebook for Liberatory Teaching*, edited by Ira Shor. Portsmouth, N.H.: Heinemann, 1987. 87–103.

Ford, Margaret I. "The Writing Process: A Strategy for Problem Solvers." *Arithmetic Teacher* (November 1990): 35–38.

Frankenstein, Marilyn. "Critical Mathematics Education: An Application of Paulo Freire's Epistemology." In *Freire for the Classroom*, edited by Shor. 180–210.

Freire, Paulo. *Pedagogy of the Oppressed*. New York: Seaview, 1971.

Freire, Paulo, and Donaldo Macedo. *Literacy: Teaching the Word and the World*. Westport, Conn.: Bergin and Garvey, 1987.

Fulwiler, Toby. "How Well Does Writing Across the Curriculum Work?" *College English* 46 (1984): 113–25.

Fulwiler, Toby, and Robert Jones. "Assigning and Evaluating Transactional Writing." In *Language Connections: Writing and Reading Across the Curriculum*, edited by Toby Fulwiler and Art Young. Urbana, Ill.: National Council of Teachers of English, 1982. 45–56.

Fulwiler, Toby, and Art Young. *Language Connections: Writing and Reading Across the Curriculum*. Urbana, Ill.: National Council of Teachers of English, 1982.

Galbraith, John Kenneth. "Writing, Typing, and Economics." In *Writing in the Social Sciences*, edited by Joyce S. Steward and Marjorie Smelstor. Glenview, Ill.: Scott, Foresman, 1984. 20–27.

Gardner, Howard. *The Unschooled Mind: How Children Think and How Schools Should Teach*. New York: Basic Books, 1991.

Geertz, Clifford. *Interpretation of Cultures*. New York: Basic Books, 1973.

Gilligan, Carol. *In a Different Voice: Psychological Theory and Women's Development*. Cambridge, Mass.: Harvard University Press, 1982.

Golub, Jeff, Beverly A. Busching, Carlota Cárdenas de Dwyer, Jane M. Hornburger, James C. Lalley, Jr., and Patricia Phelan. *Focus on Collaborative Learning: Classroom Practices in Teaching English, 1988*. Urbana, Ill.: National Council of Teachers of English, 1988.

Graff, Harvey. *The Legacies of Literacy: Continuities and Contradictions in Western Culture and Society*. Bloomington: Indiana University Press, 1987.

Graves, Richard. *Rhetoric and Composition: A Sourcebook for Teachers and Writers*. Third edition. Portsmouth, N.H.: Boynton/Cook, 1990.

Greene, Elizabeth. "SAT Scores Fail to Help Admission Officers Make Better Decisions, Analysts Contend." *The Chronicle of Higher Education* (July 27, 1988): A20.

Griffin, Susan. "Thoughts on Writing: A Diary." In *The Writer on Her Work*, edited by Janet Sternberg. New York: W. W. Norton, 1980. 107–20.

Grumet, Madeleine R. *Bitter Milk: Women and Teaching*. Amherst: University of Massachusetts Press, 1988.

Hall, Roberta. "The Classroom Climate: A Chilly One for Women?" Washington, D.C.: Project on the Status and Education of Women, Association of American Colleges, 1982.

Halpern, Diane F. "Student Outcomes Assessment: Introduction and Overview." *Student*

Outcomes Assessment: What Institutions Stand to Gain. San Francisco: Jossey-Bass, 1987. 5–8.

Halpern, Diane F., ed. *Student Outcomes Assessment: What Institutions Stand to Gain.* San Francisco: Jossey-Bass, 1987.

Halpern, Diane F., Darrell W. Krueger, Margarita L. Heisserer. "Assessment and Involvement: Investments to Enhance Learning." In *Student Outcomes Assessment: What Institutions Stand to Gain,* edited by Diane Halpern. San Francisco: Jossey-Bass, 1987. 45–56.

Hartmann, David. "Program Assessment in Sociology: The Case for the Bachelor's Paper." *Teaching Sociology* 20 (April 1992): 125–28.

Havens, Lynn. "Writing to Enhance Learning in General Mathematics." *Mathematics Teacher* (October 1989): 551–54.

Hayes, Aaron. "Putting Reading, 'Riting, and 'Rithmetic All in One Class." Unpublished. 1992.

Heath, Shirley Brice. *Ways with Words: Language, Life, and Work in Communities and Classrooms.* Cambridge: Cambridge University Press, 1983.

Hendricks, Bill. "Cultural Commonplaces and Academic Accounting: On Composition's Valuing of Difference." *The Iowa English Bulletin* 40 (Spring 1992): 39–55.

Herter, Roberta J. "Writing Portfolios: Alternatives to Testing." *English Journal* (January 1991): 90–91.

Hilgers, Thomas, and Joy Marsella. "Collaborating to Construct a Good Writing Test." *The Council Chronicle* 1, no. 5 (June 1992): 8.

Hilliard, Asa G. "Limitations of Academic Achievement Measures." In *Going to School: The African American Experience,* edited by Kofi Lomotey. Albany, N.Y.: State University of New York Press, 1990. 135–42.

Hutchings, Pat. "Assessment and the Way We Work." Closing Plenary address, Fifth AAHE Conference on Assessment. June 30, 1990. Reprinted by the American Association for Higher Education and its Assessment Forum.

Hutchings, Pat, and Ted Marchese. "Watching Assessment: Questions, Stories, Prospects." *Change* (September/October 1990): 10–38.

Hymes, Dell. *Foundations of Sociolinguistics: An Ethnographic Approach.* Philadelphia, Penn.: University of Pennsylvania Press, 1974.

Hyser, Charles P. *Writing to Learn: Specific Applications in Third Grade Social Studies.* Ph.D. diss., University of Minnesota, 1992.

Jolliffe, David A., ed. *Advances in Writing Research: Writing in Academic Disciplines.* Norwood, N.J.: Ablex, 1988.

Keller, Helen Fox. *Reflections on Gender and Science.* New Haven, Conn.: Yale University Press, 1985.

King, Barbara. "Using Writing in the Mathematics Class: Theory and Practice." In *Teaching Writing in All Disciplines,* edited by C. Williams Griffin. San Francisco: Jossey-Bass, 1982. 39–44.

Kingston, Maxine Hong. *The Woman Warrior: Memoirs of a Girlhood Among Ghosts.* New York: Vintage, 1977.

Koch, Paul, and Ronald H. Peters. "Suppression of Adult Copulatory Behaviors Mediated by Conditioned Social Aversions Elicited in Juvenile Male Rats." Paper presented at the Midwest Psychological Association, Chicago, Ill., 1992.

Kozol, Jonathan. *Savage Inequalities: Children in America's Schools.* New York: Crown, 1991.

Langer, Judith. "Relation Between Levels of Prior Knowledge and the Organization of Recall." In *Perspectives in Reading Research and Instruction*, edited by M. L. Kamil and A. J. Moe. Washington, D.C.: National Reading Conference, 1980.

Langer, Judith R. "Examining Background Knowledge and Text Comprehension." *Reading Research Quarterly* 19 (1984): 468–81.

Langer, Judith R., and Arthur N. Applebee. *How Writing Shapes Thinking: A Study of Teaching and Learning.* National Council of Teachers of English Research Report No. 22. Urbana, Ill.: NCTE, 1987.

Lather, Patti. *Getting Smart: Feminist Research and Pedagogy with/in the Postmodern.* New York: Routledge, Chapman and Hall, Inc., 1991.

Lawton, Theresa A., and Julianne C. Turner. "A Developmental Perspective on Standardized Achievement." *Educational Researcher* (June/July 1991): 12–20.

Light, Richard. *Explorations with Students and Faculty About Teaching, Learning, and Student Life: First Report.* Cambridge, Mass.: Harvard University, 1990.

Linden, Kathryn W., William LeBold, Kevin Shell, and Carolyn Jagacinski. "Predicting Engineering Retention for Undergraduate Women and Men." *U.S. Women Engineers* (November/December 1985): 36.

Loofbourrow, Peggy Trump. "Composition in the Context of CAP: A Case Study of the Interplay Between Assessment and School Life." Technical Report No. 28. University of California–Berkeley: Center for the Study of Writing, January 1992.

Lorde, Audre. "Age, Race, Class, and Sex: Women Redefining Difference." In *Race, Class, and Gender: An Anthology*, edited by Margaret Anderson and Patricia Hill Collins. Belmont, Cal.: Wadsworth, 1992. 495–502.

Lunsford, Andrea. "Reassessing Assessment: Challenges to the Tradition of Testing." Keynote address, Sixth Annual Conference of the National Testing Network in Writing, Minneapolis.

Macrorie, Ken. *Twenty Teachers.* New York: Oxford University Press, 1984.

Martin, Nancy, Pat D'Arcy, Bryan Newton, and Robert Parker. *Writing and Learning Across the Curriculum, 11–16.* London: Ward Lock Educational for the Schools Council, 1976.

Marzano, Robert J. "Standardized Tests: Do They Measure General Cognitive Abilities?" *NASSP Bulletin* (May 1990): 93–101.

Mayher, John S. *Uncommon Sense: Theoretical Practice in Language Education.* Portsmouth, N.H.: Heinemann, 1990.

McCarthy, Lucille. "A Stranger in Strange Lands: One College Student Writing Across the Curriculum." *Research in the Teaching of English* 21 (October 1987): 233–65.

McLeary, Bill. "Florida Composition Teachers Protest Workload." *Composition Chronicle* (April 1991): 7.

Michaels, Sarah. "Narrative Presentations: An Oral Preparation for Literacy with First Graders." In *The Social Construction of Literacy*, edited by Jenny Cook-Gumperz. London: Cambridge University Press, 1986: 94–116.

Mitgang, Lee. "Verbal Scores on SATs Hit Record Low." *Buffalo News* (August 27, 1991): A1–A3.

Moore, Leslie E., and Linda H. Peterson. "Convention as Connection: Linking the Composition Course to the English and College Curriculum." *College Composition and Communication* 37 (1986): 466–506.

Morrison, Toni. Keynote Address, Second Annual Chicago Humanities Festival. In *Humanities* 3 (Spring 1992): 19–20.

Murray, Donald M. *A Writer Teaches Writing.* 2d ed. Boston: Houghton Mifflin, 1985.

Myers, Miles. Keynote address, Iowa Council of Teachers of English Annual Meeting, Des Moines, Iowa, 1987.

"National Tests Can Help." *Buffalo News* Editorial (January 8, 1992): B2.

Neuleib, Janice. "The Friendly Stranger: Twenty-five Years as 'Other'." *College Composition and Communication* 43 (May 1992): 231–43.

Neuman, Susan B. *Literacy in the Television Age: The Myth of the TV Effect.* Norwood, N.J.: Ablex, 1991.

Newell, George. "Learning from Writing in Two Content Areas: A Case Study/Protocol Analysis of Writing to Learn." *Research in the Teaching of English* 18 (1984): 265–87.

Newman, Judith M. "Mealworm: Learning About Written Language Through Science Activities." In *Whole Language: Theory and Use,* edited by Judith M. Newman. Portsmouth, N.H.: Heinemann, 1985. 145–52.

Noddings, Nel. *Caring.* Berkeley: University of California Press, 1984.

Oakley, Ann. "Interviewing Women: A Contradiction in Terms." In *Doing Feminist Research,* edited by Helen Roberts. Boston: Routledge and Kegan Paul, 1981. 30–61.

Paris, Scott G., Theresa A. Lawton, Julianne C. Turner, Jodie L. Roth. "A Developmental Perspective on Standardized Achievement Testing." *Educational Researcher* (June-July 1991): 12–20.

Parker, Robert P. "Points of Development, Not Points of Failure." In *Assessment for Instruction in Early Literacy,* edited by Leslie Mandel Morrow and Jeffrey K. Smith. Englewood Cliffs, N.J.: Prentice Hall, 1990. 75–82.

Paulson, Leon F., and Pearl R. Paulson. *How Do Portfolios Measure Up? A Cognitive Model for Assessing Portfolios (Revised).* Paper presented at the Annual Meeting of the Northwest Evaluation Association, Union, Washington, August 2–4, 1990.

Perrone, Vito. "Standardized Testing in Early Grades." *The Education Digest* (January 1992): 42–46.

Perry, William. *Forms of Intellectual and Ethical Development in the College Years.* New York: Holt, Rinehart and Winston, 1970.

Polanyi, Michael. *Personal Knowledge: Towards a Post-Critical Philosophy.* New York: Harper and Row, 1958.

Porter, Connie. *All-Bright Court.* Boston: Houghton Mifflin, 1991.

"Racism 101, Frontline," Public Broadcasting System, May, 1988.

Rich, Adrienne. "Taking Women Students Seriously." *On Lies, Secrets, and Silence: Selected Prose 1966–1978.* New York: W. W. Norton, 1979. 237–45.

Riegel, Laurel Blyth. "Texas Campus Report Cards: The Story of One Blind Man and Six Elephants." Reprint of paper presented at the annual meeting of the American Educational Research Association, San Francisco, April 20, 1992.

Robinson, Adam. *Cracking the System: The LSAT.* New York: Villard Books, 1989.

Roemer, Marjorie Godlin, Lucille M. Schultz, and Russel K. Durst. "Portfolios and the Process of Change." *College Composition and Communication* (December 1991): 455–69.

Romano, Tom. "A Time for Immersion, A Time for Reflection: The Multigenre Research

Project and Portfolio Assessment." Paper presented at the Annual Spring Meeting of the National Council of Teachers of English, March 1991.

Rose, Mike. *Lives on the Boundary: A Moving Account of the Struggles and Achievements of America's Educational Underclass.* New York: Penguin, 1989.

Ruddick, Sara. "Maternal Thinking." *Feminist Studies* 6 (1980): 70–96.

Sadker, Myra, and David Sadker. "Confronting Sexism in the College Classroom." In *Gender in the Classroom: Power and Pedagogy,* edited by Susan L. Gabriel and Isaiah Smithson. Urbana, Ill.: University of Illinois Press, 1990. 176–187.

Schön, David. *The Reflective Practitioner: How Professionals Think in Action.* New York: Basic Books, 1983.

Sensenbaugh, Roger. "Assessing Writing Using Portfolios." *Composition Chronicle* 4 (1991): 8–9.

Shaughnessy, Mina. *Errors and Expectations: A Guide for the Teacher of Basic Writing.* New York: Oxford University Press, 1977.

Shor, Ira, and Paulo Freire. *A Pedagogy for Liberation.* Westport, Conn.: Bergin and Garvey, 1987.

Sims, Serbrenia J. *Student Outcomes Assessment: A Historical Review and Guide in Program Development.* Westport, Conn.: Greenwood Press, 1992.

Smith, Frank. *Joining the Literacy Club: Further Essays into Education.* Portsmouth, N.H.: Heinemann, 1988.

Smith, Frederick R., and Karen M. Feathers. "Teacher and Student Perceptions of Content Area Reading." *Journal of Reading* 26 (1983): 348–54.

Smithson, Isaiah. "Investigating Gender, Power, and Pedagogy." In *Gender in the Classroom,* edited by Gabriel and Smithson. 1–27.

Sobol, Thomas. *A New Compact for Learning: Improving Public Elementary, Middle, and Secondary Education Results in the 1990s.* Albany, N.Y.: State Education Department of New York, 1991.

Soltow, Lee, and Edward Stevens. *The Rise of Literacy in the United States: A Socio-economic Analysis to 1870.* Chicago: University of Chicago Press, 1981.

Stallman, Anne C., and P. David Pearson. "Formal Measures of Early Literacy." In *Assessment for Early Instruction,* edited by Lesley Mandel Morrow and Jeffrey K. Smith. Englewood Cliffs, N.J.: Prentice-Hall, 1990. 45–61.

Steward, Joyce S., and Marjorie Smelstor. *Writing in the Social Sciences.* Glenview, Ill.: Scott, Foresman, 1984.

Stuckey, Elspeth J., and Kenneth Alston. "Cross-Age Tutoring: The Right to Literacy." In *The Right to Literacy,* edited by Andrea Lunsford, Helen Moglin, and James Slevin. New York: Modern Language Association, 1990. 245–54.

Tchudi, Stephen N. *Teaching Writing in the Content Areas: College Level.* National Education Association, 1986.

Thaiss, Christopher. "Language Across the Curriculum." In *Rhetoric and Composition,* edited by Graves. 33–37.

Thomas, David John. *The Social Psychology of Childhood Disability.* New York: Schocken Books, 1980.

Thompson, Kirk. "Learning at Evergreen: As Assessment of Cognitive Development." Spring 1991. Available in monograph from The Washington Center for Undergraduate Education, The Evergreen State College, Olympia, Washington.

Tompkins, Jane. "Pedagogy of the Distressed." *College English* 52 (1990): 653–60.

Trachsel, Mary. *Institutionalizing Literacy: The Historical Role of College Entrance*

Examinations in English. Carbondale, Ill.: Southern Illinois University Press, 1992.

Vaughn, Charlotte. Presentation for Faculty Workshop on Assessment. St. Ambrose University, Davenport, Iowa, August, 1992.

Vygotsky, Lev S. *Thought and Language,* edited and translated by Eugene Hanfamann and Gertrude Vaker. Cambridge, Mass.: Massachusetts Institute of Technology Press, 1962.

Walvoord, Barbara Fassler. *Helping Students Write Well: A Guide for Teachers in all Disciplines.* New York: Modern Language Association, 1982.

Warriner, John E., Joseph Mersand, and Francis Griffith. *English Grammar and Composition 11.* San Diego: Harcourt, Brace, Jovanovich, 1958.

Wauters, Joan K. "Evaluation for Empowerment: A Portfolio Proposal for Alaska." In *Portfolios,* edited by Belanoff and Dickson. 57–68.

Weaver, Constance. *Reading Process and Practice: From Sociolinguistics to Whole Language.* Portsmouth, N.H.: Heinemann, 1988.

Weiler, Kathleen. *Women Teaching for Change: Gender, Class, and Race.* Westport, Conn.: Bergin and Garvey, 1988.

Wells, Gordon. *The Meaning Makers: Children Learning Language and Using Language to Learn.* Portsmouth, N.H.: Heinemann, 1986.

"Why We Still Live Best." *Money* Magazine (November 1991): 86–93.

Williams, Robert L., and James D. Long. *How to Manage Your Life.* Princeton, N.J.: Houghton Mifflin, 1991.

Willie, Charles Vert. "The Problems of Standardized Testing in a Free and Pluralistic Society." *Phi Delta Kappan* (May 1985): 626–28.

Willinsky, John. *The New Literacy: Redefining Reading and Writing in the Schools.* New York: Routledge, 1990.

Worthen, Blaine R., and Vicki Spandel. "Putting the Standardized Test Debate in Perspective." *Educational·Leadership* (February 1991): 65–69.

Zinsser, William. *Writing to Learn.* New York: Harper and Row, 1988.

Index

About the Authors

PATRICK L. COURTS is Professor of English at the State University College at Fredonia, New York. He has written several books including *Literacy and Empowerment: The Meaning Makers* (Bergin & Garvey, 1991).

KATHLEEN H. McINERNEY is a doctoral candidate in English Education at the University of Iowa and Instructor of English and Education at Augustana College in Illinois.